# WHAT IS
## AND WHAT
# OUGHT
## TO BE

# WHAT IS AND WHAT OUGHT TO BE

## The Dialectic of Experience, Theology, and Church

## Michael G. Lawler

continuum
NEW YORK • LONDON

2005

The Continuum International Publishing Group Inc
15 East 26 Street, New York, NY 10017

The Continuum International Publishing Group Ltd
The Tower Building, 11 York Road, London SE1 7NX

www.continuumbooks.com

Printed in the United States of America

**Library of Congress Cataloging-in-Publication Data**
Lawler, Michael G.
      What is and what ought to be : the dialectic of experience, theology, and
   church / Michael G. Lawler.
          p.   cm.
      Includes bibliographical references and index.
      ISBN 0-8264-1703-5 (alk. paper) – ISBN 0-8264-1704-3 (pbk. : alk. paper)
      1. Theology, Practical – Methodology.   2. Christianity and the social sciences.
   3. Catholic Church – Doctrines.   I. Title.
   BX1753.L375 2005
   230'.2'01 – dc22
                                                                      2004029169

*To my colleagues*
*in the Theology Department at Creighton University,*
*for thirty-five years of friendship, creative stimulation,*
*and support*

# Contents

# Abbreviations

AAS     *Acta Apostolicae Sedis: Commentarium Officiale* (Rome: Typis Polyglottis Vaticanis)

AG     *Ad Gentes,* Decree on the Missionary Activity of the Church

CL     *Christifideles Laici,* John Paul II, Exhortation on the Laity

DS     *Enchiridion Symbolorum Definitionum et Declarationum de Rebus Fidei et Morum,* ed. Henricus Denzinger and Adolphus Schönmetzer (Freiburg: Herder, 1965)

DV     *Dei Verbum,* Dogmatic Constitution on Divine Revelation

FC     *Familiaris Consortio,* John Paul II, Exhortation on the Role of the Christian Family

GS     *Gaudium et Spes,* Pastoral Constitution on the Church in the Modern World

HV     *Humanae Vitae,* Paul VI

LG     *Lumen Gentium,* Dogmatic Constitution on the Church

OT     *Optatam Totius,* Decree on the Training of Priests

PBC     Pontifical Biblical Commission, "The Interpretation of the Bible in the Church," 1994

PG     *Patrologiae Cursus Completus: Series Graeca,* ed. J. P. Migne

PL     *Patrologiae Cursus Completus: Series Latina,* ed. J. P. Migne

PO     *Presbyterorum Ordinis,* Decree on the Ministry and Life of Priests

SC     *Sacrosanctum Concilium,* Constitution on the Sacred Liturgy

ST     *Summa Theologiae Sancti Thomae de Aquino*

UR     *Unitatis Redintegratio,* Decree on Ecumenism

All abbreviations in the endnotes are listed without any italicized emphasis. All translation from languages other than English are the author's. All documents abbreviated are from the Second Vatican Council unless otherwise noted.

# Prologue

The seed for this book was first sown in 1961 in a seminar on theological method under the guidance of Bernard Lonergan. Lonergan was convinced that something new was happening in history and that, since a living theology is called to take part critically in whatever is going on in history, we were living in a new theological age that required a new theological approach. In this book I am concerned with three characteristics of that new approach: it is necessarily historical, empirical, and in interdisciplinary collaboration with the social sciences to elaborate and evaluate a heuristic hermeneutic of culture.

The notion of culture was central to Lonergan's search to formulate the method and structure of the new theology, and he introduced a distinction between a classicist and an empirical notion of culture. "The classicist notion of culture was normative: at least *de iure* there was but one culture that was both universal and permanent." The empirical notion of culture "is the set of meanings and values that informs a way of life. It may remain unchanged for ages. It may be in the process of slow development or rapid dissolution."[1] Classicist culture is static; empirical culture is dynamic, and theology mirrors those states. In a classicist culture, theology is a static "permanent achievement" which anyone, educated or barbarian, can learn; in an empirical culture, theology is a dynamic "ongoing process."[2] Lonergan himself was deeply rooted in an empirical notion of both culture and theology but, understanding the angst generated by change, he predicted in 1965 that "there is bound to be formed a solid right that is determined to live in a world that no longer exists. There is bound to be formed a scattered left, captivated by now this, now that new development." What will count, however, "is a perhaps not numerous center, big enough to be at home in both the old and the new, painstaking enough to work out one by one the transitions to be made, strong enough to refuse half measures and insist on complete solutions even though it has to wait."[3] In retrospection from the present socio-historical situation, one cannot but be struck by how prophetic that statement was. My intention and hope in this book is to be part of the predicted painstaking, strong center.

From the outset, I describe this book as an exercise in practical theology, the "theological discipline which is concerned with the church's self-actualization here and now — both that which *is* and that which *ought to be.*"[4] Practical theology is the *theological* reflection provoked by and in response to the church's actual situation. It does not explain from deductive theological principles the church's actual situation, but reflects critically on the actual situation to test it for relevance and significance in light of both the gospel and the socio-historical conditions of the time. Practical theology grows out of the relationship between *theoria* and *praxis* which, for the church, is the relationship between *faith,* both *fides qua creditur* and *fides quae creditur,* subjective and objective faith, and *praxis.* To explicate scientifically the church's actual situation and to perform the required theological reflection, Karl Rahner argues, "practical theology certainly requires sociology."[5]

In this book, therefore, I explore, in general, the relationship between practical theology and sociology and, in specific, the theological realities, *sensus fidei* and *reception,* and their relationship to both theoretical sociology and the empirical data of sociological research. The exploration is concretized by a consideration of the sociological data and theology of two Catholic moral doctrines, divorce and remarriage without prior annulment, and artificial contraception. A *theological* reflection on the actual situation of both doctrines in the church and a *sociological* consideration of the data suggest that a dramatic development and re-reception[6] of both doctrines is under way and that the development is in line with previous dramatic developments of doctrine in the church.

The development of these doctrines can be detected in what may be called the high tradition, comprised of believers whose grasp of the philosophical precision of the language in which Catholic doctrine is articulated enables them to understand the meanings embedded in doctrine, and the popular low tradition, comprised of believers who do not understand the language and, therefore, more often than not, misunderstand doctrine. There is an important and theologically legitimate distinction in the high tradition between the magisterium, whose task it is to speak *from* and *for* the church, and theologians, who speak only *from* the church. Because the theologian's role is to speak *from* the actual faith situation of the church, not only to hand on traditional doctrine but also to test and retest it for relevance and significance in the present socio-historical situation, sociology, which can research and manifest the present situation of doctrine, can be a tool for theological reflection as important as philosophy and history.

No Catholic theologian would deny that ecclesial faith is the primary source for theological reflection, but that faith, as the New Testament consistently teaches, always includes *praxis* or action. The Letter of James is usually advanced as *the* foundation for the Catholic claim that faith includes *praxis*. "What does it profit, my brethren," James asks, "if a man says he has faith but has not works? Can his faith save him? ... If a brother or sister is ill-clad and in lack of daily food, and one of you says to them, 'Go in peace, be warmed and filled,' without giving them the things needed for the body, what does it profit? So faith by itself, if it has not works, is dead" (2:14–17). The Reformers, of course, regretted the presence of James in the biblical canon, which enabled them to advance and sustain their slogan of "justification by faith alone," but James is far from the only New Testament book connecting faith and *praxis*. His text, indeed, resonates with loud echoes of Matthew. From his Sermon on the Mount, "You will know them by their *fruits*" (7:16) and "not everyone who says to me "Lord, Lord,' shall enter the kingdom of heaven, but he who *does* the will of my Father who is in heaven" (7:21) to the great parable of the last judgment, Matthew is incontestably clear. Genuine faith includes the good fruit of action. In the parable of the great judgment, the Judge separates people "as a shepherd separates the sheep from the goats" (Matt 25:32). "Come, O blessed of my Father," he says to those on his right hand, "inherit the kingdom prepared for you from the foundation of the world; for I was hungry and you gave me food, I was thirsty and you gave me drink, I was a stranger and you welcomed me, I was naked and you clothed me" (vv. 35–36). The question is posed as to when they had seen him hungry, thirsty, naked, or a stranger, and the Judge replies with the punch-line of the parable: "Truly, I say to you, as you did it to one of the least of these my brethren, you did it to me" (v. 40).

Both Paul and John reiterate this judgment. "The fruit of the Spirit," Paul teaches, "is love, joy, peace, patience, kindness, goodness, faithfulness, gentleness, self-control" (Gal 5:22–23). He prays that the Philippians be "filled with the fruits of righteousness, which come through Jesus Christ to the glory of God" (Phil 1:11). The Colossians are "to lead a life worthy of the Lord ... bearing fruit in every good work" (Col 1:10). "If anyone has the world's goods and sees his brother in need, yet closes his heart against him" John asks, "how does God's love abide in him?" (1 John 3:17; cp. 4:20). These texts are not advanced as proof texts for a position, but they reveal a pattern that pervades the New Testament and establish the connection between faith and action as a long-standing Catholic position. Theological inquirers can conclude from the presence of genuine faith to appropriate *praxis;* conversely, they can conclude from *praxis* to the faith that sustains it. Sociology plays an important part in that process by empirically describing actions, making it possible for theologians to conclude to faith that lies behind them.

The Second Vatican Council taught that "in pastoral care sufficient use should be made, not only of theological principles, but also of the findings of secular sciences, especially psychology and sociology." The council goes on to assert that "in this way the faithful will be brought to a purer and more mature living of the faith."[7] Lonergan's empirical principle is involved here, "there are no true factual judgments without a foundation in relevant data,"[8] and I suggest the actual faith of the church in its present situation can best be uncovered only by sociological analysis. Relevant data, required to achieve true knowledge of any kind, are required to achieve true knowledge of what the church believes. The intersection of empirically demonstrated faith-*praxis* and faith-seeking-understanding or theology is a nodal point at which Peter Berger's judgment is verified. "*Methodologically,* in terms of theology as a disembodied universe of discourse, sociology may be looked on as quite harmless — *existentially,* in terms of the theologian as a living person with a social location and a social biography, sociology can be a very dangerous business indeed."[9] My claim in this book is that, dangerous to settled theological positions or not, sociology has a key part to play in manifesting and interpreting what the church *actually* believes and *ought to* believe in both faith and *praxis.* I am advancing sociology, to borrow Aquinas's medieval terminology, as a modern handmaiden for theology.[10]

I confess again what I have confessed many times before. No author writes a book in isolation; he is subject to many influences. I am no exception to that rule, and I freely express my gratitude to all those teachers, colleagues, students, and friends with whom I have interacted over the years and from whom I have learned the craft of theology in the Catholic tradition. Since I cannot name all of them, it always seems churlish to me to name any of them. In this case, however, I break from my established practice. The influence of two of my earliest, and ongoing, theology teachers, Bernard Lonergan and Yves Congar, runs throughout the book and can be easily detected. The influence of my long-standing colleagues in the Theology Department at Creighton University also runs throughout the book, though it may not be so easily detected. To none of them, of course, is to be attributed any error or distortion I have introduced into their theological positions. To all of them, for thirty-five years of theological collaboration and encouragement in *koinonia kai eirene,* I gratefully dedicate this book.

MICHAEL G. LAWLER

*Creighton University*

# WHAT **IS** AND WHAT OUGHT TO BE

# ONE

# Theology, Sociology, and Theologians

The Prologue announced my hope and intention to be, in this book, part of a painstaking and strong center. Before I can do that, however, I have to clarify the notions of theology and sociology with which I am working. Theology and sociology are similar one to the other, and dissimilar to the physical, so-called "hard" sciences, in that the material and criteria of both are "soft." The physical sciences are "hard" because they deal with *things* which they do not control, the laws of which they discover and enunciate with apparent precision. The social sciences are "soft" because they deal not with things but with *social facts* which, as we shall see, are not determined by causes in the same way as physical things. Humans have what Anthony Giddens calls a "double involvement" in social facts: "we create society at the same time as we are created by it."[1] Theology is "soft" and fluid in much the same way as sociology, which makes it that much more difficult to establish exactly how one relates to the other. In addition, neither operates according to an undisputed paradigm. The neo-Platonic theology of Augustine is as different from the Aristotelian theology of Aquinas, and the transcendental theology of Lonergan and Rahner is as different from the neo-orthodox theology of Karl Barth, as the sociology of Emile Durkheim and Max Weber is different from the sociology of Karl Marx.

In a book about the mutual mediations of theology and sociology, therefore, Michael Baxter's legitimate question, "Whose theology? Which sociology?"[2] must be answered. In this chapter, accordingly, I set out, first, what I mean by theology and, then, what I mean by sociology. Finally, I set out something equally important and frequently ignored by theologians and sociologists alike, an understanding of the human subject-knower who does either theology or sociology or both. All three elaborations are necessary for the understanding of the theological ideas that constitute the substance of the book that follows.

1

## Theology

The controlling definition of theology in the Catholic tradition is still broadly Anselm's: faith seeking understanding. The apparent simplicity of this definition masks several questions. What is faith? What is its origin? What is its object? What is the relationship of faith and reason? What counts as understanding in general and as theological understanding in specific? Rahner's modern definition attempts to embrace these questions: "the conscious effort of the Christian to hearken to the actual verbal revelation which God has promulgated in history, to acquire a knowledge of it by the methods of scholarship, and to reflect upon its implications." Fully installed in modern historical consciousness, Rahner knows that "theology cannot be sharply distinguished against revelation, because the latter is promulgated in human terms and thus already contains an element of human reflection of which God has made use."[3] Verbal revelation, the result of human reflection on and reflexive construal of an original pre-reflexive revelation, is already theology. It, and the theologians who produce it, is a product of the socio-historical context in which it is construed.[4] I will expand on these socio-historical facts in chapter 2.

Lonergan approaches theology from a different intellectual commitment. For him, "a theology mediates between a cultural matrix and the significance and role of a religion in that matrix."[5] Christian theology is a disciplined, methodological reflection on two intimately interrelated dimensions of reality: first, the self-communication of God to humankind, a self-communication that for Christians and their theology becomes definitive and is definitively revealed in Jesus Christ; second, the cultural matrix in which Christians relate to God, to the created universe, to themselves in that universe, and to the socio-historical forces which generate both progress and decline in that universe. That theology unfolds in two phases.

A first phase, involving research, interpretation, history, and dialectic, mediates from the past to the present. This phase is *oratio obliqua,* indirect speech, that "tells what Paul and John, Augustine and Aquinas, and anyone else had to say about God and the economy of salvation." A second phase, involving foundations, doctrines, systematics, and communications, mediates from the present into the future. This phase is *oratio recta,* in which "the theologian, enlightened by the past, confronts the problems of his own day."[6] Theology in its entirety, therefore, is never only about articulating past theological and ecclesial tradition. That exercise is only preliminary to the tasks of bringing the tradition to bear on the present cultural situation, evaluating its ongoing usefulness or non-usefulness in that situation, and handing on to the future either an unchanged, still-useful tradition or a tradition nuanced in dialogue with the present situation. Systematic theologians, in particular, in the second phase of the theological enterprise, offer an understanding of the past tradition which they hold to be true and, therefore, good in the present and soon-to-be-future cultural situation. In offering that understanding they allow their own voices, albeit linked to and shaped by the voice of the church, to speak in the present as John and Paul, Augustine and Aquinas, Leo and Pius spoke in the past.[7] In the theological understanding offered, the theologian uses both general cultural and special theological categories.

General cultural categories, like man, woman, gender, body, father, mother, king, symbol, myth, community, "regard objects that come within the purview of other disciplines as well as theology." Such categories are commonly used in the general enterprise of historico-cultural understanding. Special categories, like God, Spirit, Christ, revelation, incarnation, resurrection, kingdom of God, church, faith, grace, sin, sacrament, "regard the objects proper to theology."[8] They are used only in theology that seeks a comprehensive understanding of the historico-cultural matrix by seeking specifically an understanding of its supernatural dimension. It is precisely here, as an effort to understand the present matrix comprehensively, that theology can contribute, along with other disciplines, to an overall understanding of the present situation.

This focus on the present situation raises a word of warning about the theological method of correlation so prevalent in the twentieth century. In its best known and most influential formulation by Paul Tillich, "the method of correlation explains the contents of Christian faith through existential questions and theological answers in mutual interdependence."[9] Tillich's method of correlation involves a twofold analysis, an analysis of the present situation that results in the emergence of existential questions and an analysis of the Christian tradition that results in the emergence of answers to these questions. Therein lies the problem. This method does not permit genuine correlation, only juxtaposition, for Tillich privileges the theological tradition over the present situation. The questions all come from the present situation, the answers all come from the theological tradition, ignoring any answer developed by other disciplines in the situation. I agree with Tillich that a method of genuine correlation is essential for theology, but I cannot accept his method as the one. What is needed methodologically is a method of correlation in which the meanings of revelation as mediated by the symbols of the Christian tradition, and the meanings of human experience as mediated by contemporary symbols, are mutually and critically correlated in such a way that present experience illuminates the tradition and the tradition illuminates the present experience. In such mutual mediation the tradition and present situation mutually illuminate and critique one another, which seems to me more faithful to what has, in fact, happened in history.

Two Catholic theologians, David Tracy and Roger Haight, agree that theology must be correlational. Tracy argues that there are two sources for Christian theology, Christian texts and common human experience, and that there must be some way of correlating the results of the investigations of these two sources. He judges that although "Tillich's position continues to seem peculiarly helpful" it should be rejected, because his "method does not call for a critical correlation of the results of one's investigations of the 'situation' and the 'message.' "[10] Tracy insists, as have I, that such mutually critical correlation is necessary. Haight argues that "method in theology may be called a method of correlation." For Haight, the method of correlation is based on the distinction between what he calls original revelation and dependent revelation. "Original revelation lies at the source of the religious tradition and is codified in the scriptures. Dependent revelation is the ongoing communication and reception of revelation in the [religious] community."[11] He agrees in principle with Tracy that correlation means, first, distinguishing past theological tradition and present situation and, then, bringing them together in a mutually critical way that generates a present, perhaps new, understanding of the original revelation. The problem with such a methodical correlation is that it dichotomizes the tradition and the present situation, and it is precisely with this dichotomy that I disagree. In the present age, I believe, the socio-historical situation itself is essentially theological because it is essentially graced, an assertion that requires careful explication.

The special theological category, *grace,* is commonly used but not necessarily commonly understood. It has acquired secondary meanings in theological history, but its primary meaning derives from its scriptural source, where its meaning reduces to three main ideas: "condescending love, conciliatory compassion, and fidelity. The basic sense of Christian grace, whatever its later technical connotations, should always remind us that God first loved us."[12] The theologian known as John insists that this sums up the secret of grace: "in this is love, not that we loved God, but that God first loved us" (1 John 4:10). Grace is usually distinguished, as *uncreated* or operative grace, God giving Godself in love, and *created* or cooperative grace, the effect of this personal self-gift of God which transforms men, women, and their world. Grace, therefore, has two traditional theological meanings: first, God's self-giving to men and women[13] as cause and, second, a transformation produced in men and women who accept God's self-gift as effect. These two meanings are, of course, intimately related, but the exact nature of their relationship has been a matter for theological dispute.

In the Eastern Catholic tradition the idea of uncreated grace has dominated, created grace remaining a practically unknown concept. Even in the West there was no clear formulation of created grace for eleven hundred years.[14] The Reformation disputes, however, placed created grace so squarely in the forefront of theological discussion in the West, and post-Reformation Roman Catholic theology made it so much the primary reality of grace, that the use of the word "grace" without explanation came to mean created grace, a reality different from God. Uncreated grace, God's self-gift to men and women, ceased to be the source of created grace and, instead, became its consequence or necessary fruit. Created grace became the primary reality of grace, and was assumed to yield as one of its fruits the indwelling of God or uncreated grace. How may this Western view, in which a reality different from God yields the presence of God as its necessary consequence, be harmonized with the view of the scriptures and the fathers of the church, in which created grace appears as the consequence of God's prior self-communication to men and women? An effort to solve this thorny question has been made in modern theology, and has won wide acceptance.[15] It begins with a consideration of the relationship of the state of grace to the ultimate vision of God which the blessed enjoy in heaven.

It is common theological teaching in the West that in heavenly glory there is an intimate communion between God and the blessed. This communion is of an interpersonal kind, in that it is achieved in knowledge and love. Creaturely knowledge and love of God, however, are not achieved in the normal way, that is, mediately. Rather, God is immediately united to creatures and moves them to know and love God. This communion of God and human creatures in glory is of an ontological nature, that is, it is a union of *beings* before it is a union of conscious knowledge or love. In the vision of God in glory, creatures are ontologically assimilated to God before they reflexively know or love God. In fact, it is only *because* they are ontologically united to God that they can know and love God immediately, face to face. This analysis of the presence of God to creatures in heavenly glory is applied analogically to the question of how to articulate the presence of God to them in their human lives, that is, to the question of how to talk in human terms about the presence of uncreated grace. The communion between God and men and women in their earthly life is presented in the scriptures and in the tradition of the church as the seed and root of their union in heaven. Theologians, therefore, take the theory relating to the presence of God to creatures in heavenly glory, their being possessed by and their possession of God, and relate them to the presence of God as uncreated grace in human life.

God, uncreated grace, creates men and women and offers Godself to them at their creation. It is this offer, which is above and beyond the demands of their human nature, that Rahner characterizes as a supernatural elevation or supernatural existential.[16] In this theory, men and women live always and everywhere in an economy of grace; they live in a radically graced world. Creation is but the beginning of grace, in which God creates creatures, dwells in and with them as uncreated grace, and draws them into personal, loving, self-transforming relationship. As in heaven, so also in human lives God dwells in creatures prior to their personally knowing or loving God (John 14:23; 1 John 2:6, 24, 27–28; 3:6, 24; 4:12–16; 1 Cor 6:19; Rom 5:5; 8:9–16; Gal 4:6; 1 Thess 4:8). The presence of God, of uncreated, operative grace, is not a consequence of the transformation in men and women that is called created or cooperative grace, but rather a cause of it. The transformation called created grace exists only when God is actually present and acting to transform.

This, then, raises the question: If men and women live in a fundamentally graced world, what is the specific contribution of Christian symbols to the living of a life of grace, a life of relationship with God? The answer is not difficult to find if we reflect anthropologically on the place of symbols in human lives. Boy, for instance, meets girl; boy and girl fall in love; boy  loves girl and girl loves boy. There is only one problem: it is not concretely obvious to the boy that the girl loves him. He does not recognize the love for him that is really in her, nor does she recognize the love for her that is in him until they *make love* in some symbolic action of loving. When they do make love, their mutual love is drawn into personal, concrete realization, and thereafter their relationship is one of ever-growing love to the extent that they continue to make love in the symbols with which their culture provides them. The case of God's self-communication to creatures coming to consciousness by being concretized in symbols parallels the case of the love between one human being and another.

Uncreated grace, the loving self-gift of God to all men and women, exists long prior to any symbolic, sacramental action. Every man and woman created by God is enveloped in grace, for grace "is God himself in his forgiving and divinizing love."[17] Because of this offered uncreated grace, history for every created person is a history of hidden grace and possible salvation, quite apart from any "religious" activity. As with the boy who does not concretely recognize the girl's love for him, however, so neither do men and women always concretely recognize the presence of the God who is Grace. To realize the possibility of grace, they need to *make grace*, as the boy and the girl need to make love, in some symbolic action. Religious symbols, though they are not the exclusive ways to make grace, are nevertheless established ways to make grace. When men and women engage in religious action, they proclaim and make concrete not only grace as offered by God but also grace as accepted by them. The gracious offer of God and the faithful acceptance of that offer by believers, in and through symbolic or sacramental actions, make grace. The primary grace which is made is the acknowledged presence of God; the consequence of God's acknowledged presence and action, the saving transformation of men and women known in the special theological category of created or co-operative grace, is secondary.

If this theological analysis of grace is accepted, the conclusion is the judgment that initiated this excursus: the present situation is itself essentially theological because it is essentially graced. When grace is understood as *uncreated* grace, God offering Godself in loving relationship to every woman and man at creation, there is no ungraced human being or no ungraced human situation. When grace is understood as *created* grace, the ontological transformation achieved in humans by their loving relationship with God, there are graced human beings and graced human situations only when free men and women freely accept and cooperate with God's offer of Godself.[18] Uncreated grace is always offered to men and women for their free acceptance and cooperation; it is never forced upon them. Here I agree with John Milbank: "without an acknowledgment of the supernatural our account of reality is incomplete."[19] Any method of correlation which treats the theological tradition and the present situation as completely dichotomous does not comprehensively understand either the tradition or the present situation. Since God as grace is active in both tradition and present situation, both demand an analysis that opens up a mutually dialogical and critical mediation that enables the tradition to be meaningful in both the present and the coming future situation. The future situation is described by the theological tradition as a situation more aligned to the special biblical category of the kingdom of God. I will return briefly to theology and that kingdom in a moment.

I agree entirely with all those theologians who argue in their different ways that theology has two sources, a past theological tradition and a present historical situation and that, to develop authentically, theology requires a method that correlates the two. Since, however, tradition and situation are both essentially theological, I cannot agree with those who see that correlation as a correlation of dichotomous sources. Understanding the tradition, as Lonergan has so well explained, is ultimately only *oratio obliqua,* what John, Paul, Augustine, and Aquinas have said. Systematic theology is and must be *oratio recta,* a statement by the present-day theologian of what she or he judges in faith to be true and good, not only on the basis of what John, Paul, Augustine, and Aquinas have said in the past but also on the basis of the discernment of the present situation. Such systematic theology, in Robert Doran's formulation, "is not a correlation of the categories appropriate to the tradition with the categories adequate to the situation, but an understanding of the realities named by both special and general categories, as these realities determine both the tradition and the two situations, the one to be addressed and the one to be evoked."[20] Given that the general category *correlation* has accumulated so many historical accretions, I will eschew it in this book and replace it with another category, *mediation*. Systematic theology, understood as *oratio recta,* requires more of the theologian than just an objective, historical, neutral understanding of the past. It requires the subjective, actual, conscious investment of the theologian as subject, and to that I will return in the final section of this introduction.

Because the present situation is always, in part, theological, theology is necessarily one discipline involved in its comprehensive and evaluative understanding. Because there are other dimensions of the situation beyond the theological, theology is "but one dimension, albeit an essential and foundational one, in a more comprehensive, scholarly, scientific, and evaluative understanding of human cultures."[21] I would make one addition to the adjectives describing understanding in the preceding citation, the addition of the category *transformative*. The function of authentic Christian theology, one that follows the biblical injunction of Jesus, whom it confesses as the Christ, that "not every one who *says* to me 'Lord, Lord' shall enter the kingdom of heaven, but the one who *does* the will of my Father who is in heaven" (Matt 7:21), is not only to provide comprehensive understanding of the present situation but also to transform it into a future situation more approximating the kingdom or rule of God. That transformative agency can only begin proximately with individual believers, by whose agency, in turn, it is spread to transform ecclesial and, ultimately, cultural values. It is as such a transforming agent that systematic theology becomes eminently practical, a "theological discipline which is concerned with the church's self-actualization here and now — both that which *is* and that which *ought to be.*"[22]

## Sociology

We now turn to a consideration of the other discipline involved in the dialogical and dialectical mediation under discussion in this book, namely, sociology. What is to be presented here is to be understood as a brief introductory sketch; the detail is provided in the following two chapters. Whenever we see the suffix "-logy" we know we are dealing with a discipline that is considered a science, that is, a branch of study that discovers causes

and facts and orders them in principles and theories. For those who understand the classicist culture introduced in the Prologue, in which "science"
was an important consideration, a caveat arises here. In classicist culture,
science was held to be certain knowledge of things through their four causes,
end, agent, matter, and form. That is not the case with modern science. It
attends more to empirical data than to things, to correlations rather than to
causes, and it claims to lead not to certainty but to probability. In contrast to
beliefs accepted in faith, modern science proceeds according to the scientific
method, a method rooted in replicable experiment and empirical evidence.
Auguste Comte, who coined the term "sociology" in the nineteenth century,
wanted sociology to be a science in this sense so that, by discovering the
laws governing human society, humans would be able to shape their own
destiny, much as modern science has allowed them to master and control the
natural world of things. I have already hinted at a fact that will be explicated
in detail in the following two chapters, namely, sociology is not that kind
of hard science; it is a soft science. There is broad, general agreement, however, that sociology is a science, a search for social facts and patterns, based
on a scientific method that is rooted in replicable experiment and empirical
evidence, not in faith or ideology.

Sociology is generally defined as "the scientific study of society."[23] Society itself is a system of institutionalized patterns of belief and behavior that
occur and recur across large spans of time and space. There are a multi-
tude of such institutionalized patterns in a society, but the major ones are
usually listed as family, education, economics, politics, and religion. The
general definition, then, may be further specified by specifying the realities that sociology studies. Sociology is "a social science having as its main
focus the study of the social institutions brought into being by the industrial
transformations of the past two or three centuries."[24] Since those industrial
transformations have created what we know today as contemporary society
or civilization, then sociology may be further defined as "the study of man
and society that seeks to determine their general characteristics, especially
as found in contemporary civilizations."[25] Sociology studies societies and
the individuals who comprise them, and it studies them to discover their
recurring social facts and patterns. It may be either theoretical or empirical.
Theoretical sociology provides abstract scientific theories and hypotheses
that enable people to understand their society more surely than they would
by using everyday common sense. Empirical sociology conducts research
into individuals and groups to provide relevant empirical data from which
factual conclusions may be drawn. The data provided by both theoretical
and empirical sociology may be used for the practical purpose of solving the

social problems of society. Hence Comte's famous formula: *prévoir pour pouvoir,* to predict is to control.

An obvious first dimension to the study of society is the men, women, and children who make up society; in the abstract, the individual in society. Under this heading, sociology studies culture, socialization, the self, and social groups. For sociologists, culture is "a way of life shared by a group, a system of ideas, values, beliefs, knowledge, and custom transmitted from generation to generation within a social group."[26] You remember Lonergan's definition: "the set of meanings and values that inform a way of life."[27] Men and women do all sorts of things: we know, we feel, we get exhilarated or depressed, we choose a mate, we marry, we have children, we drive our children to school, we work, we go to the sea or the mountains or the desert. We do all these things without too much thought — quite "naturally," we say — but still the question arises: why do we do those things and not others? The sociological answer to that question is revealing.

We do those things and we avoid others because we have written into us a cultural story. That story tells us who we are, what we are like, what the world is like, what beyond the world is like. It tells us what we must value and strive for, both in the world and beyond the world. When we do anything "good," we do it in accord with our story; when we do anything "bad," we do it in contravention of our story. We cannot do even the most insignificant things without imagining, at least implicitly, what reality is like, where and how I fit in that reality, and what really matters within that reality. The cultural story is learned in the simplest of ways: by being born into a particular human society and being raised and socialized to live in that society. The American learns and enacts the American story; the Iraqi learns and enacts the Iraqi story; the Buddhist learns and enacts the Buddhist story. None of this is to be understood to suggest that every single individual in America or Iraq or every Buddhist thinks the same way about everything; societies are too varied and complex for that to be true. It means only that most of the people most of the time in America share an American story which they have learned in the process of being inculturated or socialized into the American story.

Socialization names the process in and by which an individual becomes a participating member of a culture and society. Since culture is carried and transmitted in a variety of symbols, physical realities which stand for crucial abstract realities and meanings, we can say that socialization names the process in and by which individuals are imbued with a set of symbols and their correlative meanings, accept those symbols as adequate articulations of reality, and enact those symbols in their everyday lives. The meanings learned in the process of socialization are powerful meanings because they are socially validated, institutional meanings. That means they are widely known, accepted, and applied; they are enforced by strong social sanctions; they are based on sources of authority that are revered; they are deeply internalized in individual psyches; they are inculcated and reinforced early in life; they are objects of prevalent and consistent conformity. These culturally and socially transmitted meanings are not optional if one wants to live in this particular society; they are mandatory. Action contrary to the transmitted cultural story will result in social isolation, alienation, and condemnation of the individual as deviant. Such alienation, as Karl Marx so powerfully showed, leads to self-destruction.

It would be a mistake to assume that socialization is always an intentional instructional process. The cultural story that explains the way things are and how they came to be that way is not told all at once. Rather, it is "ambient"[28] in the culture. Explanations are assembled bit by bit like a jigsaw puzzle from a million and more bits of information provided in a million and more ways by others who share the story. They are provided by parents, educators, economists, politicians, theologians, books, television, movies, Sunday schools, news media, children's cartoons, and a million and more others. The ambient story is absorbed as much by human osmosis as by intellectual explanation, and once it is absorbed it is uncritically enacted as true. Indeed, it is enacted to be made true. Because *our* cultural story is embraced and enacted as true, all others are rejected as necessarily false.

If the perception of reality and truth is as culturally dependent as I have indicated, and a myriad disciplines today agree with sociology that it is, an inevitable question arises: which cultural story of the way things are, and how they got to be the way they are, is the objective and true story? Common sense dictates that, in any real situation, something is the same for every normal observer. Common sense, however, which will differ to a degree from culture to culture as a result of different socialization, does not, because it cannot, explain in what way that sameness is to be understood. The whole world, for instance, watched Nazis herd millions of people, Jews, Gypsies, homosexuals, and others into gas chambers. In the cultural story being enacted by Nazis this action was perceived as purification of the race; in other cultural stories in the watching world, it was perceived as murder of the innocent; and we can only guess how the herded people perceived it as they waited for the gas. For all three groups, the action is generally the "same," the herding of people into gas chambers. But, again for all three groups, the perception of the way things are is specifically different because the cultural stories they were enacting caused them to interpret the same action in radically different ways. Men and women in society are always enmeshed in situations which they themselves define. It is utterly futile to attempt to point out to committed actors the so-called "objective" truth of the situation. Nazis herded people to their deaths to objectively purify the race, the rest of the world called it objectively murder, and the people waiting for death probably also called it murder, or perhaps they judged it objectively meaningless and beyond understanding within their cultural stories.

However any given individual may have judged the situation, sociologists argue that their various judgments are not as objective as any of them would like to claim. Because of the double involvement of human actors alluded to at the opening of this chapter, human judgments are, at best, only partially objective; they are also partially subjective and social. It is not some abstract ontological structure that defines reality and truth for men and women, but the meanings assigned to the structure by human actors socialized into a culture and society. Theodore Roszak has argued, cogently and correctly, that objective knowledge is in the general category of mythology. "It is an arbitrary construct in which a given society in a given historical situation has invested its sense of meaningfulness and value."[29] Objective knowledge represents a human construct in which a particular society embodies its sense of meaning about women and men, about the world in which they live, about values, about the great mystery that lies beyond the world immediately known to humans. Objective knowledge is more properly called, in terms to be explained in a moment, objectivated knowledge. It derives not exclusively from some ontological structure of reality but also from a human cultural system socially externalized into objectivated meaning. Human beings are essentially in the construction business, the construction of objective reality out of internalized social reality.

Physical reality exists independently of any human activity; human reality does not. Human reality, which always has a correlative dimension of meaning, is a human product and nothing but a human product, a point that will be discussed in detail in chapter 3. However objective it may look, it has no status of reality or truth apart from the human activity that created it and sustains it. This reality, a human product, then acts back upon the humans who produced it to control them. Following Karl Mannheim, Peter Berger and Thomas Luckmann argue that the double involvement or dialectic between men, women, and society has three moments: a moment of externalization, a moment of objectivation, and a moment of internalization.[30] Men and women do not have a relationship to the world around them. They have to establish one and, as they create that relationship, they also create both a meaningful world and themselves as meaningful within that world. The world they create is called culture, the ideas, values, beliefs, customs that are meaningful, the people, things, and events that are shrouded in symbols and make everyday life possible. Culture, then, is an externalized product of human creative activity.

To speak of culture as an externalized product of human activity is already to suggest it has a certain autonomy with respect to its creators. Berger and Luckmann name the process by which human products are transformed into realities that not only derive from human activity, but also confront their human creators as objective realities outside of them, objectivation. The human product becomes something out there in the world, an object that cannot easily be wished away, something that takes on the status of objective reality. The objectivity of the material products of human activity is easily grasped. Men and women build a house, bake a cake, paint a picture, knit a sweater, and by their action increase the sum of physical objects which confront them in the world as outside of and independent of them. The objectivity of the non-material products is just as real but not as easily grasped. Men and women construct a language and then find that their perception of reality and their process of communication is controlled by that language and the rules they have made for it. They construct and prioritize values and then feel guilty when they do not live by those values. They fashion institutions, stable systems of meanings, which then confront them as powerful, objective forces in the external world apart from their human activity. Institutions such as family, education, politics, economics, religion; meaning systems such as common sense, mythology, art, science; roles and identities such as male, female, son, daughter, theologian, teacher, scientist; all these are apprehended as real and objective phenomena in the world apart from human activity, though both they and the social world which legitimates them have no existence apart from human activity.

Human consciousness, then, is confronted by the objectivated products of human activity. Internalization names the process of reabsorption of these objectivations into human consciousness in such a way that the structures of the objectivated world determine the structures of consciousness itself. Human products, which need not be enumerated again, function as the formative elements of human consciousness. To the extent that internalization has successfully taken place, the individual apprehends the elements of the objectivated world as phenomena of both the external world and the internal world of consciousness. Every society faces the problem of communicating its objectivated meanings and realities to the next generation, a task which each accomplishes in the process we have already termed socialization. This threefold social process of externalization, objectivation, and internalization raises what is for many an ugly specter, the specter, namely, of the relativity of human meaning, reality, and truth.

If you have followed the foregoing theoretical-sociological analysis, you will not doubt that human truth is relational — to a particular group of human beings who create a particular set of meanings which, in turn, fashion a particular province of meaning. This last phrase is derived from Alfred Schutz, one of the theorists in whom the sociology of knowledge is rooted. Schutz argues that "it is the meaning of our experiences and not the ontological structure of the objects which constitute [human] reality."[31] I shall leave any detailed explication of this assertion to chapter 3. For the moment, I wish to underscore two things: to say that human truth is relational is to say only that it is true in relation to a particular province of meaning; it is not to insinuate anything about its truth or falsity. To say that truth is *relational* is more correct than to say it is *relative,* for relational merely points out that it is of the nature of human truth to derive from a humanly generated province of meaning rather than from a totally objective or ontological reality. It makes no judgment whatsoever about its ultimate truth or falsity, which is what makes many people uncomfortable about the word "relative."

When we have shown the origin of a human statement, we have done just that, shown its origin. We have asserted or insinuated nothing about its truth or falsity. To assume that, because it makes sense only in this province of meaning, a statement is automatically false is to be guilty of the generic fallacy. The judgment of truth or falsity is a separate judgment from the judgment of origin. At most, illuminating the origin of a human assertion of truth might raise the suspicion that it represents only a partial point of view, which needs to be dialogically and dialectically open to other points of view to achieve a more complete view of the truth of the matter in question. An analogy may help. A man at a first-story window gets a first-story perspective on the landscape outside the window; a man at a tenth-story window gets a tenth-story perspective. The issue is not how to get a perspective-free view of the landscape, for that is not possible, but to realize that each view is a perspective and that, by juxtaposing different perspectives, a more complete, panoramic view of the landscape can be achieved. Perspective is not in itself a source of error. It is, rather, a source of truth, albeit of relational, not absolute, truth.

So far in this section, I have been considering a theoretical and abstract kind of sociology. There is another kind, more concrete, more obviously empirical, perhaps more accessible to the uninitiated. It is the empirical research side of sociology. Every scientific inquiry has two notable aspects: first, a prior theoretical explanation of the question at hand, which leads to the formation of certain hypotheses; second, empirical research which is controlled observation to see if the hypotheses are verified or falsified. Lonergan states the empirical principle at work in scientific research this way: "there are no true factual judgments without a foundation in relevant data."[32] This principle is easily illustrated. The Greek philosopher Aristotle, among the greatest thinkers who ever lived, wrote about many matters, including what we call today physics. All Aristotle knew about physics, however, he knew from pure reasoning, not from experimentation, and experimentation was needed to verify or falsify the hypotheses he arrived at by pure reason. Aristotle hypothesized that the speed of a falling object was determined by its weight divided by the resistance of the air through which it fell, a judgment which is shared intuitively by modern golfers playing in what they call a "heavy" atmosphere. But, alas poor golfers, both they and Aristotle are wrong. Some nineteen hundred years after Aristotle, Galileo stood on top of the baptistery tower in Pisa, dropped light and heavy objects, and discovered, contrary to Aristotle's hypothesis, that they landed at almost the same time. Empirical experiment forced Aristotle's hypothesis to be changed and, some years later still, further experiment led to Newton's law of gravity. In modern science, both physical and social, the empirical principle rules.

The social science of sociology shares in this empirical principle. It conducts studies of individuals and groups, in environments carefully controlled by the researcher, to discover relevant data from which factual conclusions may be drawn. Sociologists are not like physicists: they do not peer through electron microscopes, or measure the distance between neighboring stars, or drop heavy objects from the baptistery tower of Pisa. They do, however, share with physicists the purpose of discovering and explaining relationships between a variety of variables, which may or may not be dependent one on the other, and on the basis of what they find they further seek to make generalizations that apply to entire classes. As Galileo did not seek to discover the rate at which only these particular weights fell from the tower of Pisa but how all weights would fall from it, the sociologist seeks to discover the impact, for instance, of divorce not only on this particular couple but also on all couples.

To achieve such representativeness, the sociologist-researchers must take care that the cases they study are typical of the whole class of similar cases about which they want to generalize. To put it another way, the sample they choose to actually study must be representative of the entire population about which they want to learn and generalize. The most common way to achieve the desired representativeness is to construct a random sample, one in which every individual in the population to be studied, and indeed every combination of individuals, has an equal chance of being selected for study. Random samples can be constructed, for instance, by getting the names of everyone in the population to be studied and then using some random device for selecting individuals for the sample. Everything else being equal, the larger the sample the more confidence the researcher can have that the results will approximate the true patterns of the entire population to be studied, though an authentically randomized sample of two thousand persons will yield accurate statistical patterns for a population of ten thousand or ten million. In the end, however, what must always be remembered, is that the result of sociological research is the same as the result of all scientific research, namely, probability and not absoluteness. Statistical rules inform the researcher about the level of probability.

There are canonized rules for scientific research. I paraphrase from Jerry Rose the rules that apply to sociological research.[33] A first rule, in terms of the integrity of the research an essential rule, is that the researcher must have freedom from pressure to have his research findings conform to the presuppositions or desires of people who can reward or punish him for his work. The researcher must be free to find what he finds, not what his employers or financial sponsors want him to find. A second common rule is that the freedom and privacy of the individuals in the study sample must be fully respected. This is usually achieved by asking for their informed consent, by assuring them of complete confidentiality, and by never revealing their names in any report of the research. A third rule is that the description and explanation of human behavior deriving from research should be in the most general and abstract terms. This rule is simply the specification of what was argued earlier about sociology as a *generalizing* social science. The researcher wants to know, not only about this or that particular divorced couple but about all divorced couples. A fourth rule is that the observations made in the course of sociological investigation must be reliable and valid representations of the data related to the matter under investigation. The key terms in this rule are the terms "reliable," which refers to a research method which can yield the information sought and can be replicated either by the researcher herself or by any other researcher, and "valid," which refers to statements that are accurate representations of the sociological "facts." Following our discussion of the importance of sampling, a fifth rule is that the researcher's generalizations must be based on representative samples of the population under study. A sixth and final rule states that, in explaining why and how things happen in society, the sociologist must take account of the simultaneous operation of the variety of social forces operating in society. These forces are usually distinguished in a research project as either independent variables, which are assumed to be the cause of whatever is uncovered, and dependent variables, which depend on the independent variable and are assumed to be its effects.

## The Subject

At the opening of this chapter I presented the distinction between classicist and empirical culture. The classicist notion of culture is static. There is
but one culture that is universal, permanent, and objective, and it is to be
learned. The empirical notion of culture is dynamic. It is the set of meanings
and values that inform a way of life, it may be in the process of development or dissolution, and it is to be created in an ongoing, historical process.
The empirical notion of culture developed within the modern frameworks
of historical consciousness and experimental science. Traditional Catholic
theology prior to the Second Vatican Council was at odds with this modern
framework; it was enclosed within the classicist framework, it was universal, permanent, objective, and to be learned. That explains its evident lack
of creativity. One of the achievements of Bernard Lonergan was to point
the way beyond this classicist-rooted theology to a historically conscious,
empirical, dialectical, and critical theology. "It may be lamented, of course,
that some recent Roman Catholic theology seems determined to live in a
world that no longer exists,"[34] but I forego that lamentation and choose the
way forward Lonergan has marked in detail.

From René Descartes onward, modern European philosophy was progressively turning away from the position of true knowledge as entirely
objective to a position that assigned more importance in knowledge to the
knowing subject. Lonergan brilliantly completed that project in his densely
magisterial *Insight*.[35] There I am asked to affirm of myself that I am a
knower, a conscious unity, identity, whole whose consciousness unfolds on
four intimately interconnected levels: an empirical level on which I sense,
perceive, and imagine data that are presented to me; an intelligent level
on which I inquire into the sense data, grasp an intelligibility immanent in
and emergent from the data, come to understand, and formulate my understanding; a rational level on which I reflect, marshal the evidence, and pass
judgment on the truth or falsity, certainty or probability, of my understanding; a responsible level on which I deliberate about possible courses of action,
evaluate them, make a decision and carry it out.[36]

All of these operations are transitive, they have objects: I sense something, understand something, judge something to be true, decide something.
All are also operations of an operator, who is named subject in two senses:
first, in the sense that the operator is the subject of verbs, *I* sense, *I* understand, *I* judge, *I* decide; secondly, in the sense that the operator operates
consciously. As I sense, understand, and judge, I am conscious of myself as
a subject sensing, understanding, and judging. "As operations by their inten-
tionality make objects present to the subject, so also by consciousness they

make the operating subject present to himself."[37] The human subject's operations in the process of knowing yield transcendentals. "If we objectify the
content of intelligible intending, we form the transcendental concept of the
intelligible. If we objectify the content of reasonable intending, we form the
transcendental concepts of the true and the real. If we objectify the content
of responsible intending, we get the transcendental concept of value, of the
truly good."[38] To reach these transcendentals, I must conscientiously follow
the transcendental imperatives: be attentive, be intelligent, be rational, be
decisive. A fifth imperative, be in love, will be introduced once the notion
of conversion has been considered.

Horizon is an important category in Lonergan's philosophy and theology.
In its general use, it denotes the line at which the earth and the sky appear
to meet, the outer limit of physical vision. Horizon is not fixed. It moves as
I move, either receding in front of me or encroaching behind me. It is determined by my standpoint and, in turn, determines what I can and cannot see.
"Beyond the horizon lie the objects that, at least for the moment, cannot be
seen. Within the horizon lie the objects that can now be seen."[39] Physical
horizon provides an easy analogy for the personal horizon of knowledge.
What lies within my personal horizon is, to a greater or lesser degree, an
object of interest and of knowledge: I can be attentive to it, understand it,
make a judgment about its truth, make a decision about it. What lies outside
my horizon lies outside the range of my interest and knowledge. Even more
than the physical horizon, the personal horizon of knowledge is a standpoint, the product of both past socialization and individual achievement, at
once the condition and the limitation of further development In the sociological words of the preceding section, personal horizon is a human product,
and different products, different horizons, different provinces of meaning as
I have already called them, may be opposed dialectically. An understanding,
a judgment, and a decision that is intelligible and true in one horizon may
be quite unintelligible and false in another. As I have the freedom to move
within a horizon, so also do I have the freedom to move from one horizon
to another. This move from one horizon to another is what Lonergan means
by conversion.

Conversion, the movement from one horizon to another, may be either
intellectual, moral, or religious. Intellectual conversion is "the elimination of
an exceedingly stubborn and misleading myth concerning reality, objectivity,
and knowledge. The myth is that knowing is like looking, that objectivity
is seeing what is out there to be seen and not seeing what is not there, and
that the real is what is out there to be looked at."[40] This myth confuses the
physical world of sensation, the sum of what is experientially seen, heard,
touched, tasted, smelled, with the world mediated by meaning, which is a

world known, not by the act of sensation alone, but by the cognitive process of sensation, understanding, and judgment. Knowing is not seeing, hearing, touching, tasting, smelling; it is sensing, understanding, and judging. Until the moment of judgment that understanding is true or false, there is no true knowledge. The myth that is to be clarified and eliminated has many possible consequences. It can lead to naive realism, thinking that the world of meaning can be known simply by looking at it, thinking that I achieve true knowledge simply by looking at and learning what Paul or John, Augustine or Aquinas, Pius IX or John Paul II, Durkheim, or Weber or Marx, said and wrote. Once intellectually converted from this prevalent myth, I come to understand that knowing is not only sensing but also understanding and judging. I come to understand that what Augustine or John Paul or Marx state is only *oratio obliqua,* a first step in the process of my coming to know, to be followed by *oratio recta,* my own understanding and judgment, not only of what was said but also, and especially, of what is true. This converted horizon is what Lonergan means by critical realism.

Conversion may be also either moral or religious. Following judgment in the process of knowing is the decision about what to do. Moral conversion "changes the criterion of one's decisions and choices from satisfactions to values."[41] Moral conversion involves progressively understanding the present situation, exposing and eradicating both my individual and society's bias, constantly evaluating and re-evaluating my scale of preferred values, paying attention to criticism and protest, and listening to others. Neither one instance of moral conversion nor one moral decision leads to moral perfection, for after one conversion there remains the possibility of either relapse or another conversion and after moral decision there is still required moral action. Conversion is not to be conceived as a one-off moment but as an on-going process. Religious conversion "is being grasped by ultimate concern. It is other-worldly falling in love. It is total and permanent self-surrender without conditions, qualifications, reservations."[42] In Christian terms, religious conversion is falling in love with God; it is the gift of grace, both operative and cooperative. Robert Doran, Lonergan's most authentic and creative interpreter, has beautifully described the love that is religious conversion. "Love alone releases one to be creatively self-transcendent. It is love that reveals values we would not otherwise see, commands commitments, dissolves bias, breaks the bonds of psychological and social determinisms, and so conditions the very emergence of the creative capacities for insight, judgment, and decision. The self-transcendence of intelligent, reasonable, responsible persons becomes a way of life . . . only to the extent that we are in love."[43] When we are in love, especially with God, a new principle takes over, life begins anew, and love becomes the all-controlling horizon.

Doran has also argued that there is an important dimension of individual interiority in addition to Lonergan's intellectual, moral, and religious dimensions, namely, the dimension which modern depth psychology calls the psyche. He has, therefore, called also for psychic conversion. For Doran, the notion of psychic conversion is postulated by the resources of depth psychology, particularly that of Jung, which aid the clarification of the human subject, particularly that subject who is so central in this book and who is the foundational reality in all theological endeavor, namely, the theologian. If Lonergan's cognitive analysis moves the individual to be authentically attentive, intelligent, rational, and responsible, so also does depth psychology move him to be fully self-conscious and to choose consciously an authentic life direction. Psychic conversion is required for self-directed self-consciousness. It is, in depth psychology terms, a "transformation of the psychic component of what Freud calls the 'censor' from a repressive to a constructive agency in a person's development."[44] The psyche is the locus of imagination, insight, understanding, judgment, and decision, and also the locus of the restrictive and oppressive forces which limit our imagination, insight, and understanding and from which we need to be released by conversion. Psychic conversion is a reorientation of the omnipresent psychic censor from the exercise of a repressive function to the exercise of a constructive function over the self-direction of my own personal development. Such conversion, with which Lonergan at least twice expressed his agreement,[45] frees subjects to engage unfettered in the construction of a fully human world and themselves within that world.

The final question for this chapter is an obvious one: what does any of this have to do with theology or sociology? The answer is as sweeping as the question: everything. The intentional operations of seeing, hearing, touching, smelling, tasting, inquiring, imagining, understanding, reflecting, judging, evaluating, deciding, discerning are the operations of a subject-operator. When the operations are about theological data, the subject is operating as a theologian; when they are about sociology, the subject is operating as a sociologist. Theologians are simply specific cases of the persons we have been talking about in general; and, to attain the theological true and real, they have to be attentive, intelligent, rational, and responsible. Since, however, their theological imagining, understanding, judging, and deciding is as restricted by their horizons as any other individual, they are in constant need of conversion. Theologians are in need of intellectual conversion, movement from the prevalent myth that objective knowledge is simply looking carefully at something to the realization that knowledge is sensing, understanding, and judging. They are in need of moral conversion, movement from making decisions on the basis of personal or ecclesial satisfactions to making them on the basis of a set of evaluated and decided values. They are in need of religious conversion, movement away from human love to the unconditional love of God and to all that the God they believe in stands for in the human world. They are in need of psychic conversion, liberation from the repressive censor that limits their access to insights the censor does not want them to have access.

Intellectually, morally, religiously, and psychically converted theologians will have different images, insights, understandings, judgments, and decisions than unconverted theologians. They will do theology, research, interpretation, history, dialectic, foundations, doctrines, systematics, communications, differently. Theology produced by converted theologians will be different from theology produced by unconverted theologians. Converted theologians will not know for sure whether their converted theology or their opponents' unconverted theology is true theology, but they will be open to dialogue with others, to be convinced by them in debate if need be, to further conversion. In special theological categories, converted theologians will be open to the impulses of the Spirit of God, to the instantiations and negations of the reign of God in the world, to the possibilities of ever more approximating the biblical reign of God in the affairs of the world. The converted theologian will be a free human being, freely, consciously, responsibly exercising the task to which he is called, the task of the Christian theologian. Over the centuries, converted theologians have, on many occasions, converted also the ecclesial theology and tradition of the church, as I shall show in chapter 7. I defer examination of the relationship of sociology and the converted theologian to the next chapter.

## Conclusion

This chapter has been an introduction to theology, sociology, and the human subjects who pursue them to achieve converted understandings of themselves, their world, and the Mystery-God some confess as the Creator of the world and all that is in it. It is to be understood not only as theology and sociology *in oratione obliqua,* not only what John and Paul, Augustine and Aquinas, Comte, Durkheim, and Weber said in the past, but also as theology and sociology *in oratione recta,* what the author, who in this case is both theologian and social scientist, says in the present as he confronts actual situations with the accumulated wisdom of the past. This direct theological and sociological speech provide's an answer to Baxter's legitimate question: "Whose Theology? Which Sociology?"[46] The answer in this book is "the author's."

The theology presented here is a theology that "mediates between a cultural matrix and the significance and role of a religion in that matrix."[47] It is disciplined, methodological reflection on two intimately related dimensions of reality: the self-communication of God to humankind and the cultural matrix in which Christians specifically relate to God, the created world, themselves in that world, and the socio-historical forces which generate progress and decline in that world. Such theological reflection embraces a twofold mediation, of the past theological tradition to the present socio-historical matrix, and of the present matrix to the past theological tradition, with a view to fostering a theological and social future that better approximates the kingdom or rule of God in the world. The theological reflection that takes place in this chapter and throughout this book seeks to be transformative, therefore, of the present ecclesial, theological, and social situations. It is concerned not only with what *is* in the present situation but also with what *ought to be*.

The sociology presented in this chapter is also to be understood as transformative. Though I do not subscribe fully to Comte's ancient formula, *prévoir pour pouvoir*, to predict is to control, I do believe that to understand the human context more fully puts one in a better position for making factual judgments about what ought to be both theologically and ecclesially. The idea of sociology operative in this book conceives it as "the study of man and society that seeks to determine their general characteristics."[48] It is either theoretical or empirical. Theoretical sociology provides abstract theories and analyses which enable men and women to understand more fully the social facts and patterns in their society in general and in the present social matrix in particular. The theoretical sociology presented in this chapter and throughout this book is a sociology that highlights the double involvement of humans and human institutions, an involvement that means that humans create and recreate society and are created and recreated by it, a mutual process that unfolds in three steps of objectivation, externalization, and internalization. That social process, which creates a social story that is then enacted to be made true, has important implications for theologians and their theologies. Empirical sociology conducts scientific research into individuals, groups, and societies to provide factual data from which factual conclusions, including theological and ecclesial conclusions, may be drawn. Empirical sociology also has important implications for theologians to the degree that it illuminates what *is* on the basis of which the theologian may reflect on what factually *ought to be*. Empirical sociology will feature prominently in the concluding chapter of the book.

The final movement in this chapter was a consideration of the human subject who knows, whether she be theologian, sociologist, hard scientist, or busy mother of a family. Following Lonergan, the human knower was presented as a conscious unity, identity, and whole whose consciousness unfolds on four intimately connected levels: an empirical level on which I sense and imagine data presented to me; an intelligent level, on which I inquire into the data, come to understand it, and formulate my understanding of it; a rational level on which I reflect, marshal the evidence, and pass judgment on the truth or falsity, certainty or probability, of my understanding; a responsible level on which I deliberate about possible courses of action, evaluate them, make a decision, and enact it. No matter what John or Paul, Augustine or Aquinas, Durkheim, Weber, or Marx said, I know nothing until I have reached the level of judgment that what they said is true or false, and only then can I enact a responsible decision. My knowing creates for me a personal horizon akin to the physical horizon. The physical horizon marks the outer limit of my vision; what lies within the horizon I can see, what lies beyond it I cannot see. So it is with my personal horizon. What lies within my personal horizon is of interest and can be known; what lies outside it cannot be of interest or be known. Neither physical nor personal horizon is fixed; both move as I move, either receding in front of me or encroaching behind me. I can move from horizon to horizon. The movement from personal horizon to personal horizon Lonergan calls conversion, a notion which will be important throughout this book, for the converted theologian will produce a theology that is different from that of the unconverted theologian. The use of sociology in what follows has as its end the conversion of theologians, who will then both embrace and enact a different theological and ecclesial story. To that end we move forward.

## Questions for Discussion

1. The traditional definition of theology, "faith seeking understanding," needs to be carefully unpacked for full understanding. What do you think of Lonergan's way of unpacking it? How do you personally unpack it?

2. How do you understand the difference between uncreated grace and created grace? What does it mean to you to claim that the social situation is always also a graced and, therefore, theological situation?

3. If a broad definition of sociology is "the scientific study of society," what concrete things would sociology study? What are the broad divisions of the science of sociology?

4. What do you understand by the sociology of knowledge's claim that human meaning and reality are socially constructed? What are the implications of this claim in general? What are its implications specifically for theology?

5. What is the distinction between objective and subjective knowledge? Where do you personally stand in this distinction? Where would you stand if intellectually converted in Lonergan's meaning of the word?

TWO

# Theology and Sociology: Mutual Mediations

## Radical Orthodoxy

This chapter is about the mutual and mutually critical mediations between theology and sociology introduced in the opening chapter. There can be no talk of such mediations today, by either theologian or social scientist, without consideration of John Milbank's damning rejection of all mediation in his *Theology and Social Theory*.[1] That, therefore, is where we begin. Milbank stands in bold opposition to every modern and postmodern effort to delineate a place, called "the secular," which is free from divine purpose. He argues that, since all human reality is governed by the vocation to fellowship with God, there is no such place, and that the person oriented to God, indeed the Christian person oriented to God in Christ, is the fully real person.[2]

Following Maurice Blondel, a Milbank theological hero, who argues that "participation in the eternal generation of the *logos* is that to which *omnia intendunt assimilari deo* properly applies,"[3] Milbank argues what I argued in the opening chapter, namely, that "without an acknowledgment of the supernatural, our account of reality is incomplete."[4] But he goes further. There is no need for mediation: theology is already a social science, indeed it alone is its own adequate social science, and social science is already theology.[5] Without theology, there is no adequate social scientific explanation, while theology needs no mediation by the social sciences.[6] Theology, "which has frequently sought to borrow from elsewhere a fundamental account of society or history and then to see what theological insights will cohere with it . . . will have to provide its own account of the final causes at work in human history, on the basis of its own particular and historically specific faith."[7] Milbank's disjunction is stark: either radical orthodoxy or nihilism. It is a strong thesis, strongly held, and it has generated equally strong passions for and against.

25

English sociologist David Martin complains that "for all its architectonic brilliance, Milbank's book is less useful to practitioners and less convincing because he devised a metadiscourse far above the analyses we actually carry out. Milbank engaged in obliteration bombing in which the whole discipline was obscured in a pall of smoke."[8] It is a fair comment. American sociologist John Coleman judges that Milbank's project is to have theology auto-generate its own sociology, believing "that theology always encounters in sociology only another form of theology in disguise."[9] Coleman's judgment is echoed from a theological perspective by English theologian Aidan Nichols, who complains that "despite numerous true judgments, good maxims, and beautiful insights to be scattered throughout this book, its overall message is deplorable. His objections can be summed up in two words: 'hermeticism' and 'theocracy.'"[10] By hermeticism Nichols means the complete isolation of Christian discourse and action within a separate universe of thought and action where they are free from the influence of any secular wisdom. This protest against hermeticism is an eminently Catholic *theological* objection which needs to be more fully explicated, and I shall return to it in a moment. By theocracy, he means the restoration of Augustine's *civitas Dei* or, perhaps more tellingly for Anglican Milbank, Richard Hooker's *Respublica Christiana* with its three pillars of Scripture, Tradition, and Reason. Gregory Baum, the Canadian theologian who has done more than any other Catholic theologian to incorporate sociology into his theology, describes Milbank's work as an "outstanding intellectual achievement," but immediately adds that "because I find his postmodern deconstruction of reason and truth unconvincing, the book also disturbs me."[11] I agree.

American theologian Michael Baxter is more personally in tune with Milbank's overall project of radical orthodoxy. He suggests that Coleman has not really come to terms with Milbank's argument. Milbank, he argues, would concede that sociology can be of assistance to theology. "But he [Milbank] would also argue that the validity of all sociological descriptions and explanations and their positions within the overall Christian narrative must ultimately be determined by theology . . . which is why theology must be restored to its position of 'queen of the sciences.'"[12] Baxter points out that Coleman's, or anyone's, understanding of the relation between theology and sociology needs to be argued *theologically,* and appears to go further to argue, following Don Browning, that sociology should be situated within a broader practical theology and that practical theology should be situated within Milbank's radical orthodoxy.[13] As a Catholic theologian, I accept Baxter's challenge to reflect on Milbank's project theologically, and leave to sociologists the sociological critique.[14]

*Theology and Social Theory* is not a stand-alone book, nor is its project a stand-alone project. Both book and project are part of a larger project of a group of young, Cambridge-trained theologians to establish, yet again, a *nouvelle théologie* to confront and deconstruct the trendiest and most influential European thinkers of the modern and postmodern eras. Their project is set out programmatically in an edited collection of essays under the revealing title *Radical Orthodoxy: A New Theology*,[15] and may be described as the articulation of an all-encompassing Christian perspective to supersede and reign over all modern and postmodern secularisms, which Milbank reduces to nihilism. Hence the disjunction: either this new radical theology, which is orthodox, Augustinian, and Christianly neo-Platonic, or nihilism; either the eternal *civitas Dei* or the ephemeral *civitas mundi*. Theological perspective is "the only non-nihilistic perspective and the only perspective able to uphold even finite reality."[16]

The Catholic theologian is reminded of the nineteenth-century controversies surrounding Louis Bautain and Félicité Robert de Lamennais, the former's fideism proclaiming that revelation, received in faith, is the primary guiding force of all truth, the latter's traditionalism holding that the seeker of truth must rely on faith alone as communicated in the tradition of the Catholic Church. Both teachings were reactions against the extreme rationalism of the time; both also, however, succeeded only in standing rationalism on its head. Orthodox Catholicism rejected both fideism and traditionalism along with the rationalism that spawned them. Against rationalism, the First Vatican Council taught that belief in revealed truth is "not because its intrinsic truth is seen in the natural light of reason, but because of the authority of God who reveals it."[17] Against fideism and traditionalism, it taught that the submission of faith must be "consonant with reason"[18] and that "the assent of faith is in no way a blind impulse."[19]

Popes Pius XII and John Paul II, each in his own way, confirmed this position as thoroughly Catholic and further explicated it for modern times in their respective encyclicals *Humani Generis* and *Fides et Ratio*. John Paul specifically warns against the resurgent fideism which disdains "the classical philosophy from which the terms of both the understanding of faith and the actual formulation of dogmas have been drawn."[20] Milbank, somewhat sheepishly, confesses that "not without distress do I realize that some of my conclusions here coincide with those of reactionaries in the Vatican."[21] That confession, however, does injustice to even the most reactionary of Vatican reactionaries. An unbridgeable chasm stands between the fideist and speculatively traditionalist views of radical orthodoxy and the views of even the most ultramontane of Vatican denizens. The chasm divides suspicion of exaggerated reason and elimination of all reason by obliteration bombing.

In their programmatic *Radical Orthodoxy,* John Milbank, Catherine Pickstock, and Graham Ward explain how their new theology is radical. It is radical, first, "in the sense of a return to patristic and medieval roots, and especially to the Augustinian vision of all knowledge as divine illumination — a notion which transcends the modern bastard dualisms of faith and reason, grace and nature." It is radical, second, "in the sense of seeking to deploy this recovered vision systematically to criticize modern society, culture, politics, art, science and philosophy with an unprecedented boldness." It is radical, third, in the sense that "via such engagements we *do* have also to rethink the tradition."[22] It is radical in a fourth sense which they do not mention though it is obvious, important, and fully explicative of their overall project, and so I mention it for them: Not only are the proponents of radical orthodoxy all Cambridge-trained theologians, they are also all Anglicans of that persuasion known as Anglo-Catholicism, which grew out of a twofold root, a profound commitment to Christian tradition and a deep dissatisfaction with the concrete Anglican and Roman Catholic historical incarnations of that tradition. By conviction, Anglo-Catholics are committed to tradition; by judgment, neither historical Anglicanism nor Roman Catholicism provide an adequate institutional basis for faithfulness to the Christian tradition. "Therefore," R. R. Reno, an American Episcopal theologian, comments "a tradition had to be invented. Of course, this invention was denied."[23]

Anglo-Catholicism is characterized "by an extensive archaeology of patristic and medieval texts, endless recoveries of Catholic-leaning figures in early Anglicanism, as well as extensive borrowings from post-Tridentine Roman theology and sacramental practice. Yet, however ancient the pieces, however venerable the raw material, the actual structure and form of Anglo-Catholicism emerged out of an idealized picture of catholic faith and practice."[24] For Anglo-Catholics, there is no choice but to turn to a speculative ideal, because the concrete word and sacrament in which the tradition is historically enshrined is inadequate. The "new" theology of radical orthodoxy embraces this ideal tradition free from all the manifest imperfections of the historical Christian forms. Nichols judges that, in Milbank's case, "*malgré lui,* with the discovery of his Anglicanism," the term "ideal" must be reinstated.[25]

Unfortunately, among the concrete historical forms from which the ideal tradition and the new theology free Christians are the forms that define God, as mediated in the concrete Jewish Christ, as mediated in the historical Christian church, which is his body, however dirty, damaged, and misshapen it might be. As a Catholic theologian in that body, I see no real choice in history but to echo Peter's "Lord, to whom shall we go?" (John

6:68). Reno is utterly correct. "To escape the patterns of theological modernism, therefore, the first task is not to reject, imagine and invent. Instead, we must train ourselves in that which modernity rejects most thoroughly and fatally: the discipline of receiving [and, I would add in agreement with Milbank, purifying] that which has been given. We must eat the scrolls that the Lord has given us, and dwell amid his people."[26] There are multiple correct judgments, brilliant insights, and bright ideas in Milbank's project. Sadly, however, as Bernard Lonergan trenchantly informed me in his seminar, not every bright idea is a right idea, and, in the final analysis, the radical orthodoxy project is *theologically* fatally flawed because it is at odds theologically with the very Christian tradition it seeks to promote. It is, therefore, to be theologically rejected.

## Theology and Social Context

Milbank is not the first English scholar to concern himself with the mutual mediations of theology and sociology. Two others, one a distinguished theologian, Robin Gill, the other a distinguished sociologist and Anglican priest, David Martin, have long examined connections between the two. It is one of the greater puzzles in Milbank's book that he makes no mention of either, though both are overtly Christian thinkers whose projects are intimately related to his own. Gill, citing Berger with approval, points out what every sociologist takes for granted, namely, that however much theologians may strive to influence society, they themselves are inevitably first influenced by the society in which they live. Long before they start doing theology, and while they are doing theology, theologians are persons living in and formed by a particular socio-historical context. Their personal context, they themselves, and the theology they produce, are all products of that socio-historical context and can, therefore, be "illuminated by the lighting apparatus of the sociologist."[27] Milbank acknowledges the import of social context when he locates himself in an Augustinian context; I acknowledge it when I locate him in an Anglo-Catholic context. Here is one way in which sociology can be helpful to theology, by providing social, contextual information which theologians cannot afford to ignore if they wish to understand themselves, be credible in a postmodern world, and communicate effectively in the world in which they live.

This same point has been made by Robert Doran in his monumental explication and extension of Lonergan's meta-methodology of theology. For Lonergan, as I have already explained, the total enterprise of theology unfolds in two phases. A first phase, which includes the functional specialities

of research, interpretation, history, and dialectic, is indirect discourse and
mediates the past to the present. A second phase, which includes the specialties of foundations, doctrines, systematics, and communications, is direct
discourse and mediates the present to the future. "There is a theology *in
oratione obliqua* that tells what Paul and John, Augustine and Aquinas, and
anyone else had to say about God and the economy of salvation. But there
is also a theology *in oratione recta* in which the theologian, enlightened by
the past, confronts the problems of his own day."[28] In Lonergan's inten-
tionality analysis, the functional specialty *foundations* occurs on the fourth
level of human consciousness, the level of deliberation and decision. It is
"a fully conscious decision about one's horizon, one's outlook, one's world-
view. It deliberately selects the framework in which doctrines have their
meanings."[29] Doran adds that an essential part of horizon and outlook
is the self-appropriation of the theologian which results from intellectual,
moral, religious, and psychic conversion.[30] Social science can illuminate the
converted theologian's horizon.

Gill suggests that sociology can illuminate not only the theologian's personally converted horizon but also the social context of her or his theology
in three different ways. First, if theologians wish to communicate to society at large, and not just to the choir of convinced believers, sociology can
clarify for them the *social context* in which their theology is both construed
and effectively received. If they wish, however, to communicate only to the
community of believers, they can ignore social context and communicate
exclusively in the special, sometimes arcane, categories of traditional theology. Second, in assessing the mutual correlation between faith and praxis,
sociology can clarify what may be called the *social structure* of theology, the
actual *is* of a religious or theological situation rather than the *ought to be*.
As long as sociologists stay within the limits of their discipline to describe
the *is* and do not intrude on theological prescription of the *ought to be*, they
can be of great help to the theologian assessing faith in practice. Third, sociology can also help the theologian assess the *social consequences* of theology
as long as, again, it is restricted to assessing, and not evaluating, those consequences. Evaluation of theological consequences is the task of theology,
but sociology can greatly assist theological evaluation by supplying detailed
assessment of them.[31] Sociology, then, can illuminate theologians and their
theologies in four different ways: by illuminating the intellectually, morally,
religiously, and psychically converted theologian's horizon, by illuminating
her or his social context and social structure, and by illuminating the social
consequences of her or his theology. All four ways will recur throughout
this book.

Karl Rahner presents practical theology as a descriptive/critical discipline, very much in line with Gill's presentation of sociological description followed by theological prescription. "Practical theology is that theological discipline which is concerned with the Church's self-actualisation here and now — both that which *is* and that which *ought to be*."[32] The task of practical theology embraces both description and evaluation of the present situation, including the present situation of doctrine. For description, it relies on social science; for evaluation, theology critically distills this social scientific data through theological and ecclesial filters. The assistance received from the social sciences is description of the present situation; theology alone then carries out the task of theological and religious evaluation. Rahner explains why theology needs the social sciences for assessment. The present theological or ecclesial situation cannot be deduced abstractly from prior dogmatic and theological knowledge; it can be concretely described only by practical analysis of the situation. This is in accord with Lonergan's empirical principle: "there are no true *factual* judgments without a foundation in relevant data,"[33] and the relevant empirical data are supplied by social scientific research. The social sciences offer a range of scientific tools for that analysis, and theology, drawing on its own tradition and principles, can then suggest courses of action consonant with that tradition and those principles. The Second Vatican Council articulated the very same principle on, one can safely assume, the very same foundation. "In pastoral care, sufficient use should be made not only of theological principles but also of the secular sciences, especially sociology and psychology."[34]

This approach shows a family resemblance to Don Browning's "descriptive theology." Descriptive theology is, broadly, "horizon analysis; it attempts to analyze the horizon of cultural and religious meanings that surround our religious and secular practices."[35] Since this horizon embraces the human actors in the practice, including the researcher-actor, what Anton Boisen called "the human document,"[36] descriptive theology cannot be just a sociological task, if sociology is understood as a narrowly empirical science. If sociology, however, is understood as a hermeneutical discipline, as it is in the sociology of knowledge, which I will consider in the next chapter, descriptive theology and hermeneutical sociology merge into one another. Hermeneutical sociology sees its task as dialogue between the concrete realities and practices which the researcher studies and the multiple theories and pre-understandings embedded in the human document. Material, psychological, and social realities that determine the researchers are placed within the larger meanings that direct their actions, research, and conclusions.[37] "These larger meanings that constitute the theory embedded in our practices," Browning argues, "invariably have a religious dimension. This is why hermeneutic sociology, when properly conceived, fades into descriptive theology."[38] If, as I argued in the previous chapter, every human situation is a graced situation, then every sociological effort to describe the present situation comprehensively will ultimately have to transition or fade from sociological to theological analysis. The former will describe the empirical facets of the situation, the latter the theological facets.

This fading of sociology into theology will not be easily accepted by the sociologist, nor will the fading of theology into sociology be easily accepted by the theologian, but I believe Browning's formulation is an important contribution to the mediation of the two disciplines. His later contribution to the national debate on family in the United States, *From Culture Wars to Common Ground,* is a brilliant exemplar of both descriptive theology and the successful integration of sociology and theology. This work, Browning suggests, differs from a standard theological text in that "we work hard not only to state the theological and ethical ideals that should govern families, but also to speak of the actual development and social conditions that allow them to be made manifest in the lives of persons."[39] In other words, he and his co-authors work hard to illuminate the socio-historical contexts in which theological and ethical ideals might flourish. Browning's argument, and mine in this book, is that such illumination requires the contributions of disciplines beyond theology and that theologians ignore these contributions on peril of failing to communicate in the real world and becoming irrelevant.

The ethical life of real people is an obvious place for sociology to assess scientifically the social consequences of theological doctrine and principle, and Robin Gill brilliantly exemplifies the correlational methodology involved in his *Churchgoing and Christian Ethics.* Intrigued by the turn toward character and virtue in ethics and puzzled by the fact that virtue ethicists, principally Stanley Hauerwas and, I would add, Milbank, demonstrate a remarkable ambivalence about the ethical communities required to socialize people in character and virtue, Gill seeks to assess the difference historical church communities make. Hauerwas enunciates his, and surely also Milbank's, dilemma. "We must admit that the church has not been a society of trust and virtue. At most, people identify the church as a place where the young learn 'morals,' but the 'morals' often prove to be little more than conventional pieties coupled with a few unintelligible 'don't's.'"[40] The church as it *ought to be* can enshrine Christian virtues properly, but unfortunately the church as it *is* in history does not do so properly. In Hauerwas's judgment, the church as it ought to be, read as Hauerwas believes it should be, has not yet happened in its two-thousand-year history. The sociologist interested in the social context of theology cannot help but notice that Hauerwas's attitude to the churches that *are* hardened, and his attitude to the church that *could be* became ever more hyperbolic and abstract, with his move from the University of Notre Dame to Duke University.[41] David Fergusson notes correctly that "the church advocated by Hauerwas nowhere exists. It is a fantasy community, the conception of which fails to reflect the ways in which the members of the church are also positioned within civil society."[42]

Gill proposes a different approach, rooted in the churches that historically are. He proposes to assess real churches as socializers of virtue by sociologically assessing the ethical values of those who may legitimately be called churchgoers. Churchgoing discriminates between those who attend church and those who do not, and, by employing churchgoing as an independent or explanatory variable, Gill can correlate the various values, virtues, and behaviors of churchgoers and non-churchgoers. Using large data sets from Britain, Ireland, Australia, and the United States, embracing Catholics, Anglicans, and Evangelicals, Gill is able to show that "there are broad patterns of Christian beliefs, teleology, and altruism which distinguish churchgoers as a whole from non-churchgoers."[43] Churchgoers in all these traditions show more concern for the needy than non-churchgoers; they are more opposed to abortion, capital punishment, and euthanasia; they are more likely to see purpose in life; they are more likely to support social and moral order; they are more concerned with the environment; they are less racist; they have a greater sense of having and being able to make a positive contribution to world problems; they are more engaged in political life (voting, for instance); they are more engaged in voluntary activities within their communities; they are more likely to show concern for what they see as declining moral standards. In spite of their far-from-perfect churches, the distinctiveness of churchgoers across the Christian traditions is documentably real.

The distinctiveness of churchgoers is also relative, that is, the values, virtues, and behaviors of churchgoers are shared to a degree by non-churchgoers. Gill demonstrates not that churchgoing is the *only* cause of specific values, virtues, and behaviors but that these virtues and behaviors are more present in churchgoers than in non-churchgoers. That is sufficient sociological description for the theologian to proceed to the theological prescription that churchgoing is good and ought to be. The picture that emerges from Gill's study is much like the picture postulated theoretically by Alasdair McIntyre. Eschewing the dichotomy between church and society embraced by Hauerwas and Milbank, McIntyre argues that real society, as distinct from ideal society, is "a *mélange* of moral thoughts and practice ... fragments from the tradition — virtue concepts for the most part — are still to be found alongside characteristically modern and individualist concepts such as those of rights or utility."[44] In the real world, churches are partially distinct from and partially overlap with non-church, "secular," communities. The values, virtues, and behaviors of churchgoers, therefore, those who belong to the churches with greater commitment and intensity, would intuitively be expected to be both partially distinct from and partially overlapping with those of non-churchgoers. That is exactly what Gill's scientific assessment demonstrates. "The distinctiveness of churchgoers is real but relative."[45]

Gill's overall conclusion is an important conclusion also for this book. Virtue ethics makes claims about moral communities which can be empirically tested for truth. Sociology, with its scientific assessment, not theoretical ethics with sweeping, hyperbolic, idealistic claims, can provide that testing. "Of course, actual, as distinct from idealized, communities are likely to be ambiguous and messy moral carriers. People argue and fight, they disagree and conflict, and even in the most conformist communities there are always idiosyncratic nonconformists. Church communities are no exceptions."[46] As Gill, and Andrew Greeley,[47] have shown, however, historical churches, Christianly ambiguous and messy though they may be, are genuine carriers of value, virtue, and behavior. Making grand, idealistic claims is so easy that it is ultimately unhelpful to practical theologians. Making claims that fit the real situation is more difficult, time consuming, and to some scary, but a truthful description of what *is* is the minimum starting point for any theological prescription of both what *ought to be* and how it might come to be. This argument will recur later when we consider Catholic ethical prescriptions related to contraception and divorce and remarriage without annulment.

David Martin is another who believes that mediation between theology and sociology is not only possible but also mutually enriching, though he warns of the difficulties such mediation faces. Theology and sociology are similar to the degree that, in distinction from the *hard* sciences, the material and criteria of both are *soft* and this similarity makes it difficult to establish how the one relates to the other. "Those trying to relate the precarious to the precarious may well lose their footing."[48] Martin articulates the condition of mutual mediation as an exposition of "the socio-logic informing a symbol system" and the consideration of the light that can throw on "the form and the development of the theo-logic." When the correspondences are examined with care, and neither discipline is reduced to the other, "the result may be mutual enrichment rather than a mutual destruction."[49] Another problem arises for mediation between sociology and theology: neither discipline operates according to an undisputed paradigm. There are multiple ways of doing theology, for example, neo-Platonic Augustine and Aristotelian Aquinas, transcendental Rahner and neo-Orthodox Barth, and there are multiple ways of doing sociology, Durkheim and Weber variously open to religion, Marx totally closed to it. The procedures and operation in each discipline are far from univocal; they are related only by family likenesses which enable one to recognize that both Rahner and Barth are doing theology and Durkheim and Marx are doing sociology. This paradigmatic multivalence makes Baxter's question inescapable: "Whose theology? Which sociology?"[50] The answer to both those questions is a precondition for any discussion of mediation between theology and sociology.

Martin insists that religion always takes place in a social context and under conditions which "yield sociological rules as to the average likelihood of conversion. Religions tend not to phrase their accounts of conversion in this way, but rather to envisage religious change as a *deus ex machina*. The *ex* is overemphasized."[51] He has illustrated this connection between social context and religious faith in two major sociological studies. In his *General Theory of Secularization*,[52] Martin draws a map of Europe, displaying where religion is vibrant as judged by standard religiosity measures, adherence to doctrine, church attendance, and strong religious identity. Where religion flourishes on this map, in Ireland, Poland, Croatia, the Basque country of Spain, Brittany, Flanders, it flourishes in correlation with the same social context and under the same conditions. There is in all these regions: first, historic opposition to a "secular" capital; second, the support of a distinctive language and myth of a nation or cultural enclave within a nation; third, a historic border with another country or culture. "The peninsula of Brittany defends a distinctive language and faith against secular Paris; likewise the Basques defend their faith, language and land against what they call 'atheist' Madrid. Flemish-speaking Flanders defends itself against French-speaking Brussels.... [The influence of religion] finally acquires maximum influence in the ultimate island of Ireland. And there, of course, lies the border of the great confessions, as well as a border of ethnic groups and historic myths."[53]

There is good and bad news here for religion and theologians. The good news is that there are enclaves of culturally sustained religious flourishing. The bad news is that almost all these religio-cultural enclaves, with the possible exceptions of northwest Ireland, and Croatia, Serbia, Bosnia, are now more of historical than genuinely religious interest. The sociological evidence shows that the great European secular centers, London, Paris, Brussels, Madrid, strengthen, and their religious peripheries weaken. Martin advances only minor evidence in support of this claim. "Catholics in Glasgow suddenly felt no special obligation to go to church. The rate of reproduction in Catholic southern Europe has now dropped below the rate in Protestant northern Europe, and in some areas is below replacement."[54]

He could have selected multiple data in reference to his enclaves, sociological descriptive assessment which, again, provides realistic information for theological prescription.[55]

As his *General Theory* maps European religiousness and details its relationship to social context, David Martin's *Tongues of Fire*[56] charts the spread of Pentecostal sects throughout Latin America. He raises three preliminary questions from general sociological theory. What is the socio-historical situation: what religious traditions are actually available in Latin America? What are the social conditions that might lead to a change of dominant tradition? What geographical locations are most vulnerable to the supplanting of the dominant tradition? He correlates his answers to social context. In Latin America, the Pentecostal teaching of the universal action of the Holy Spirit is close enough to the dominant Catholic doctrine of the action of the Spirit to make Latin America fertile soil for Pentecostalism. Mobility is an important social factor that makes it easy to hear and embrace previously unheard messages, and therefore to challenge the dominance of Catholicism, and in Latin America there is mobility of every kind, from rural countryside to urban megalopolis, from one religious enclave to another, from one country to another, from the center of life to the margins. The inroad of new Pentecostal messages can actually be detailed in both time and place. "Chile and Brazil are respectively 20 and 13 per cent evangelical, Guatemala 30 per cent, Mexico 6–7 per cent. The Andean republics are relatively resistant with the proportion of evangelicals at about 5 per cent."[57]

All of these variations, Martin argues, are to be understood in terms of social context, in terms of the response of evangelical Pentecostalism to the demographic, economic, and moral changes in Latin America. Two American studies are in a somewhat similar vein. Rodney Stark and William Bainbridge show the statistical probabilities in the United States for conversion to New Age, evangelical sects, or cults, and provide a set of indicators that show who is particularly vulnerable to recruitment by such groups.[58] Patricia Wittberg shows that the religious denominations and orders that are flourishing in the United States are flourishing to the degree to which they respond innovatively to the hungers, strains, and stresses of modern American society. She urges all religious organizations to look carefully at the specific hungers and stresses of society before deciding on any prescription to respond to them.[59] She urges in the concrete what I have urged several times already in the abstract: description before prescription.

A reductionist interpretation lurks here, and is to be resisted. It is one thing to show that theological ideas arise in social contexts, and a totally other thing to claim that they are *only* reflections of and are sufficiently explained by that social context. Conclusion from the contextual origin of an idea to its falsity commits the simplest of logical errors known as the generic fallacy. Research and analysis can show the contextual origins of an idea, but only a reasoned judgment can declare the idea to be true or false. It is perfectly possible that an idea, in any province of meaning, can be shown to be correlated with a given social context *and* still be true. Not only sociologists can be guilty of reductionism; so also can theologians. Theologians are tempted, for instance, to assign everything religious to the grace of the Holy Spirit, or the demon, depending on who is talking and what they are talking about. Martin agrees theologically about the universal grace of the Spirit, but also points out that "the lava of the Spirit runs along the lines of social fault, and the wind of the Spirit blows according to a chart of high and low pressures."[60] Wittberg adds that "not only does the lava of the Holy Spirit flow through existing societal fault lines, the mustard seed of ecclesial structures subsequently sprouts and grows in the same volcanic soil."[61] It is a modern version of the classic Thomistic principle that grace builds on nature. I am arguing at this point, both philosophically and theologically, that even if the Spirit does follow, and can be shown to be following, social fault lines, theological truth can grow in those faults and in that volcanic soil.

Wittberg complains, with justification, about the blithe willingness of some theologians "to make statements and predictions in ignorance of the way societal 'fault lines' affect the phenomena they are describing."[62] Lonergan's empirical principle recurs again: there are no true factual judgments without a foundation in relevant data. The social scientist urges the theologian to learn this principle, to take it seriously, and to look to the sociologist for the factual description of the relevant social data. To refuse to take the empirical principle seriously, to construct a theology that ignores sociological description of the facts, opens theology to the charge that it is arcane and anachronistic, a charge many students of sociology take as already proven. The theologian must learn that, though theological ideas are not wholly determined by social fault lines, social context, or history, they are nevertheless rooted in and sustained by those fault lines and contexts. It goes without saying that the sociologist must equally learn that, while sociological ideas are not wholly determined by either social context or history, they are inescapably related to the social and historical bases that sustain them.

Neither sociology nor theology originates in a vacuum. The natural sciences take for granted "objective" knowledge and the separation of a neutral observing subject and observed object; the human sciences take for granted an interconnection of an active, involved subject and object. "Both the social scientist and the social action studied by them have been produced by the same history. Social scientists do not stand on neutral ground; they

find themselves in a position that has been affected by the object they intend to study."[63] Irish poet William Butler Yeats makes the same point
in more poetic language: "Whatever flames upon the night / man's own
resinous heart has fed."[64] Michael Polanyi articulates the same thing in
his now widely accepted thesis of personal knowledge: all knowledge is
the knowledge of an active, involved subject, and it rests on tacit, un-
proven assumptions and bases.[65] This is put in "religious" language thus:
all knowledge rests on some prior faith. Social scientists are tempted to forget this, and they are to be called to acknowledge it, every bit as much as
theologians.

## Symbolic Realism

The final movement in this chapter begins with sociologist Robert Bellah
and what he calls *symbolic realism*. Bellah shares his interest in, though
not necessarily his understanding of, symbol with a host of other major
commentators, all of whom agree that the human animal is a symbolic animal.[66] The human animal is active, that is, in the transformation of sensuous
realities into more than sensuous symbols embodying abstract reality and
meaning, a process that is called symbolic transformation. The agent of
symbolic transformation is human society. "The potter, and not the pot,"
Alfred North Whitehead comments, "is responsible for the shape of the
pot."[67] He also articulates the commonly held answer to the question of
symbolic transformation and symbolism, an answer which may be subsumed
under two statements. Symbolism organizes "the miscellaneous crowd into a
smoothly running community," and it achieves this organization by making
"connected thought possible by expressing it, while at the same time it automatically directs action."[68] Symbols move the human animal to thought,
action, and feelings consonant with the thought and action. The critical
question for our purposes in this book, however, is neither the shape of the
pot or symbol nor its function, but what the symbol represents or means.
Interpretation is needed here, and where there is interpretation there will
perforce be dialectic.

   Symbols and their meanings are correlative, that is, though a symbol and
its meanings are distinguishable they are inseparable, a knowing subject
cannot know one without simultaneously knowing the other. Ernst Cassirer
puts this forcefully. Symbols "are not imitations but *organs* of reality, since it
is solely by their agency that anything real becomes an object for intellectual
apprehension, and as such is made visible to us."[69] For all human purposes
a symbol *is* the meanings and reality it symbolizes in representation. The
flag *is* the country in representation, the water of baptism *is* death to old

and rebirth to new life in representation, a kiss *is* the love between lovers in representation. Symbols also differ from signs. A sign is related to what it signifies in a fixed and unique way, a symbol is characterized "not by its uniformity but by its versatility. It is not rigid or inflexible but mobile."[70] It is precisely the versatility or multivalency of symbols that make them more complex and opaque than simple signs. This opacity "constitutes the depth of the symbol which, it will be said, is inexhaustible."[71] Both the multivalency and opacity of symbols demand that they be interpreted and create the possibility that interpretation itself will be multivalent. The multivalent interpretation of symbols is abundantly documented throughout history.

There are multiple modern definitions of religion, but many betray a family resemblance: "religion is a system of symbols." Bellah, for instance, defines religion as "a set of symbols providing the most general level of orientation to reality."[72] Anthropologist Clifford Geertz defines it as "a system of symbols which acts to ... [formulate] conceptions of a general order of existence...."[73] Theologian Herbert Richardson defines it as that symbol system which evokes "the felt-whole."[74] The sociological, anthropological, philosophical, and theological discovery of the importance of myth, ritual, and symbol in the nineteenth century, led to a change of attitude toward religion. Alongside the post-Enlightenment conviction that religion could not be taken seriously on its own terms, there developed another approach which held that the symbols of religion were not entirely false but contained a kernel of truth. The student of religion always has to determine what that truth is.

For Marx, and his explanatory principle of class struggle, both the truth and falsity of religion were easy to express: the symbols of religion are opiates for heartless and soulless conditions, nothing more. "Religion is the sigh of the oppressed creature, the heart of a heartless world, and the soul of soulless conditions. It is the opium of the people."[75] For Freud, and his discovery of the unconscious, the symbols of religion express the universal Oedipus complex. The biblical God is the primordial father toward whom sons feel both rebellion and guilt because of this feeling. The wish to kill the father, the wish to be killed for this unspeakable desire, and the wish to be raised to the right hand of the father are all summed up in the biblical Christ.[76] Religious symbols mean no more than that. Emile Durkheim, one of the founding fathers of the sociology of religion, disagreed with Freud. The reality lying behind religious symbols is not the Oedipus complex but society and the morality that expresses it. The appropriate morality for modern society is a developed individualism, which was nurtured by Christianity but no longer needs Christian symbols to sustain it.[77] Max Weber, sociology

of religion's second father, made no claim to know the meaning lying behind religious symbols. His perspective was, rather, that the beliefs behind
the symbols could not be taken seriously by the scientist but that the social consequences of those beliefs had to be taken seriously. This approach
spawned the brilliant analysis in his classic *Protestant Ethic and the Spirit
of Capitalism.*[78]

Bellah dubs all these approaches "symbolic reductionism," and opposes
them to his own approach named "symbolic realism," which holds that
religious symbols "express reality and are not reducible to empirical propositions."[79] Symbolic realism moves along the path traced by Paul Ricoeur:
symbols are opaque and their depth of meaning is inexhaustible. Some social scientists, Bellah argues, have come to believe that there are depths in
religious symbols that they have scarcely begun to fathom, and that even
"the great symbols that justify science itself rest on unprovable assumptions
sustained at the deepest levels of our consciousness."[80] The same suggestion of the non-literality, depth, and irreducibility of symbols in general,
and therefore of religious symbols in specific, has been made by a number
of other thinkers from a variety of disciplines. Psychologist Liam Hudson
has argued it,[81] as have philosopher Max Black,[82] scientist Ian Barbour,[83]
and theologians Karl Rahner,[84] Michael Lawler,[85] and Ian Ramsey.[86] This
convergence of methodologies, Bellah judges, can only be beneficial to both
the sociologist and theologian. "If the theologian comes to his subject with
the assumption of symbolic realism, as many seem to be doing, then we are
in a situation where for the first time in centuries theologian and secular
intellectual can speak the same language."[87] I approve the boon in that, but
I also see a methodological problem.

Bellah makes two claims: symbolic realism is "the only adequate basis
for the social scientific study of religion" and religion "is *sui generis.*"[88]
Both these claims cry out for demonstration, but no demonstration is forth-
coming. This non-demonstration, indeed the implied impossibility of any
demonstration, raises the specter that the claims derive from ideology and
not science. As a theologian, I am totally committed to the symbolic realist approach to religious and theological interpretation, but I share Gill's
concern about Bellah's symbolic realism. If, indeed, symbolic realism becomes an ideology sociologically, it may be "of considerable use to the
theologian, but of distinctly less use to the sociologist."[89] The kind of mediation between sociology and theology which I have outlined already in
this book requires the disciplines to remain disciplinarily separate and to
make their distinctive contributions, the one as scientifically descriptive the
other as theologically prescriptive based on this description. Any conflation

of sociology and theology, which seems to me to be implicit in Bellah's approach, makes the sociology of religion less relevant to general sociology and, therefore, of necessity, also to theology.

I am more attracted to the methodological mediation between sociology and theology Gill suggests, a mediation which depends on an *als ob* or *as if* methodology, with the essential proviso that this approach is to be fully understood as methodological and in no way ontological. Using such a methodology, "the sociologist would work *as if* there were social determinants of all human [including religious] interactions — believing as an individual, though, that there may not be."[90] Sociologists would, that is, treat all religious phenomena as exclusively social phenomena, whether they believe there is epistemological truth embedded in them or not. They have to believe not that religious phenomena are exclusively social phenomena, that would be sociological imperialism, only that they cannot exclude any such phenomena from social examination. Theologians would also work with an *as if* methodology, but with different assumptions. They would work *as if* all religious and theological language had a transcendental cause and referent; they must "take seriously the possible reality of reference in the term 'God.'"[91] They have to believe methodologically not that religious phenomena are explained exclusively by transcendental causes, that would be theological imperialism, only that they cannot exclude transcendental causes from their analysis. This methodology does not conflate the task of sociologist and theologian, but leaves both free to pursue their specific analyses according to the research canons of their respective disciplines.

Gill's methodological suggestion is analogous to one that Maurice Wiles proposed to theologians speaking of the doctrine of creation. Miles argued that theologians speaking of creation are obliged to employ two stories, the one scientific, the other theological. On the one hand, they tell the scientific story of evolution; on the other hand, they tell the symbolic, mythological story of the Spirit of God moving over the chaotic waters to bring order. "If we know what we are doing we can weave the two stories together in poetically creative ways — as indeed the poet combines logically disparate images into new and illuminating wholes."[92] The one thing theologians should not do, Miles warns and I agree, is attempt to conflate or harmonize the two stories. They are two distinct, yet complementary, stories about the one reality. I take Miles's point to be one that Gill is also making and that I approve. Science, natural or social, and theology are not to be conflated; they are distinct disciplines which, nevertheless, can be complementary.

## Conclusion

This chapter focused on possible mediations between theology and sociology. It began with a consideration and rejection, on theological grounds, of
Milbank's nineteenth-century-replicating radical orthodoxy project, with its
exaltation of a hermetically isolated theology, and its denial of any possible
mediation between theology and any modern science. Radical orthodoxy
was rejected on theological grounds for not being radical enough, that is,
for not being rooted in the real, historical, ecclesial, and theological world.
Grand, sweeping, idealist theological claims are easy to make, but if they
are to communicate to real people they will have consequences which can
be verified in the historical world, and the assessment of anything in that
world, including anything religious and theological, is a task for scientific
sociology, not for speculative and historically unrooted theology. That judgment, it was argued, does not yield to sociology any of the prescriptive,
ought-to-be, functions of theology. It asserts only that for the theological
*prescription* of what *ought to be* to be realistic it should be preceded by the
sociological *description* of what *is*. Karl Rahner puts it well. The task of
practical theology is both description and evaluation of the present world
and ecclesial situation. For description, theology relies on social science; for
evaluation of the present situation, theology distills this description in the
still of ecclesial and theological perspective.

The distinction between what *is* and what *ought to be* led to reflection on
the social context in which theologians do their theologies and the influence
it has on both them and their theologies. This, in turn, introduced mediational methodologies which focus on the empirical description of what *is* as
a required precedent of what theologically *ought to be*. The methodologies
of Gill, Martin, and Browning were considered, all of which have positive
contributions to the kind of mediation that there might be between theology and sociology. A preference was expressed for the *as if* methodology
suggested by Gill, because it did not conflate the two disciplines but left
each free to pursue its own specialized tasks. Methodologically, sociologists
treat all religious and theological phenomena as if they are exclusively social
phenomena, even though they believe, as Gill and Martin do, that they are
more than social phenomena. Theologians, for their part, treat all religious
and theological phenomena as if they have exclusively transcendental causes
and referents, even though they believe they may have other, social causes
and referents.

It is important to understand that this *as if* strategy is purely *methodological* and does not suggest anything *ontological*. The beginning of
consideration was also given to that version of the widely held symbolic

realist approach to religious and theological phenomena that does not collapse theology into sociology. There is a convergent agreement in social science and theology on symbolic realism, that is, the position that there are depths in religious symbols that we have barely begun to fathom. Religious symbols, following Ricoeur, have a depth of meaning that is inexhaustible. The sociological approach that is most useful here is the approach of hermeneutical sociology, which is best exemplified in the sociology of knowledge. It is to that sociology we now turn in chapter 3.

## Questions for Discussion

1. What do you think of Milbank's disjunction: either his radical orthodoxy, which is Augustinian and Christian, or nihilism; either the eternal city of God or the transient city of this world? Have you any alternative to offer to this disjunction?

2. How do you understand Gill's suggestion that sociology can illuminate the social nature of theology in three ways: by clarifying its social context, its social structure, and its social consequences? If this is true, what are the implications for theologians and their theologies?

3. Practical theology is concerned with the socio-historical here and now, with both what *is* and what *ought to be*. Can sociology offer theologians any help in their practical tasks?

4. "Conclusion from the contextual origin of an idea to its falsity commits the simplest of logical errors known as the generic fallacy." Discuss this assertion and examples of the generic fallacy you might have encountered in your experience.

5. What do you understand by the notion of symbol? How do symbols function in human life? What do you understand by symbolic realism and, in particular, its application to religion?

# THREE

# Sociology of Knowledge and Theology

This chapter is about the sociology of knowledge, the branch of sociology that analyses the relation between socio-historical existence and knowledge, and the possible benefits that it offers to theologians and their theologies. The sociology of knowledge is, on the one hand, a sociological theory of the social determination of the process of knowing and the end product of that process, knowledge. It is, on the other, a socio-historical method of empirical research. Its distinctive theory, that knowing and knowledge, along with human meaning and reality, are socially constructed, was introduced in general in the opening chapter. In this chapter, the specific detail of that theory is filled in.

## The Social Construction of Meaning

We begin with an essential insight of sociology: human consciousness is produced by the social, economic, and political institutions which women and men create for their common life. "Life is not determined by consciousness," Karl Marx wrote, "but consciousness by life."[1] A materialistic-reductionist understanding of this social determination of consciousness, as if social determination leaves no room for personal freedom, is to be rejected from the start. Not even Marx ever argued this reductionist position. He always believed that, though the institutions humans create for their life in common then act in them to produce a determinate consciousness, this social determination left room for personal freedom, creativity, and the possibility of reshaping the movement of history. This perspective will have to be kept clearly in mind throughout this chapter.

George Herbert Mead, a significant figure in the history of the social sciences in the United States, took up the consideration of the social origin of consciousness and is credited with the transformation of men and women from passive to active subjects in social processes. His research led him to his distinctive understanding of the social self. "The self, as that which can be a reflexive object to itself," Strauss argued in his analysis of Mead, "is essentially a social structure and it arises in social experience."[2] This social self emerges, together with consciousness or what Mead calls "mind," in social interaction. Self, mind, and society are all socially generated.[3] It is absurd, he asserts, to consider mind only from the standpoint of the biological organism, for it originates and develops only in the social processes of interaction with others individuals.

Key words in Mead's analysis of mind are *gesture* and *significant gesture*. A gesture becomes a significant or meaningful gesture in a process of interaction between two individuals. A Self comes to be through the interpretation which an Other offers to the Self's gesture. An I points to something and an Other interprets this gesture and responds to it. The I simultaneously experiences itself making the gesture and the Other responding to it, which makes the gesture meaningful for both of them. The I discovers what the gesture means in social, as distinct from individual, reality because it discovers what the Other interprets it to mean. Meaning arises in a social process of interaction between an I and an Other. It is a social creation, arising in the triadic structure of communication: an I's gesture, a pointing, the sharing of bread, the giving of a ring; an Other's response; and the assumption of the role of the Other by the I" through which the meaning of the gesture is grasped.[4]

This analysis, of course, is a purely formal analysis of the origin of meaning. Mead's achievement, which has been outlined here only to the extent needed to show his theory of the social origin of meaning, self, and society, suffers from the ambiguities of its behaviorist framework. The major problem in his account, Winter points out, "comes down to an inadequate notion of the self as a centered being, as an 'I.' "[5] Mead gave a brilliant account of the social self, the self as reflected through the eyes of an Other, what social psychology calls the "me," but his theory always ran the risk of reducing the self to the social self, of absorbing the individual I into the social "me." This reduction of the self to the social self vitiates the triadic structure which Mead postulates as the basis of meaning: gesture, interpretive response, perceived meaning of the gesture through the response. The social self cannot be the source of the gesture, since it comes to be precisely through the perceived meaning of the gesture. The gesture presupposes an individual I who gestures and another individual I who interprets the gesture. Sociality is presupposed, not explained, in Mead's theory of meaning and the social self. His proper break with an exclusively mechanistic model yielded an inadequate polar model in which the two poles were an intentional self or I and a social self or me, completely ignoring the social we which is ontologically prior to any relation between the I and the me.

Georges Gurvitch introduces this social We into the question of the relation between an I and an Other, yielding a tripolar dialectical process in the psychic phenomenon, the three poles being an I, an Other, and a We. In any communication, an I communicates with an Other or Others through signs and symbols which are necessarily founded in a social We which is socially prior to both the I and the Other and gives effective validity to them and the meaning they share. Consciousness consists in the tensions between these three terms and in their various combinations. "Consciousness is a dialectical relationship between 'I,' 'Other,' and 'We,' which partially interpenetrate each other and partially converge through opposition."[6] Gurvitch argues there are two basic forms of sociality, partial fusion in a social We, and partial opposition between an I and an Other. The active character of sociality, which is our concern here following Mead's break with passive, mechanistic models, "manifests itself especially in the affirmation of a common task to be accomplished, which is more clearly evident when it concerns a We than when it concerns relations with an Other."[7]

Alfred Schutz, who also sought the presuppositions, structures, and meanings of the world of everyday reality, comes close to Gurvitch's insistence on the priority of the We. Schutz judges that Mead tended to identify meaning with its semantic expression and to consider language, speech, symbols, significant gestures as the fundamental condition of social intercourse.[8] He further judges that Mead's solution only appears to answer the question whether the communicative process is the foundation of all possible human relationships or whether it presupposes some other social interaction which, though it is the condition of all possible communication, does not itself enter the communication process. He proposes such a social interaction on which all communication is grounded, calls it a "mutual tuning-in relationship,"[9] and argues that it is in this mutual tuning-in that both I and Other are experienced by the participants as a vividly present We.

The Other is a taken-for-granted constant in the taken-for-granted world of everyday reality and is pre-given in any reflection on that world, thus establishing social relatedness. Schutz explains consciousness of the Other and founds his social theory in a general thesis of *alter ego*. This thesis implies that the Other is like me, capable of thinking and acting, and that the Other's thinking shows the same connectedness as mine. Both I and Other can experience each other's thoughts and acts in the vivid present, whereas each can grasp his or her own only in reflection and only, therefore, as past. "This present, common to both of us, is the sphere of the pure We.... We participate without an act of reflection in the vivid simultaneity of the We, whereas the I appears only after reflective turning."[10]

The We-relation highlights the social interdependence of the I and the Other. The I actualizes his *now* as vivid present through the Other, even as the Other actualizes his *now* as vivid present through the I. The We-relation is the matrix of the simultaneous self-actualization of both the I and the Other. It is the matrix of social interdependence in which the I and the Other together construct mind, self, and social reality. The We-relation founds for Schutz the thesis that the world of everyday, taken-for-granted reality is a socially constructed world. This thesis leads him to confront the problem which initiated this section: what is the source of the human theoretical or conceptual organization of reality? What is the source of the paradigms which cause humans to view reality within perspectives, rather than face to face?

Schutz is concerned with the understanding of social action as having the meaning subjects involved in the action bestow upon it. Actors, he maintains, are responsible for defining the meaning of their actions, as well as for defining the meaning of the situation of which their actions are part. "It is the meaning of our experiences and not the ontological structure of the objects which constitutes reality."[11] We recall Whitehead's comment from the previous chapter: "the potter, and not the pot, is responsible for the shape of the pot."[12] Thomas Luckmann agrees: "Subjective experience considered in isolation is restricted to mere actuality and is void of meaning. Meaning is not an inherent quality of subjective processes but is bestowed on it in interpretive acts."[13] The point is that meaning is bestowed in interpretive *social* acts. Winter puts it decisively: "The decisive criterion for the 'meaning of action' is the project of the actor — the anticipated state of affairs in his own pre-remembrance or the retrospective recovery of that project as elapsed; that is, meaning is 'what is meant' or 'what was meant.' "[14]

If "the decisive criterion for the 'meaning of action' is the project of the actor," then there arises an immediate problem. An Other may define the "same" situation in a radically different way than an I, and the question then arises as to which definition is true. Common sense dictates that something is the "same" for every normal observer, but that is not to say how this sameness is to be understood. As discussed in the preceding chapter, the entire world watched the Nazis herd Jews, Gypsies, and homosexuals into gas chambers. The Nazis perceived it as purification of the race; the rest of the world perceived it as murder; and we are left to guess how the people waiting for the gas perceived it. For all three groups of participants the action was, indeed, the "same," namely, the herding of designated people into gas chambers. But the meaning of this "same" action for all three groups was completely different. Humans are enmeshed in situations as *they* define them. It is utterly futile to point out to committed actors the "objective" situation. Nazis herded despised men and women to their death to "objectively" purify the race; the rest of the world saw it as "objectively" murder; the people waiting for death may have seen it as "objectively" murder of the innocent, or as simply meaningless. Schutz's thesis would seem to be correct: it is not some ontological structure that defines reality, but the meaning assigned to it by the actor.

William James argues that reality bespeaks relation to the human animal's emotional and active life.[15] To designate something as real is to say that it stands in a certain relationship to the human. All reality originates subjectively; whatever excites and stimulates our interest is real. There are many and various orders of reality, each with its own particular style of existence. James calls these "sub-universes," and cites as examples the world of physical things (which is the paramount reality), the world of mythology, the world of religion, the world of science, the world of the "idols of the tribe."[16] Everything we think of is ultimately referred to one of these sub-universes. "Each world whilst it is attended to is real after its own fashion; only the reality lapses with the attention."[17] Rather than speak of sub-universes of reality, Schutz speaks of "finite provinces of meaning," because "it is the meaning of our experiences and not the ontological structure of the objects which constitutes reality."[18] The world of everyday life is, as for James, the paramount reality, the one that seems to us to be the natural one, the unquestionable one, the one that we do not readily abandon. But it is by no means the only reality or the only province of meaning; it is only one among many accessible to us. Schutz condenses the characteristics of these various provinces of meaning into a number of theses.

First, all these worlds, the world of everyday reality, the world of art, the world of religion, the world of science, for instance, are finite provinces of meaning. All have a peculiar cognitive style, and, with respect to this cognitive style, all experiences within each of these worlds are consistent in themselves and compatible with one another. Second, consistency and compatibility of experiences with respect to their peculiar cognitive style subsists merely *within* a particular province of meaning to which those experiences belong. By no means will that which is compatible within the province of meaning of science be compatible also within the province of meaning of religion. On the contrary, seen from the perspective of science, taken-for-granted as real, religion and all the experiences belonging to it would appear as fictitious, incompatible, and inconsistent; and vice versa. Third, we are thus entitled to talk of *finite* provinces of meaning, finiteness implying that there is no possibility of referring one province of meaning to another via some formula of transformation. Passage from one to another can be achieved only by Lonergan's conversion or Søren Kierkegaard's leap of faith, always accompanied by the subjective experience of shock. Fourth, to the cognitive style peculiar to each province of meaning belongs a specific tension of consciousness and, consequently, also a specific *epoche,* a prevalent form of spontaneity, a specific form of self experience, a specific form of sociality, and a specific time perspective.[19]

In each of these provinces of meaning humans are equipped with a stock of knowledge, only a minimal amount of which originates in their individual experiences. The greater part of it is socially derived and, more importantly, socially approved. Sumner's classical theory expresses well the human attitude to this socially derived knowledge: the folkways of the in-group, that is, the socially derived and approved knowledge, both theoretical and practical, are unquestioningly accepted by its members as the only true, good, efficient, and morally right way of life.[20] It is utterly irrelevant whether such socially approved knowledge is ontologically "true." All its elements are believed to be true and are, therefore, real components of the definition of any situation. Social science expresses the practical reality of this socially approved stock of knowledge in the so-called Thomas Theorem: "If men define situations as real, they are real in their consequences."[21] Every different province of meaning embodies a claim to rightness. As Martin comments: "*this* line of conduct is seen as appropriate or even as natural; *that* line of conduct as inappropriate or unnatural."[22] Translated to Schutz's terminology, this means that if any item of knowledge is socially approved, then that item is taken for granted as a real and true element of the world.

To return to the example of the Nazis. Part of the socially approved stock of knowledge available to Nazis was the belief that Jews, Gypsies, and homosexuals were a source of impurity in the race. To argue that such a postulate is manifest nonsense misses the mark, for in the province of meaning in which convinced Nazis moved it was accepted as unquestionable fact. Within the Nazi conceptual organization such a thesis was defined as real, and its social consequences were all too tragically real. Examples could be multiplied from various provinces of meaning, for instance, the established theological world's reaction to Aquinas, the scientific world's reaction to Copernicus and Galileo, the academic art world's reaction to the Impressionists, but for the moment this one will suffice.

The question of how truth and reality are settled in a world in which humans live within provinces of meaning rather than face to face with reality can now be resolved. In the light of the preceding analysis, the solution to this important question can be condensed into several theses: First, humans live within various provinces of meaning or perspectives, among which we name everyday life, mythology, religion, art, and science. Second, each of these provinces of meaning receives from the actors involved in them a particular accent of reality, a particular cognitive style, and a particular internal consistency and compatibility. Third, consistency and compatibility exist only *within* a province of meaning and in no way function from one province to another. What is consistent and compatible, for instance, within the province of religion will not necessarily be compatible within the province of science, and vice versa. Fourth, within each province of meaning there is a specific *epoche,* or suspension of doubt, about the truth and reality of the meaning proposed in the province.

In sum, the question of truth and reality in the *human* world is settled within and in relation to provinces of meaning which are established by human actors, within and in relation to perspectives adopted by human actors. Such a solution to the question inevitably raises the specter of relativity, which is frightening to many. If truth and reality are settled in relation to provinces of meaning or perspectives, is this not to advance the postulate that all human truth is relative? The answer is that, indeed, all human truth is relative. But this answer requires careful elaboration. Before proceeding to this elaboration, however, the analysis of the social origin of truth and reality must be concluded by taking it one further, systematic step.

## Sociology of Knowledge

Peter Berger and Thomas Luckmann, following Karl Mannheim, have codified the preceding analysis into a systematic sociology of knowledge.[23] They have highlighted one facet of the problem of social reality which has been in the background to this point, namely, that the individual and the society in which he lives are not two totally independent realities. Rather they are realities which work in an ongoing dialectic of interdependence. Human society is a human product and nothing but a human product. "Despite the objectivity that marks the social world in human experience, it does not thereby acquire an ontological status apart from the human activity that produced it."[24] And yet this humanly produced social world constantly acts upon its producers, conforming them to itself and controlling them. On the one hand, in their social life expressions, Mead's "me," humans are social products which then, on the other hand, act upon the society which produced them to modify it and give it new form. The relationship between men and women, the producers, and the social world, their product, is dialectical. Society is a product of human activity, and humans, at least in part, are products of society. "The problem of human science is to formulate the parameters of the intersubjective world in such a way that the self-transcendence of the intentional consciousness (the "I") is held in tension with the structures of the social and cultural world [including the social self or the "me"]."[25] Berger and Luckmann argue that the tension between individual and society has three moments: a moment of externalization, a moment of objectivation, and a moment of internalization.

Humans do not have a given relationship to the world; they must establish one. In the process of establishing this relationship to the world, humans simultaneously produce both a world which is a human world and themselves as social beings in this world. The world that is produced is called, broadly, culture, the totality of human products, both material and non-material.[26] Men and women produce tools of every kind. They produce, also, language and via this language, complex constructions of meaning that permeate every aspect of their lives. In Schutz's terms, they produce complex, and finite, provinces of meanings. Society is part of that complex of meanings, that part of it that structures men's and women's ongoing relations with their fellow men and women. Individuals become persons, that is, individuals-in-relation, by taking up the cues historically offered to them in the social drama that unfolds around them. They define themselves, and are socially defined, through the opportunities and constraints others set before them as either socially appropriate and right or socially inappropriate and wrong. "It is human nature to grow real in the mirror of other people's eyes."[27] As an element of the cultural meaning complex, society fully shares in culture's character as a human product. Society and its citizens are both constituted and maintained by the activity of human beings, and have no reality apart from such activity.

Society, then, is an externalized product of the human, symbolic animal. To speak, however, of an externalized product is already to imply that the product achieves a certain autonomy from its producer. The process of transformation of human products into a world that not only derives from humans but also confronts them as an objective reality apart from them is called objectivation. The human product becomes something *out there,*[28] something that cannot easily be wished away, something that has the status of objective reality. For the material products of human activity, that objectivity is readily grasped. Men and women construct houses, automobiles, shirts, and cakes, and by their actions increase the totality of physical objects in the world and of objects which confront them as *out there,* independent of them. It is similar with the human products they produce. They construct a language and then find that their verbal communication is dominated by that language and its rules of syntax. They construct values and then feel guilty when they contravene them. They fashion institutions, which then confront them as powerful forces in the external world apart from their activities. Institutions such as family, education, politics, economics, religion; meaning structures such as mythology, religion, philosophy, science; roles and identities such as parent, child, theologian, scientist; all these are apprehended as real and true phenomena in the social world apart from human activity, though both they and the social world are nothing but the products of creative human activity. Eric Voegelin puts what I have been saying strongly. Human society, he says, "is illuminated from within by the human beings who continuously create and bear it as the mode and condition of their self-realization. It is illuminated through an elaborate symbolism ... from rite, through myth, to theory ... and this symbolism illuminates it with meaning so far as the symbols make the internal structure of such a cosmion, the relations between its members and groups of members, as well as its existence as a whole, transparent for the mystery of human existence."[29] Persons embraced into a society that humans have created experience the society, not as something merely convenient or accidental, but as something that is of their human essence.

Human consciousness, then, is confronted by its own objectivated products, non-physical as well as physical. Internalization is the process of reabsorption of these objectivations into consciousness in such a way that the humanly created structures of the objectivated world, in turn, create the structures of human consciousness. Human products, and they need not be enumerated again, function as the formative elements of human consciousness. Insofar as internalization has taken place, individuals apprehend the elements of the objectivated world as both phenomena of the external world and phenomena internal to their consciousness. Every society faces the problem of communicating its objectivated meanings to succeeding generations, a task which is accomplished through the broad process of education called socialization.[30] Berger advances the foregoing dialectic understanding of human and social reality as a synthesis of the theories of the two fathers of classical sociology, Max Weber and Emile Durkheim. Weber understood social reality as constituted by human meaning; Durkheim understood it as having the character of facticity over against the individual. They intended respectively the subjective origin and the objective facticity of social reality.[31] Berger's theory preserves both these ideas in dialectical tension. It also raises the critical, and to many threatening, question of relativity. It is that to which we now turn.

## Truth Within Perspective

It is time to take up the question which was bracketed earlier, namely, the question of the relativity of human truth. Our previous analysis concluded that human truth is acknowledged from within a province of meaning which is humanly constructed. Each province of meaning has its own accent of reality, its own cognitive style, and its own consistency and compatibility, none of which function in any other province. Outside of any given province of meaning there is no possibility of grasping the truth believed within that province. To understand the truth believed in religion, for instance, it is necessary to enter into religion with all its theoretical presuppositions. Berger argues it this way: "Each world requires a social 'base' for its continuing existence as a world that is real to actual human beings. This base may be called its plausibility structure."[32] Without participating in the plausibility structure of religion, religion will not be seen as real and valid. This view that there is a relationship between forms of thought and certain social groups in which alone they can arise, be elaborated and, consequently, understood has been a commonplace in the sociology of knowledge since Max Scheler,[33] though Scheler himself seriously compromised his move toward the social relativism of knowledge by trying to establish a hierarchy of knowledge crowned by theological knowledge.

Truth is relative to a given province of meaning and a given plausibility structure. There is a social correlate corresponding to every system of knowledge, and only in relation to this correlate can the knowledge be perceived to be true. On the basis of this social correlate, Karl Mannheim distinguishes between "relativism" and "relationalism," eschews the more common word "relative," and argues for the "relational" character of knowledge. Relativism acknowledges that all human truth is inseparably bound to the socio-historical location of the thinker, and concludes that such truth is relative and, therefore, unreliable. Relationalism acknowledges that human truth is bound to the socio-historical location of the thinker, but does not conclude that such truth is relative and unreliable. There are two conditions for the possibility of relativism, two necessary correlates on which it depends. The first is the modern insight that all historical human thinking is bound up with the thinker's socio-historical location in life, the second the confrontation of this insight with an older theory of knowledge in which knowledge is modeled after static prototypes of the type 2+2=4. This older model of knowledge, which regarded examples such as 2+2=4 as the model of all thought, has necessarily led to the rejection of all those forms of knowledge which were dependent upon the socio-historical location and subjective standpoint of the thinker.

Relativism owes its very existence to the discrepancy between a pre-modern theory of knowledge immune from all socio-historical influence and a modern theory of knowledge that acknowledges socio-historical influence on all thought processes. A modern theory of knowledge, which takes account of the *relational* as distinct from the *relative* character of all human knowledge, starts with the assumption that there are spheres of thought, or provinces of meaning, in which it is impossible to conceive of truth existing independently of the socio-historical context of the knower. Not even a god could formulate a proposition on historical subjects like 2+2=4, for what is intelligible in history can be formulated only with reference to images and conceptual constructions which themselves arise in the flux of socio-historical experience. Mannheim differentiates relativism and relationalism thus. An acceptance of the social dependency of truth and a static view of truth yields relativism; an acceptance of the social dependency of truth and a dynamic view of truth yield relationalism.

Lonergan, whose epistemology we are following in this book because, on reflection, I judge it to match accurately the human experience of coming to know, prefers to speak of *perspectivism* rather than of relativism. "Where relativism has lost hope about the attainment of truth, perspectivism stresses the complexity of what the historian is writing about and, as well, the specific difference of historical from mathematical, scientific and philosophic knowledge."[34] While relativism concludes to the falsity of a judgment, perspectivism concludes to its truth, albeit partial truth. According to Lonergan, perspectivism in human knowledge arises from three factors. First, human knowers are finite, their information is incomplete, and they do not attend to or master all the data available to them. Second, the knowers are selective, given their past socialization and personal experience and the range of data offered to them. Third, knowers are individually different, and we can expect them to make different selections. The theologian-knower trained in the philosophy of Plato/Augustine for instance, will attend to different data, achieve different understanding, make different judgments and different decisions from the theologian-knower trained in the philosophy of Aristotle/Aquinas, for instance. They will produce different theologies, which will not be necessarily contradictory and will be necessarily incomplete explanation and partial portrayals of a very complex reality. They are much like the viewers at first-story and tenth-story windows, introduced in the opening chapter. Each gets a different and limited view of the total panorama outside the building. Every judgment of truth, including, perhaps especially, every judgment of theological truth, is a limited judgment and commitment based on limited data and understanding. "So far from resting on knowledge of the universe, [a judgment] is to the effect that, no matter what the rest of the universe may prove to be, at least *this* is so."[35] It is precisely the necessarily limited nature of human, socio-historical sensations, understandings, judgments, and ultimately knowledge that leads to relationalism or perspectivism, not, to repeat again, as a source of falsity but as a source of partial truth. Though he said it on the basis of God's incomprehensibility, Augustine's restating of earlier Greek theologians is apropos and accurate here: "*Si comprehendis non est Deus*, if you have understood, what you have understood is not God."[36] Aquinas agrees: "Now we cannot know what God is, but only what God is not; we must, therefore, consider the ways in which God does not exist rather than the ways in which God does."[37]

Relationalism, then, does not signify, as does the commonly accepted nuance of relativism, that there are no criteria of rightness or wrongness for judging truth. It simply emphasizes that it is in the nature of human assertions that they can be formulated, not absolutely, but only in terms of a socio-historical perspective or province of meaning. A major question arises at this point. What does relationalism tell us about the validity of an assertion that we would not have known if we had not known that it was related to a province of meaning in which the assertor stands? Concretely, what is established about the truth or falsity of an assertion when it is established that it is derived from Catholicism, for instance, or from Marxism? Mannheim offers three possible responses to this question.

First, it may be said that the truth of an assertion is denied *ipso facto* when its origin in and structural relationship to a given socio-historical context has been shown. In this sense there is a current in the sociology of knowledge and in the theory of ideology which accepts the demonstration of origin as a refutation of the truth of an assertion, and which would use this method as a device for denying the truth of all assertions. I have named this error the generic fallacy. Secondly, counter to the first possibility, there is another possibility, namely, that the relational connection the sociology of knowledge establishes between a statement and the province of meaning or perspective of its assertor tells us nothing about the truth of the assertion, since a statement's origin tells us nothing about its truth. Whether an assertion is scientific or religious, liberal or conservative, in and of itself gives no indication of its truth value.

There is a third possibility for judging the truth of propositions, which represents both Mannheim's point of view and mine. It differs from the first view in that the mere identification and description of the socio-historical location of the assertor does not allow us to deny the truth of her or his assertion. It suggests only the suspicion that the assertion might represent only a partial view of the situation. It differs from the second alternative in that it maintains that it would be incorrect to regard the sociology of knowledge as giving no more than a description of the socio-historical conditions in and from which an assertion is made. "Every complete and thorough sociological analysis of knowledge delimits, in content as well as structure, the view to be analyzed."[38] If this possibility is the correct one, and the knowledge of human reality is dependent on the socio-historical location of the knower, and I believe that it is, then scholars, including theologians, will have to recognize that their positions, no matter how well researched, documented, and accepted, are only perspectives determined by their socio-historical location and in need of, at least, complementation and expansion or, at most, correction by other perspectives. Mannheim calls this "openness to totality."[39]

The sociological analysis of knowledge establishes that every assertion is made from the perspective of the assertor, from within a province of meaning in which the assertor uncritically stands. The application of this theory to a given assertion can contribute to determining the truth-value of the assertion, as Mannheim affirms, by warning that it may be a partial and non-exclusive truth and by precising the content and structure of that which must be judged true or false. The vexing problem with the general theory lies, not in trying to apologize for the perspectivistic and relational quality of assertions, but in showing that, given contextual relationship, true knowledge and objectivity are still possible. The real problem faced by our friends at a first-story and a tenth-story window is not how to get an unrestricted, non-perspectivistic view of the landscape, which is impossible, but how to realize that each view is only a perspective and, by juxtaposing several perspectives, reach a new and more complete level of objectivity. In other words, the unrealistic and false ideal of a detached, objective point of view must be replaced by an essentially human point of view, which is perspectivistic. This subjective point of view or perspective is not a source of error, but a source of limited truth.

The social correlate corresponding to each type and system of knowledge, which is placed in the foreground by the sociology of knowledge, should not be considered an obstacle to knowledge. The sociology of knowledge cannot invalidate knowledge, "demystify" or "disalienate" it, as Marx wanted to do. First, it is not the function of the sociology of knowledge to decide on the truth of an assertion; it does not claim to and cannot take the place of epistemology. Secondly, the "disalienation" of knowledge, understood as the freeing of all ties between knowledge and social framework, even if it is projected as something possible only in the future, can represent for the sociologist *only an intellectualist utopia of disincarnate knowledge.*[40] If knowledge is dependent on the socio-historical location of the knower, then this so-called "objectivity" is, in reality, only partial truth in need of complementation. Objective knowledge, as I have already noted, is like a mythology: "it is an arbitrary construct in which a given society in a given historical situation has invested its sense of meaningfulness and value."[41] In terms of the argument of this chapter, "objective conscious-ness" is more correctly termed "objectivated consciousness." It is not some ontological structure of reality but human meaning socially constructed into objectivated truth, meaning, value, and reality. From the perspective of the sociology of knowledge, so-called "objective reality" is more properly called "objectivated reality," "social reality," or reality invested with "social exis-tence." "We are, if you like, subject to the subject matter, which is precisely what we mean by objectivity."[42]

Such a formulation, of course, has no place in a classicist ontology which recognizes only the duality of ontological being and non-being, and which ties truth, meaning, value, and reality only to ontological being. Mannheim argues that "social being" or "social existence" lies somewhere along a con-tinuum between ontological being and non-being and suggests that it be called "being invested with meaning" or "being oriented to meaning."[43] Such an approach to the relationship of being and meaning forbids the absolute connection of meaning and reality with ontological being, and al-lows being and meaning to have a plurality of relationships deriving from a multiplicity of perspectives.

## Theology and Perspective

Theology "is a disciplined, methodologically tutored reflection on two inter-related dimensions of reality, where each of these dimensions is understood in relation to the other." The two dimensions of reality are "the supernatural communication of God in grace to historically emergent mankind" and "the existential relationships of persons to God, to one another in culture and community, to their very own selves, to the created universe, and to the principal transformative forces operative of progress and decline in human history."[44] Such theology, in Lonergan's words, "mediates between a cul-tural matrix and the significance and role of religion in that matrix"[45] and, therefore, it offers not only an understanding of God (theology) but also an understanding of man (anthropology) and an understanding of the world (cosmology). Its understanding claims to be an overarching one, within which the whole of human experience is illuminated and made meaning-ful. Such a claim differentiates theology from the social sciences which make more limited claims, offering understanding of the meaning, value, and function of particular, empirically verifiable and testable segments of human experience. The proposal of this section is, while acknowledging such obvious differentiation, to consider the interrelationship of theology and the social sciences in general, and of theology and the sociology of knowledge in particular.

The sociology of knowledge studies the functional correlations which can be established between the different types, forms, and systems of knowledge and the socio-historical contexts within which they arise.[46] In Schutzian terms, it attempts to identify the various provinces of meaning and perspectives within which humans are located and out of which they assert propositional truth. It can, therefore, be of enormous help to the theologian. It can illuminate both who the theologian is and what is the perspective out of which she or he makes assertions. It can show that the theologian is a social self inserted into a province of meaning called Christian faith and working out of that province to produce faith-rooted propositions called beliefs. It can lead theologians to the healthy realization that they advance their anthropology, cosmology, and theology from a particular province of meaning. By so doing the sociology of knowledge promotes in theologians a deeper self-understanding, which cannot but have a profound effect on both the method they employ in their theologizing and the tenacity with which they hold their theological conclusions.

The etymology of theology is easy: theology, *logos tou theou*, means word of God. Not so easy is a semantic question: is the genitive *tou theou* subjective genitive, God's own word about Godself, or objective genitive, someone else's word about God. In Christian history, *theology* has been used in both senses. Augustine used it in the fifth century to mean word about God, Dionysius the Areopagite used it in the sixth century to mean God's own word, particularly as expressed in the sacred scriptures. Scripture, he argued, in a claim that became uncritically legendary, is not just words about God but God's very own words. Both meanings passed into Christian history, which makes critical discrimination necessary when reading "theology." Though the dominant acceptation of *theology* today is the Augustinian one,[47] Dionysius continues to lurk uncritically in many quarters.

Augustine suggested and Anselm legitimated the definition which has dominated Roman Catholic theological thinking to our day. Theology is *fides quaerens intellectum*, faith seeking understanding[48] Rahner's contemporary definition, "the conscious effort of the Christian to hearken to the actual verbal revelation which God has promulgated in history, to acquire a knowledge of it by the methods of scholarship, and to reflect upon its implications"[49] further explicates Anselm. Following the Lonergan-Doran definition given above, I suggest a more Christian-specific definition. Theology is the human construal[50] of all divine and human reality in the light of the immediate self-communication of God in grace to historically emergent humankind. This self-communication, which is called by some immediate revelation, is believed in the Christian province of meaning to be historically mediated primarily in Jesus of Nazareth and secondarily in historically interpretive teachings called scripture and ecclesial doctrine. Such an approach to theology founds it on an awareness of, and makes it responsible to, the truth of God who discloses Godself to humans, but acknowledges also the constructive contribution of theologians working out of the socio-historical Christian tradition. It is God, Gordon D. Kaufman comments, "with whom the theologian *qua* theologian has to do, and since God himself has acted to make himself known, it is obvious that the ultimate court of appeal for all theological work will have to be God's revelation."[51] I agree with what Kaufman says, but something he does not say needs to be said. There is another subject in the total theological process with whom the theologian *qua* theologian and social animal has to do, namely, the theologian herself or himself who always stands in and works out of an identifiable province of meaning. As reflection, perhaps intellectually, morally, religiously, and psychically converted reflection, of a socio-historical human being on the realities of ecclesial faith, theology can never be only ecclesial, it is always also personal, historical, and social.[52]

I shall return to consider theology in greater detail in the next chapter. For the moment, I wish only to state that, though theology, as disciplined, methodologically tutored reflection on faith, is distinct from faith, it remains immovably rooted in faith,[53] and that is where the sociology of knowledge can be helpful because it focuses its analysis, not on the propositions theologians construct, but on the faith out of which they construct them. Critical socio-historical theory and analysis, now fully accepted and integrated into Catholic biblical-theological research, warn that the special theological categories "faith," "grace," "revelation," "word of God," "truth of God," in all the above affirmations must be carefully understood. Both historical and social scientific research have thrown into relief the historicity of all truth assertions, including the truth of religious and theological assertions, making extremely problematic as the ultimate court of theological appeal some unconditioned, non-perspectivistic and non-relational "God's truth." The fundamentalist may urge that the Bible is "God's truth" in an unconditioned sense, but the Catholic tradition is not fundamentalist. Catholic critical research acknowledges that the Bible is demonstrably a collection of human documents, and a very syncretist collection at that, reflecting the socio-political histories of Egypt, of Babylon, of Persia, of Greece, as well as of Israel. Far from being an unconditioned "God's truth," the Bible is the resultant of the interaction of a particular cultural history with other cultural histories in a distant Mediterranean culture. The theologian may, indeed, claim the Bible as God's truth, but only as God's truth embodied and expressed within a particular cultural context.[54]

There has been an important change of perspective in contemporary Catholic theology which sees the divine as transcendent *Mystery* present in and to the world as horizon and ground of existence.[55] This Mystery-God has been revealed in Israel and Jesus the Christ as salvation, as the One who summons women and men to recognize their personal and social sins, to repent of them, and to move forward in history to be reconciled and saved. The Mystery has not, however, been revealed from outside human history. The Mystery is communicated to every man and woman created and born into the world, and remains embedded in their world as a "supernatural existential" at the very heart of the flow of history.[56] Divine transcendence is not above the historical process but at its very heart; divine infinity is not something over and above human finiteness, but something that is "in and through the finite as its unfolding forward movement."[57] Revelation is not new propositional truths uttered into human history from the outside. Revelation is the personal, pre-reflexive, pre-propositional self-communication of the Mystery-God who is then reflexively discerned speaking in "deeds and words"[58] from within human history. Faith in this revealed Mystery-Truth establishes believers in a new consciousness, a new perspective, a new province of meaning, out of which they act toward their own and the world's salvation. If revealed Mystery-Truth is redemptive, it is not because it is static, unchanging, and to be learned but because it is dynamic, transforming, and to be lived. When believers cooperate with this dynamic operative Grace, they can be transformed, they can be intellectually, morally, religiously, and psychically converted, and either deepen their faith perspective or move to a more critical, decisive, and responsible stance with respect to it. Christian truth is not verified by philosophical analysis, it is verified by transformed human lives. "You will know them by their fruits," Jesus proclaims (Matt 7:16, 20), and his third-century follower, Cyprian, bishop of Carthage, agrees. In an exhortation to newly initiated Christians, he argues that it is the truth of Christian life that counts, not true propositions. "To put on the name of Christ and not continue along the way of Christ, what is that but a lie?"[59] If we have put on Christ, "we ought to go forward according to the example of Christ."[60]

It is no easier for the theologian to locate an unconditioned "God's truth" in Jesus of Nazareth. Christian theology must constantly be on its guard against Docetism, the perspective that taught that Jesus was never really a man but only seemed (*dokein*) to be a man. Docetism was rejected as a Christian approach to truth at the great early councils, a rejection that culminated in the credal teaching that Jesus was "truly God and truly man."[61] The social sciences insist that any such confession of the true humanity of Jesus, any confession that he was true man, leads inescapably to the conclusion that he was a man shaped by the socio-historical truths, meanings, and values of his time. It is a simple further step to eliminate any ongoing group of people, or church, as the repository of an unconditioned "God's truth," for the arguments which relationalize and limit the Bible and Jesus relationalize and limit every church as well, a point which Milbank needs to consider in his judgments of the churches which historically embody the Christian tradition. An absolute theological source, independent of and unconditioned by any socio-historical influence, is simply an abstract dream. Theological activity, in all ages of history, participates in and is dependent upon the rest of human cultural activity. It is not an isolated discipline, but one that is practiced in relation with other cultural activities, by which it is influenced and which it, in turn, influences.

The social sciences and theology are not isolated from, but inseparably bound to, one another, in as much as they derive from the same socio-historical matrix. Catholic theology has to learn from the sociology of knowledge that there is a variety of points of view or perspectives on the ultimate questions humans ask and the answers which they accept, including the ultimate questions and answers they ask in that institution called religion.[62] Each of these perspectives and provinces of meaning has its own internal truth, meaning, value, and consistency for its adherents. "In certain areas of historical-social knowledge it should be regarded as inevitable that a given finding should contain the traces of the position of the knower. The problem lies not in trying to hide these perspectives or in apologizing for them, but of inquiring into the question of how, granted these perspectives, knowledge and objectivity are still possible."[63]

Perspective is not a source of error as much as it is a source of partial, non-exclusive truth. The epistemological problem is not how to avoid perspectival knowledge, but how to recognize it as such and, by juxtaposing various perspectives, arrive at an expanded level of objectivity. The idea that there is a sphere of truth-in-itself is an ideological hypothesis, which the sociology of knowledge demands be replaced by the idea of an essentially human point of view seeking to enlarge itself. A theology informed by such theory will recognize that it, too, is perspectivistic, and also that it is one perspective among many. A specifically Christian theology will recognize that it is a perspective which, over the centuries, has emerged out of Christian

62

Sociology of Knowledge and Theology

socio-historical circumstances as the followers of the Christ came succes-sively in contact with Greco-Roman, northern European, and New World perspectives, and continues to emerge as the established tradition from the past confronts new social and cultural contexts.

Implicit in this dynamic, perspectival concept of truth, or the openness of every truth to the totality of truth, is what Mannheim calls a "politi-cal elan,"[64] a social order in which the complementation and expansion of perspectival truth is possible. That complementation can be achieved only through the medium of a genuine dialogue, or dialectic in the Habermasian sense, "an exercise of reflective judgment in which both parties mutually instruct each other . . . for the purposes of attaining a consensus among politi-cally active citizens."[65] In this dialogue, different perspectives and provinces of meaning listen to one another from a position of methodologically as-signed equality, for "true dialogue takes place only among equals."[66] In our day, the Catholic Church and its theology embrace the demands of such mutually-equal dialogue in the socio-historical contexts of the world religions.

In an address to the peoples of Asia in 1981, Pope John Paul II asserts that the church today "feels a profound need to enter into contact and dia-logue with all of these religions."[67] All Christians are to be committed to this dialogue, he explains, "so that mutual understanding and collabora-tion may grow, so that moral values may be strengthened, so that God may be praised in all creation."[68] In his important encyclical letter, *Redemptoris Missio,* the pope continues these thoughts, insisting that inter-religious dia-logue is "a method and a means of mutual knowledge and enrichment,"[69] that it "can enrich each side" in the dialogue, and that it "leads to inner purification and conversion."[70] Jacques Dupuis comments with justification that "there is question here, not of the conversion of the others to Chris-tianity, but of the conversion toward God of both partners of dialogue, the Christian and the other."[71] The subsequent letter from the Pontifical Coun-cil for Inter-Religious Dialogue, *Dialogue and Proclamation,* while firmly insisting on the unchanging mission of the church to proclaim the gospel of Jesus Christ, continues and fully elaborates the demand for dialogue, teach-ing that "the fullness of truth received in Jesus Christ does not give the individual Christian the guarantee that they have grasped the truth fully. In the last analysis truth is not a thing we possess, but a person by whom we must allow ourselves to be possessed."[72] I shall return to this personal truth in the next chapter. For the moment, I note only that Catholic theological propositions about God are acknowledged today, as they have consistently been acknowledged in the Catholic tradition, as partial, non-exclusive truth, open to complementation and expansion.[73] The designated Catholic road to that complementation and expansion is the road of dialogue between friends and equals.

The traditional description of Roman Catholic theology introduced at the beginning of this section is, then, incomplete. It requires an important addition. Roman Catholic theology not only offers an interpretation of God, the world, and the human, but it offers such an interpretation *from a Roman Catholic perspective.* The past and present history of this perspective are to be seen in the context of the socio-historical environment in which they developed and by which they were influenced in many respects. "All of the tools of social, cultural and intellectual history must be brought to bear, then, on the Hebraic-Christian history from which the Christian perspective emerged and in which it continued to be formed. . . . The value of such studies to the theologian is that they help him to see more clearly and vividly just what the Christian understanding of God, man and the world has been in the past so that he is in a better position to grapple with its appropriate formulation for the present."[74]

Roman Catholic theology, it should now be clear, is a Mannheimian perspective or a Schutzian province of meaning. It is an attempt to develop a consistent and compatible interpretation of God, the world, and the human from a Catholic perspective socio-historically conditioned in particular ways. Importantly, in Berger's terms, though it is reflection on God's self-communication and self-revelation, it is a humanly constructed interpretation. If such be the case, and if the objective consciousness of theology is really objectivated consciousness, partial truth in need of complementation and expansion by other perspectives, then theology must honestly face a problem. It can be called into question and superseded by cultural movements which find meaning and value elsewhere and provide a different socio-historical location. Pierre Thibault provides a brilliantly analyzed example in the case of Scholasticism. In the Middle Ages, when it came to prominence and flourished, Scholasticism was a highly respected and dynamic new cultural and philosophic achievement. When it was revived in the nineteenth century, under the auspices of a beleaguered papacy, it became a static philosophy which promoted the power of the church and the social order which supported it.[75] When that social order gave way, it was inevitable that the Scholasticism that rested on it would also give way, as Walter Kasper testifies that it did. "There is no doubt that the outstanding event in the catholic theology of our century is the surmounting of neo-Scholasticism."[76]

Baum offers another example of the influence of cultural change on the Catholic doctrine of human nature. For centuries, the Catholic tradition held that the subordination of women to men was of the order of nature.

Any exercise of leadership in the church by women, therefore, would be "unnatural." Today, that teaching has changed and we are told that the subordination of women to men is not according to nature, and, therefore, women are not barred from exercising leadership positions in society, including the church. They are barred, however, from holding the priestly office because of a new, modern Catholic teaching, namely, since Christ was a male, the priest who represents him must be a male.[77] Baum comments that this new view is "obviously related to the actual social change that has taken place in Western society: it dawned upon theologians only after women have become conscious of their inferior position, organized a movement to change the structure of society, and achieved considerable success."[78] It is an important concrete case of doctrine dependent on socio-historical location.

If Catholic theology is an expression of socio-historical context perspective, Kaufman's judgment would appear to be unavoidable. "We will have to admit that its social and cultural power derive in a similar way from its persuasiveness in dealing with human problems (and not simply from its being in some undialectical sense, the expression of God's truth), and that it, too, will likely come to an end when it is no longer genuinely illuminating of man's condition. This perspective, then, like any other, is apprehended as 'true' so far as it succeeds in actually illuminating man's situation in the world; it becomes questionable, and finally 'false,' when there are compelling experiences with which it cannot deal."[79] The above examples adduced by Thibault and Baum show the influence of changing socio-historical contexts on Catholic teaching. These are only two examples of the increased influence the expansion of modern knowledge has had on theological studies. "Without usually becoming expert in such disciplines, theologians have recognized how vulnerable is their discipline to influences from outside — of which archaeology, comparative religion, anthropology, psychology, and sociology are perhaps the most relevant."[80]

In a postmodern context, the job of Catholic theologians is more critical than mere commentary on sources. Following research, interpretation, history, and dialectic, which mediate the past, there is required foundations, doctrines, systematics, and communication, which mediate the past to the present situation and provoke the future. The task of Roman Catholic theologians in the present situation is always to show that Roman Catholic categories, perhaps unchanged or perhaps transformed by changing socio-historical context, can and do make contemporary experience meaningful. We proceed now to that task in chapter 4.

## Conclusion

This chapter has been about the sociology of knowledge, its distinctive theory of the social construction of reality, and the implications of such a theory for theologians and their theologies. The sociology of knowledge shows that men and women live within various provinces of meaning or perspectives, among which are numbered the provinces of common sense, mythology, science, religion, and art. Each of these provinces of meaning receives from the human actors in them a particular accent of reality which is taken for granted, a particular cognitive style which is unchallenged, and a particular internal consistency and compatibility which is uncritical. What is consistent within one province of meaning, religion for instance, will not necessarily be compatible within another province, science for instance, and vice versa. Within each province of meaning, there is a specific *epoche* or suspension of doubt about the truth and reality of the meaning taken for granted within the province. This sociological claim that questions of truth and reality in the human world are settled within and in relation to provinces of meaning socially constructed by human actors inevitably raises the threatening question about the relativity of truth in the human world. The answer to that question requires careful explanation.

Human truth is, indeed, relative. That is to say, however, not that it is false and unreliable, which is how the phrase "relative truth" is usually interpreted, but that it is true and reliable in relation to a particular province of meaning. I prefer a distinction suggested by Mannheim, human truth is *relational* rather than *relative*. Relativism acknowledges that all human truth is inseparably bound to the socio-historical location of the thinker, and concludes that such truth is, therefore, unreliable. Relationalism acknowledges that human truth is bound to the socio-historical location of the thinker, but concludes not that such truth is unreliable but that it is only partially true and in need of complementation to achieve a more total view on truth and reality. If this sociological analysis is correct, and human knowledge of truth and reality is dependent on the socio-historical location of the knower, and I believe it is, then all human knowers, including both sociologists and theologians, will have to recognize that their positions, no matter how thoroughly researched, interpreted, and undialectically accepted, are perspectives determined by their socio-historical perspectives and in need of, at least, complementation and expansion and, at most, correction by other perspectives. They must have, that is, an "openness to totality."[81] The problem with relational knowledge for all human knowers lies not in trying to hide the perspectives in which their knowledge is true but in inquiring into the question of how, given the perspectives, true knowledge and consensus is possible.

The complementation which perspectival knowledge always requires can be achieved only through the medium of genuine dialogue, an attentive, intelligent, rational, responsible process in which both parties respectfully instruct one another for the purpose of attaining more complete knowledge and consensus. In the socio-historical context of the modern world, Catholic theologians must embrace the demands of such mutually equal dialogue with respect to one another and with respect to theologians of other perspectival provinces of meaning, and the Catholic Church must embrace them with respect to other world religions. Addressing the peoples of Asia in 1981 Pope John Paul II clearly stated as much: the church "feels a profound need to enter into contact and dialogue with all of these religions."[82] This irenic dialogue, he went on to explain is necessary "so that mutual understanding and collaboration may grow, so that moral values may be strengthened, so that God may be praised in all creation."[83] A genuine dialogue, in which the partners are treated as equals, is not for the conversion of one to the other's position, but for mutual enrichment, purification, and conversion in the Lonerganian sense. A religious or theological dialogue is not for the necessary conversion of one of the partners to the other's position but for the conversion of both to God and the totality of the limited truth about God that humans may attain in a world ever delimited by perspectives and provinces of meaning. In a world of acknowledged perspectives and provinces of meaning, the task of the Catholic theologian is more critical than mere commentary on traditional sources. The task is to show that special Roman Catholic categories and symbols, perhaps changed by changed socio-historical contexts, can and do make contemporary experience meaningful. We approach that task in the next chapter.

## Questions for Discussion

1. "The decisive criterion for the meaning of human action is the project of the actor." Discuss this statement and its implications for discerning human meaning and reality.

2. What do you understand by the phrases "perspective" and "province of meaning?" Can you name any common provinces of meaning that are active in your own life? What do the phrases, and the reality that underlies them, contribute to human understanding? Do they have anything to do with Lonergan's notion of conversion?

3. What do you understand by the terms "externalization," "objectivation," "internalization." What is the overall effect of the process to which these terms refer?

4. "Truth is relative to a given province of meaning and a given plausibility structure." Discuss this statement with particular reference to Mannheim's distinction between truth as relative and truth as relational.

5. Is the socio-historical fact that there are competing systems of theology in the Catholic Church in any way connected with the reflection you have done for the above questions? Why are there competing theologies, even competing religions? Is not the "word of God" obvious to anyone who simply pays attention?

# FOUR

# Theology, Sociology, and Scripture

This chapter continues reflection on theology and social context, specifying the reflection to the correlation between theology, sacred scripture, and their social contexts. It argues that the theology of the second and third generation followers of the Christ, which resulted from their reflection on the immediate revelation of God achieved in the first generation's experience of Jesus, eventually became by socio-ecclesial decision the ecclesial scripture of the church. From this relationship it then draws principles for the use and authority of scripture in theology. The chapter is key to the overall project of the book, which argues that all theologians and the theologies they produce are socially constructed, including those theologians and theologies that were canonized in the second century as the ecclesial scriptures of the church. Because the first Christian theologians and their theologies are necessarily embedded in the ambient socio-historical contexts of their times and places, any subsequent attempt to translate and interpret the meanings of their words will have to first illuminate their social context. Such illumination, I have already argued, cannot be provided by theology alone or sacred scripture alone; it requires also social scientific analysis.

## Why Sacred Scripture?

We begin our consideration of scripture with the question that first faced the early Christian communities, at least implicitly: do we need to write the story of Jesus and, if yes, why? The answer to that question, and particularly why Matthew, Mark, Luke, and John wrote "gospels," theological narratives of "the things that have been accomplished among us" (Luke 1:1) in the life, death, and resurrection of Jesus of Nazareth, is a powerful exemplar of the influence of socio-historical contexts on even the gospels. A standard scholarly answer to the question is that the evangelists wrote in response to the "needs" of the Jesus groups, a social need occasioned by the deaths of the eyewitnesses, and a social-control need occasioned by the competing interpretations of Jesus' life, death, and resurrection advanced by emerging prophets and charismatics. Though I find this answer creatively intuitive, I believe there is another explanation, one that is more scientific and compelling, one that derives from a well-established socio-historical principle, the *principle of third generation*.[1] /

The principle of third generation was first articulated by the historian Marcus L. Hansen. The principle of third generation, Hansen wrote, "is applicable in all fields of historical study. It explains the recurrence of movements that seemingly are dead; it is a factor that should be kept in mind particularly in literary or cultural history. . . . The theory is derived from the almost universal phenomenon that what the son wishes to forget the grandson wishes to remember."[2] The principle embraces three generations: an "ancestor" or "father," representative of an original socio-historical situation; a "descendant" or "son," representative of a radically changed situation; a third-generation "grandson," representative of yet another new socio-historical situation. Hansen applies the principle to the analysis of immigrant experience; Will Herberg applies it to the immigrant religious community.[3] The first generation immigrant came from another country, the "old country," and maintained warm, frequently romanticized, feelings toward it. The second generation, the original immigrant's children, have no clear memories of the old country. They are too absorbed in the struggle to become acculturated to the new country, and in particular, perhaps, to learn a new language that will enable them to function in the new culture. The third generation, the children's children, are fully acculturated, they can speak the language, they understand and can function in the culture, and they now have questions about ethnic roots that are crucial for self-identity. Engaged in a search for roots, everything about their origin in the old country is important to them and they wish to learn about it and preserve it. I apply the same principle to the analysis of the experience of the early followers of Jesus.

The earliest followers of Jesus, those who constituted his core group, who perhaps traveled with him and were eyewitnesses of what he did and said, along with their families and believing friends, are the first Jesus' generation. They are contemporary with Jesus, and are described in the Synoptics as "this generation" (Matt 12:41–42; Mark 8:12; Luke 11:29–32). Paul and his contemporaries are the second Jesus generation. They are not eyewitnesses to what Jesus said and did. Rather, they delivered (*paredōka*), handed down, "to you as of first importance what [they] also received, that Christ died for our sins in accordance with the scriptures, that he was buried, that he was raised on the third day in accordance with the scriptures, and that he appeared to Cephas, then to the twelve" (1 Cor 15:3). The authors of the gospels are the third Jesus generation, as Luke himself clearly testifies in his Prologue. "Inasmuch as many have undertaken to compile a narrative of the things which have been accomplished among us, just as they were delivered (*paredosan*) to us by those who from the beginning were eyewitnesses and ministers of the word, it seemed good to me also ... to write an orderly account for you, most excellent Theophilus, that you may know the truth concerning the things of which you have been informed" (Luke 1:1–4). The key word in Luke's text, as it is also in Paul's, is *paredosan,* to deliver or, more accurately, to hand down. The one who hands down is different from the one who is an eyewitness. The eyewitness attests to a hearer what she has seen and heard; the hearer then hands down to a third person what has been attested to him. Three generations: the first, the eyewitnesses; the second, those to whom the eyewitnesses attest and who, in their turn, hand down what has been attested; the third, those who receive what is handed down. Luke is in this third generation, and so are Matthew, Mark, and John. The line of demarcation between the generations is, of course, fluid, not rigid. As I overlap in time with my children and my grandchildren, so also the three generations of Jesus' followers might have overlapped. Generation as I use it here is not about rigid chronology but about the radically changed socio-historical situation. Which raises a crucial question: how were the socio-historical situations of the three generations different?

"From a generational perspective, the most significant, irreversible social change for Jesus groups was the radical institutional transition from first generation Jesus group concerns with political religion (the kingdom of God/heaven) to emerging second generation concerns with fictive kinship religion (living in Christ)."[4] Jesus' fundamental preaching in the Synoptics is his proclamation that "the kingdom of God is at hand" (Mark 1:15; Matt 4:17). "Kingdom of God" or, in Matthew's pious Jewish equivalent, "Kingdom of heaven," occurs one hundred and four times in the Synoptics, a high distribution which, "along with the content, justifies considering the formula a theological theme."[5] This kingdom of God is not a geographical place, either in heaven or on earth; it is a rule, a theocratic rule, God's rule. Kingdom of God is what God does, and kingdom of God is what the first generation of Jesus' followers looked for after they were convinced of his resurrection. God, they believed, had made Jesus "Lord and Christ" (Acts 2:36), Israel's Messiah soon to come in power. The expected theocracy, however, did not materialize and, as the first generation waited in vain for it to come, a second Jesus generation arose in an entirely new socio-historical situation with an entirely new focus.

The first Jesus generation had attested to the second generation Jesus' fundamental proclamation of the Kingdom of God that was to come; God had set the divine seal on Jesus and his activity by raising him from the dead; and yet the proclaimed kingdom had not arrived. The second generation asked "why?" and answered that the kingdom had not yet come because it had not yet been proclaimed to all Israel, that all Israel was not yet prepared for the kingdom of God, and that, therefore, the kingdom had to be proclaimed. It had been attested to them that Jesus said "The good news [of the kingdom of God] must first be preached to [all Israelites in] all nations" (Mark 13:10). Paul, the representative second-generation Jesus follower, took up this charge and made it explicit. "How are men to call upon him in whom they have not believed? And how are they to believe in him of whom they have never heard? And how are they to hear without a preacher? And how can men preach unless they are sent? As it is written, 'how beautiful are the feet of those who proclaim the good news [of the kingdom of God]' " (Rom 10:14–15). Though he does on occasion cite words of Jesus (1 Cor 7:10; 9:14; 11:23), Paul shows no interest in Jesus' life. Rather than asking "what did Jesus say and do in his career?" he tends to ask "what should *we* say and do now that we are 'in Christ'?" (e.g. Rom 8:1; 9:1; 12:5; 15:17; 16:03; 1 Cor 1:2; 1:30; 3:1; 4:10; 4:17; 15:18; 16:24). His answer to that question when applied to marriage among the Corinthians, as we shall see in detail in chapter 7, even goes against the words of Jesus (1 Cor 7:15).

Third generation followers of Jesus, in contradistinction to Paul and his generation, were interested, almost had to be interested, in the story of what Jesus said and did, what some people in Jerusalem did to him, and ultimately what God did to him, not so much to sustain a hope for a coming theocratic kingdom as much to clarify "the truth concerning the things of which you have been informed" (Luke 1:4). The orderly accounts or gospels of Matthew, Mark, Luke, and John, different though these accounts are because they were written in different socio-historical contexts, presented the roots for the required clarification. The gospels, that is, in Hansen's terminology, are exemplars of the principle of third generation, "the almost universal phenomenon that what the son wishes to forget the grandson wishes to remember."[6]

Another factor motivating the third generation's search for its roots was a common one, namely, many of them were the grandchildren of immigrant Israelites. The last wave of Jesus followers left Jerusalem and Judea during the Roman onslaught of 67 CE, which culminated in the destruction of the temple in 70 CE. They became "exiles of the dispersion in Pontus, Galatia, Cappadocia, Asia, and Bythinia" (1 Pet 1:1). They became, that is, immigrants in new lands and new cultures, and they experienced all the travails traditionally experienced by immigrants. The first generation of these immigrants, who were already the third generation of Jesus followers, experienced the sense of alienation brought on by the inevitable sense of foreignness, and the consequent effort to overcome that alienation through social acceptance by "forgetting" the old country. Their grandchildren, who had become acculturated in their new cultures, sought to remember the Israeliteness that their grandfathers and grandmothers had forgotten, only now it was an Israeliteness filtered through the handed down memories of the "King of Israel" (Matt 27:42; Mark 15:32; John 1:49), "the living stone rejected by men but in God's sight chosen and precious" (1 Pet 2:4). They could think of themselves as Israelites every bit as much as were those who were returning to the Israeliteness of Torah, Temple worship, and political religion. They could, therefore, be assured in ancient Israelite images that "you are a chosen race, a royal priesthood, a holy nation, God's own people" (1 Pet 2:9). Their socialization into a Hellenistic culture, their consequent inclusive embracing of Gentiles into the Jesus movement, and their return to their Israelite roots as filtered through their "memories" of Jesus transformed the Jesus movement from its original Judean socio-historical setting into a Hellenistic cultural setting. From there, of course, as is well-known, it underwent a series of further transformations, into Roman and northern European cultural settings. None of that needs detailing here. The only question at issue here is the one that opened this section: why gospels? Gospels came into existence because the third generation followers of Jesus sought to remember what the second generation had forgotten, namely, the roots of the Jesus movement in the first generation and their experience of Jesus.

## The Origin of Scripture

The preceding section responded to the question: *why* were the gospels written? This section responds to the question: *how* were the New Testament scriptures written? This question is really a question of how theologians, in general, construe[7] scripture, and what authority, in specific, they assign to it. The standard answer for Christian theologians is that scripture is construed as a normative authority for the Christian church and, therefore, also for Christian theology. David Kelsey's detailed case study of seven Protestant theologians, however, demonstrates the diversity of ways in which that authority is construed.[8] It is construed with equal diversity by Catholic theologians. I begin my analysis with a statement of what I believe scripture to be and, alternatively, of how the followers of the Christ came to call certain writings *sacred scripture*. I suggest a standard four-stage process: a first-generation of Jesus followers who construed their experience of Jesus as religious and revelatory of God; the growth of interpretive traditions about that experience; the preservation of those traditions in written form in the third generation;[9] the canonization of certain writings as authoritative ecclesial scripture. How theologians understand this four-stage process, I suggest, determines how they construe scripture and its authority in theology.

The first stage of the formation of scriptures is a historical experience construed as religious, that is, as the revelation of the divine Mystery. It is impossible now to reconstruct in secure detail what the originating historical experience was, what it was that historically happened, for instance, in the death and resurrection of Jesus of Nazareth that led to its construal as religious and revelatory. Nor does it matter. What matters for the sociology of knowledge is not the empirical details of the event but the socially construed religious meaning of the event. A historical experience, perhaps even a *fictionally* historical experience,[10] is construed as a religious experience, as the *pre-reflexive foundational revelation* of God.[11] This foundational revelation of God to the first generation of Jesus followers is the *pre-text,* first, for the creation of socially constructed and approved meanings of this revelation in the second and third generations and, later, for the writings eventually called sacred scripture. It is also, to anticipate, the subject matter of all subsequent interpretation in theological history.

The second stage of the formation of scripture is the growth of interpretive traditions about foundational revelation. These traditions were initially oral, in poem and song, prayer and hymn, myth and story. At this oral stage, the traditions were fluid and easily accommodated to new situations. In the third stage, oral traditions were committed to writing, and the now-written traditions reflexively codified the originally pre-reflexive experience, socially construed as revelatory, and replaced it as immediate basis for reflection and commentary. The Second Vatican Council's Dogmatic Constitution on Divine Revelation, *Dei Verbum,* legitimated these three stages and explained the essential connection between them. "The sacred authors, in writing the four gospels, selected certain of the many elements which had been handed on, either orally or already in written form, others they synthesized or explained with an eye to the situation of the churches, the while sustaining the form of preaching, but always in such a fashion that they have told us the honest truth about Jesus."[12] The written traditions that derived from these three stages provide the *texts*[13] that became ecclesial scripture.

The fourth and final stage of the development of scripture is the selection of certain written traditions as privileged reflections on the original pre-reflexive revelation. The selection of certain texts from the many available in early Christian experience yielded privileged texts received in the community of believers as the classical expression of the understanding of God and of God's self-communication and self-revelation. The community judgment called canonization, which took place very slowly for the Hebrew scriptures and relatively quickly for the Christian, located the selected texts in a socio-historical perspective in which written ecclesial traditions were transformed into sacred ecclesial scripture. It is to be noted that, for the recipients of the original, pre-reflexive revelation, whoever they might have been, scripture was not original revelation but secondary, reflexive revelation, because it derived from social reflection on the original, pre-reflexive, revelatory experience. For all later generations of believers, however, it may be called secondary foundational revelation. From the perspective of believers, among whom are included Christian theologians, both the selection and canonization of texts is said in special theological language to be the inspiration of the Holy Spirit of God and is, therefore, a non-human work beyond empirical verification. From the perspective of the sociology of knowledge, however, both the selection and the canonization are easily explained as the standard work of a particular social community of believers and, therefore, open to the kind of sociological analysis that links knowledge to existence and mental structures to socio-historical contexts. Christian theologians look upon the selected writings as ecclesial sacred scripture and exegete-theologians achieve "the true goal of their work"[14] only when they have explained the meaning of scripture *as* sacred scripture. Sociologists look upon them as social, historical, and literary documents, and they achieve their goal when they have exegeted the documents as they would any other socio-historical document. I note here for the record, but to maintain focus do not deal with it, that the original revelation is expressed not only reflexively in words in sacred scripture but also non-reflexively, ritually in liturgy. Hence, the Second Vatican Council speaks of believers receiving nourishment "at the twofold table of sacred scripture and the eucharist."[15]

I suggest two imaginative ways for construing sacred scripture, the one suggested by James Barr, the second by Karl Rahner. Barr suggests the canonization of certain writings by the church was "a decision to assign a special status to the material" they contained "as the classic model for the understanding of God."[16] Scripture has special status in the community of believers because early believers assigned it that status as a classic representation of the God believed to be both source and subject of the original, pre-reflexive revelation. Rahner suggests the scripture functions also as community constitution,[17] which the Biblical Commission elaborates by explicating that "in discerning the canon of scripture, the Church was also discerning and defining her own identity."[18] *Constitution* here is to be understood, not as a legally binding document but as self-definition. The Christian church defines itself as a communion of believers in the God revealed in Jesus and expresses its understanding of that God in its canonized scripture. It is precisely "by being the self-defining classical expression of the object of the community's faith," Roger Haight writes, "that the scriptures become the constitution of the Church."[19] Scripture expresses in written form, in a specific socio-historical context, the Christian community's "rule of faith,"[20] its faith in and understanding of the God of Abraham, Isaac, and Jesus. It functions, therefore, also as the classic norm of the church's faithfulness as it seeks to express and communicate the original revelatory experience in every new socio-historical context.

## A Further Account of Theology

In the above theory, the first stage is immediate, pre-reflexive, interpersonal encounter; the second and third stages are reflexive, interpretive, and constructive human action. Since the reflection and interpretation that take place in the second and third stages are reflection on and interpretation of the revelation and presence of God, they are *theological* stages. That claim necessitates some reflection on and interpretation of the apparently innocent word "theology," for with the widespread loss of the classical languages, the ambiguity of the word is no longer transparent.

In the last chapter, I introduced both the classical definition of theology and an ambiguity embedded in the word "theology," *logos tou theou.* The ambiguity revolves around the genitive *tou theou,* of God. I asked whether that genitive is subjective, God's own word, or objective, someone else's word about God, and answered with Augustine that it is a word about God. The classical definition, "faith seeking [reflexive] understanding," continues, in one form or another, to be the accepted definition. I suggested a more Christian-specific definition. Christian theology is the construal of all reality in the light of the revelation of God, believed by Christians to be historically mediated primarily in Jesus of Nazareth and secondarily in canonized writings called scripture. The point here is that, though theology, as systematic, conceptual and verbal expression of faith, is distinct from faith, it remains rooted in faith, a Schutzian province of meaning and a Lonerganian perspective.[21] No matter how scientific it pretends to be, no matter how well its does its research, interpretation, history, dialectic, foundations, doctrines, and systematics, theology's claims to truth are rooted in faith and share faith's analogical, metaphorical, fragile knowledge of transcendent divine mystery.[22] In every age, therefore, theologians have had to face the scorn of rationalists-scientists. Augustine, as Origen before him and Aquinas after him, sought to respond to this scorn by relating theology to

Greek philosophy; later theologians have related it to a host of other disciplines. Aquinas opens his *Summa* with the question. "Whether, besides the
philosophical disciplines, any further doctrine is required?" and answers unequivocally that "it was necessary for man's salvation that there should be a
*doctrine* revealed by God, besides the philosophical disciplines investigated
by reason."[23] Philosophical knowledge is available only to a privileged few;
the knowledge provided by revelation and by *sacra doctrina* can be made
available to all.

Notice the term *sacra doctrina*. The thirteenth century was a historical
moment when faith and the word of God in scripture were so organically
linked that faith seeking understanding was essentially explanatory commentary on scripture, *commentarium in sacra pagina*. This commentary
yielded *sacra doctrina* or *theologia,* sacred doctrine or theology. The term
*theologia* asserted itself only when the thirteenth-century Scholastics added
to the technique of commentary the rationalism imported to the West with
Aristotle, a move which enabled them to distinguish philosophy and theology, nature and supernature, reason and faith, and to install theology as
the Queen of Sciences.[24] Aquinas asks "Whether sacred doctrine [theology]
is a science?" and answers that it is, "because it proceeds from principles
made known by the light of a higher science, the science of God and the
blessed. Just as music accepts on authority the principles taught by the arith-
metician, so sacred doctrine [theology] accepts the principles revealed by
God."[25] The epistemological problem, at the root of the modern tension
between scripture as the word of God and scripture as literarily, formally,
and socio-historically the words of humans, is: what are those principles
and how does the theologian come to know them?

Aquinas's articulation of a hermeneutic for *commentarium in sacra pagina* summarizes the medieval approach, and is still good advice for exegetes.
He asks "Whether in holy scripture a word may have several meanings?"
and replies that it may. There is a first meaning in which words signify
things, and that meaning is "the historical or literal meaning." The word
"fire," for instance, means the thing we see leaping and hear crackling in
the fireplace. There is a second meaning in which things signified by words
themselves have meaning to a writer, and that meaning is the spiritual meaning, *"which is based on the literal and presupposes it."*[26] *Fire,* for instance, as
in Exodus's "flame of fire out of the midst of a bush" (3:3) or Luke's "I came
to cast fire upon the earth" (12:49), does not mean only the reality leaping
and crackling in the fireplace. It also is a socially established Hebrew symbol
for the presence of God. The priority of the literal meaning as a basis for
every other meaning remains the authentic Catholic position, emphasized in
every document from *Divino Afflante* (1943) to *The Interpretation of the*

*Bible in the Church* (1993).[27] The literal meaning of the word, and any spiritual meaning socially rooted in it, is the meaning intended by the author in his socio-historical context. It is to be found only "by means of a careful analysis of the text within its literary and [socio-]historical context," and "is not to be confused with the 'literalist' sense to which fundamentalists are attached."[28] The meaning of a word is not necessarily found and expounded in a mere word-for-word translation.

If this standard theory of the formation of scripture is correct, and if Stages 2–4 are as critically constructive as I claim, several things follow. To keep sharp focus, I will deal with only three: the traditions, the writings, and the sacred scriptures expressing foundational revelation are all socially constructed; as constructive, imaginative outcome of human construal, scripture is socio-historically conditioned; if scripture is a normative authority for church and theologian and theology, it is neither an absolute nor an absolutely external authority. A consideration of these three points in turn will provide the outline of my constructive proposal for an answer to the question of the use of scripture in theology. The generic fallacy has to be recalled here, lest the claim that the interpretive traditions and the sacred scriptures which derive from them are social construals be read reductively to mean they are *only* social construals and nothing more. In the *as if* methodology I have embraced, the theologian will read the claim as if they had transcendent origins and the sociologist as if they were, indeed, nothing more than social construals.

## Scripture as the Result of Human Construal

I consider, first, foundational revelation and its reflexive expression in writings canonized as sacred scripture. The Second Vatican Council's document on revelation reflected a critical shift in the Catholic understanding of revelation, a shift from an *objectivist* to a *subjectivist* understanding.[29] An objectivist understanding equates revelation with propositional forms, in Christianity usually scriptural propositional forms. Revelation is regarded as objective knowledge about God, objectively expressed in scripture, received as the objective word of God in the Dionysian sense. That is the approach of biblical fundamentalism. The Catholic Church pursues its own doctrinal fundamentalism, which holds that revelation, objective knowledge about God, is objectively expressed also in church doctrine. Both biblical and doctrinal fundamentalism were firmly rejected by the Catholic Church at the Second Vatican Council.

Revelation is not the communication of objective knowledge *about* God, but the communication of a subject-*God* to human subjects as to friends.[30] God does not reveal books or propositions or words; God reveals Godself. This self-revelation, Christians confess, takes place definitively not in words about God but in the subject-Word of God incarnate, Jesus of Nazareth. Revelation is, therefore, subjective not objective; better, it is inter-subjective, the self-communication of a divine subject to human subjects, operative Grace seeking human co-operation. When that self-communication is received in faith, it is also self-revelation. Subjective revelation is a form of conscious human experience and, to that extent, it is knowledge. It is not, however, reflexive knowledge, not scientific knowledge in clear and distinct Cartesian ideas. It is experiential knowledge, immediate, pre-reflexive and undifferentiated, as in its best human analogy, interpersonal encounter, especially encounter between lovers. Christians confess that subject encounter with a subject God is mediated to them in the historical subject, Jesus of Nazareth. In this encounter, there is both communication and reception of that communication, the making of a conscious impression and the spontaneous, implicit interpretation of that impression. Pure, unconstrued experience, does not exist. Pure passivity, that is, the unconstrued reception of an impression, does not exist. Human experience is always actively, if only implicitly, construed. "That which is on the one hand 'received' is on the other hand 'thought' in terms of a language which contains concepts and religious notions that feed into the interpretation."[31] When it is *real* and effective encounter, experiential encounter has to be constructively received by the recipients in a socio-historically conditioned way.

The initial construal of encounter is implicit and pre-reflexive. It can be further critically construed and interpreted by explicit reflection. By being attentive to the experience, by asking intelligent questions about it, by making judgments and decisions about it,[32] humans can actively unpack the pre-reflexive encounter and represent it in reflexive metaphor, in poem and song, prayer and hymn, myth and narrative. This reflexive, critical, and constructive activity depends on both the original experience and the cultural "language" available to express it. Had the pre-reflexive self-revelation of God been reflexively construed in a cultural context other than the Mediterranean, it would certainly have been differently construed. Underlying every construal of experience are the socio-historical experiences of the group which are taken for granted and unchallenged. The construal of the encounter that is believed to be the original, foundational revelation of God, the reflection going on noetically, is faith seeking understanding, that is, theology. The language in which the reflection issues, oral or written, is human words-about-God, *logoi tou theou,* theology. It is of necessity poetic, analogical, symbolic language,[33] language which refers to something other than its referent in everyday reality, which must be negated and transcended to disclose it's referent in the province of theological meaning. There is presently an ongoing tension between biblical studies and theology precisely because biblical studies has shown that biblical language is analogical, poetic, and symbolic, and the institutional Christian churches and their theologians have not fully come to terms with broken myths, images, and symbolic representations.

Sacred scripture, then, is in the special category of theology, reflexive and secondary, not foundational, revelation. "The New Testament is made up of theological tracts. Each book of the New Testament is in its own way a methodical [theological] interpretation of the Christian experience of revelation."[34] Not only is the New Testament made up of different theological tracts, but these tracts contain different forms, sometimes history, sometimes poetry, sometimes myth. So, too, does the Old Testament. To understand scripture, therefore, the Second Vatican Council teaches, the interpreter must "have regard for literary forms."[35] Written construal of original revelation is necessarily pluralistic, in plural language in the broadest sense, as humans struggle to express the divine infinite in language apt only to express the finite. Canonization has no effect on this pluralism or on the human limitations which spawn it. It does not erase pluralism; it does not alchemically convert the plural forms into one univocal form; it does not offer the option of one hermeneutical key. "Pluralism is inevitable"[36] in every human construal of the self-revelation of God, in the initial construal that is scripture and every subsequent construal derived from it.

A scan of scripture shows that its construals are pluralistic and sometimes contradictory. The creation narratives of Genesis 1 and Genesis 2 are seriously different. Paul and Luke report Jesus' words over the ritual cup differently from Matthew and Mark. Luke's preference for "you poor" (6:20), combined with his "woe to you that are rich" (6:24), is not Matthew's preference for the "poor in spirit" (5:3), though both Matthew and Luke, and the Hebrew Bible, are selectively conflated by contemporary theologians as if they spoke with one voice about poverty.[37] Paul's teaching in his letters to the Romans and Galatians on justification by faith apart from works of the law, so beloved of the Reformers, is at serious variance with James's teaching, so un-canonized by the Reformers, that faith without works is dead (2:17). Paul and Luke are as canonical as Matthew and Mark; John and James are as canonical as any of them. None of this is to be taken in the sense of what Tracy calls an "empty pluralism of sheer differences."[38] It is to be taken in the sense of both theological evidence and demand for Christian diversity, pluralism and ecumenicity. As Ernst Käsemann remarked forty years ago: "the variability of the kerygma in the New Testament is an expression of the fact that in primitive Christianity a wealth of different confessions were already in existence, constantly replacing one another, combining with each other and undergoing mutual delimitation."[39] The sociologist of knowledge nods his head and thinks different confessions because different perspectives, different provinces of meaning.

Theological pluralism should not come as a surprise, given both the Jewish and the Christian belief in the transcendent Mystery-God whom "no one has ever seen" (John 1:18; cp. Ex 33:20), a belief I have hinted at several times. On the one hand, the absolute transcendence of God vis-à-vis the human is such that no human language can comprehensively or even adequately image or encompass God. We recall Augustine: "*Si Deus comprehendis non est Deus,* if you understand it is not God you understand."[40] On the other hand, a plurality of images suggests the richness of the reality of God. Both the pluralism of form and the internal contradictions in scripture rule out any *bibliolatry,* any naive claim to verbal inerrancy, and any citation of a single text to establish a theological claim. The practice of proof-texting, *pace* Aquinas,[41] is not possible when scripture is recognized as plural and internally contradictory.

Original revelation, the pre-reflexive self-communication of God to humans, and scripture are not the same thing. Revelation and scripture are organically connected as pre-reflexive experiential root and reflexive cognitive flower; but they are not identical. Scripture and theology, on the other hand, are identical, in the sense that all scripture is theology, the result of critical reflection in faith on foundational revelation. Not all theology, however, is scripture, but only that theology which has been canonized as such by the community. It is that canonical authority assigned to scripture that is in question when we ask about the use of scripture in theology. We begin to clarify that authority as we confront our other two questions.

## Scripture as Socio-Historically Conditioned

Scripture is the result of reflexive, critical, human construal and has to be, therefore, as socio-historically conditioned as its construers. It cannot be otherwise. If God is to be really revealed to concrete, historical women and men, there is no alternative but for the revelation to be mediated in socio-historical symbols. If foundational revelation is to be expressed in human language, oral or written, there is no alternative but for the expression to be in a language that is socio-historically mediated. There is no synchronic, transhistorical, transcultural language valid for all times and for all peoples. The condition for the possibility of real human encounter with God, transcendentalists like Martin Heidegger, Karl Rahner, and Bernard Lonergan will say, *pace* Milbank, is precisely that it be socio-historically mediated. Since the scriptural rule of faith and the critical writings selectively derived from it are historically and culturally conditioned, and therefore relational in the Mannheimian sense, they will require interpretation and elaboration to truly disclose God in any different historical and cultural situation. Since the interpreters may stand in different socio-historical contexts, their interpretations of the classic tradition will almost certainly be pluriform, which will lead to dialectic. That dialectic will be resolved only by intellectually, morally, religiously, and psychically converted theologians in respectful dialogue.

Foundational revelation and scripture are not identical. Foundational revelation is the immediate, experiential, pre-reflexive self-communication of God to historical women and men. Scripture is the mediate, critical, reflexive construal of that revelation in the cultural symbols and language of a specific time and place. The purpose of this elaboration is the reflexive disclosure of the revelation experience and the differentiation of its multiple meanings. *The* problem with scripture, indeed with every theology, arises here. Does any human language have the capacity to disclose the revelatory experience completely, with no remainder? Both the Jewish and Christian traditions answer no. No human person (not Moses, not Jesus, not Aquinas, not John Paul II), no human event (not Creation, not Exodus, not Incarnation), no human language (not Hebrew, not Greek, not Latin, not Kikuyu) is capable of fully disclosing the self-communication of God to humans. Every human person, every human experience, every human language which purports to complement that disclosure by expressing it does so only in socially accepted analogy, symbol, poetry, and myth. Every human person, every human experience, every human language requires reflection, interpretation, and elaboration so that, first, its undifferentiated meanings may be reflexively differentiated and, secondly, the foundational revelation of God which it expresses may be disclosed.

Foundational revelation and scripture are not the same thing. They are related, not as identical but as immediate, pre-reflexive experience and mediate, reflexive interpretation and elaboration of that experience. Because of its organic connection to original revelation, I have suggested that scripture is for later generations of believers secondary foundational revelation. It is secondary revelation, however, only to the extent that it makes possible the revelation of God, and only to the extent that it manifests the presence of God in human history. If it does not reveal God's presence, or if it ceases to reveal God's presence in a new socio-historical context, it is not revelation in even this derived and secondary sense, no matter how canonical its symbols may be. The task of the theologian is precisely to shape, re-shape, and ongoingly nuance the classic tradition so that, in fact, the revelation of God may be reflexively and effectively communicated to the men and women of every time and place. That task, in Lonergan's language, can be accomplished only *in oratione directa,* in the direct speech of the contemporary theologian. Any *oratio obliqua,* indirect speech of what Paul, John, Augustine, or Pius said, is merely preparatory for that converted direct speech.

Hermeneutics raises its ugly head again here, for scripture is not exactly what I have so far suggested, namely, the canonized reflexive elaboration in "human language" of foundational revelation. There is no such thing as "human language" in the abstract any more than there is any such thing as "human" in the abstract. As there is only *this* concrete woman or *that* concrete man, so also is there only *this* or *that* concrete language, Hebrew or Greek or Latin or Kikuyu, for example. The difference between "human language" and Hebrew, Greek, Latin, and Kikuyu is that "human language" is an abstract, all-language-embracing idea in the interior world, and Hebrew, Greek, Latin, and Kikuyu are each a concrete, one-language-embracing reality in the exterior world. Hebrew, Greek, Latin, and Kikuyu, and every other empirical language, suffer from the same drawback that Roman Catholicism and Anglicanism suffer from for Milbank, they are messy embodiments of the ideal, abstract, all-embracing language or church.

That Hebrew, for example, is a concrete reality in the socio-historical world means that it is a history-specific and culture-specific reality, with no transhistorical or transcultural connotations. To disclose the original revelatory encounter with God, even to the original recipients, Hebrew language, that is, Hebrew imagination, understanding, judgment, decision, and culture construed in metaphor, symbol, poetry, and myth, requires ongoing interpretation. To disclose it to any non-original recipient will require minimally the same effort at interpretation and maximally much more. This will be especially true for anyone in a different time, a different culture, and a different socio-historical context. In his discussion of the sociology of knowledge, Mannheim offers the example of a peasant boy who has spent his entire life in a small village so that the manner of speaking and thinking of the village, a rural culture, is something he takes entirely for granted. Should he move to the city and slowly adapt to city life, an urban culture, the rural mode of thinking and speaking would no longer be taken for granted and would be gradually laid aside. That which within a given group, in the case in point a rural group, is accepted as absolute appears to the outsider, in this case someone in an urban group, as conditioned by the group and, therefore, relational and partial.[42] So it is even with sacred scripture. That which appears absolute to those within the group of recipients of original revelation will appear socially conditioned and partial to anyone outside that group. Any theologian-exegete interpreting sacred scripture in a socio-historical context other than the original will always have to be aware of this social fact.

Theology, as I have explicated it, is the experiential, intellectual, judgmental, and decisive construal of foundational revelation. It is also the reflexive construal in the theologian's direct speech of secondary revelation or scripture, never its mere recitation or simple verbal translation. Elaboration of scripture in a different time, a different culture, and a different situation is a three-step process: translation, interpretation, inculturation.[43] Such elaboration yields new meanings, the relationship of which to foundational revelation or to scripture brings us to our final question, the authority of scripture in and for this elaboration and these new meanings.

## Scripture as Authority for Theology

In this section we reach the heart of our question: the relationship of scripture and theology, specifically the authority of scripture in theology. In Catholic theology, Leo XIII's metaphor has become a kind of a proof-text itself: scripture is "the soul of theology."[44] Even with papal statements, however, proof-texting and *oratio obliqua* are not helpful for the effective communication of God's self-revelation; even papal metaphors require *oratio recta* interpretation. I understand Leo's metaphor to mean that scripture is the animating life-force of theology, but what does that mean in the concrete for the theologian actually doing theology? I begin with two negative observations, stating the kind of authority scripture is not.

First, scripture is written, socio-historically conditioned language, the result of socio-historically conditioned reflection on an original experiential revelation. As so socio-historically conditioned, it's authority in the converted human world can only be relational, never absolute. There is no absolute or absolutely revealed scripture, no objective revelation in the sense of a verbal revelation valid for all times and for all places. If scripture was an absolute authority for theology, then theologians would be no more than tape-recorders, and theology would be nothing but the playing of texts, *sacra pagina* rather than *commentarium in sacra pagina,* and *sacra doctrina* rather than *theologia.* Even contemporary fundamentalist theologians concede that recitation of texts is never enough, for their recitation is always accompanied by some form of perspectival selection and interpretation. Secondly, scripture is not an authority absolutely external to theology, for scripture is itself the result of theological reflection on pre-reflexive original revelation. Scripture cannot be separated absolutely from theology, for it is itself theology. It can be distinguished only in a way that acknowledges that the theology canonized in scripture is the classical expression of the understanding of God and, therefore, the rule of faith for every future theological elaboration. Though scripture is neither an absolute nor an absolutely external authority for theology, it is an authority. Its authority, however, is *social* and *socially approved* authority, derived not from scripture itself but from the community of believers, for that community has, first, canonized and, then, accepted scripture as its classical representation of the God encountered in the immediate experience of Jesus, and established it as secondary revelation. This authority may be stated both negatively and positively.

As a socio-historically conditioned construal and reflexive expression of an original experiential revelation of God, scripture will always demand further construal and elaboration in new socio-historical contexts. Scripture is both the classic foundation on which subsequent theological interpretations are construed and the socio-religious authority which judges what counts as a genuinely Christian interpretation. This authority can be both easily stated and easily misunderstood: no theological elaboration can contradict scripture. This statement should not be construed as prohibiting the contradiction of any scriptural *verbal proposition,* for scripture itself does that. It should be construed, rather, as prohibiting the contradiction of any theological *theme* which is expressed throughout the canonical scripture. It is for this reason that there is among scholars, across the Christian traditions, a movement away from what we might call a "biblical rules" approach to theology. "Realizing the impossibility of transposing rules from biblical times to our own, interpreters look for larger themes, values, or ideals which can inform moral reflection without determining specific practices in advance."[45]

Any theology which presents God as an impersonal some*thing,* as only a phenomenon of the natural world, for instance, will be judged by sacred scripture as not genuinely Christian. Any theology which presents Paul or John or Matthew, not Jesus, as the Christian medium of the self-revelation of God will be judged not genuinely Christian. Any theology which seeks to sustain itself by the bald citation of one scriptural proposition, ignoring equally scriptural contradictory propositions — for instance, Mark's report on the words of Jesus about divorce and remarriage rather than Matthew's or Paul's — will be judged not genuinely Christian. The ultimate problem with proof-texting citation is that it promotes one proposition in an evidently pluralistic canon over other equally canonical propositions. That distorts the classical self-revelation of God expressed in the scripture, for the only authentic Christian rule of faith is not an individual scriptural proposition but the canonical scripture as a whole.

Negative authority, however, is not the only authority exercised by scripture. It exercises also a positive authority. As there is no abstract and universal "human," neither is there any abstract and universal "theologian." There is only the concrete, socio-historically conditioned theologian. An essential social characteristic of all Christian theologians is their Christian province of meaning, what I choose to call their Christian subjectivity and, especially, imaginativity. That subjectivity is inescapably shaped by their social context as *Christian* theologians, as that context has itself been inescapably shaped by scripture and its later historical elaborations. The Christian context or perspective inevitably provides theologians with the data to which they are attentive, with the metaphors, symbols, and myths in which they image this data, with the rational concepts in which they articulate the experienced data, and with the judgments in which they affirm its truth. The Christian perspective conditions every aspect of every Christian construal of revelation in every new socio-historical context. In this way, scripture makes possible and controls the ongoing revelation of God in every historical time and place.

Scripture controls not only the Christian theologians who elaborate it anew in each new generation; it controls also their theologies. It can be found in those theologies as both that which is their classic foundation and that which is the norm of their faithfulness to that foundation. Those Jewish theologians who initially sought to construe their experience of God in their experience of Jesus of Nazareth did so in terms of their Jewish subjectivity, imaginatively shaped by their Jewish context. Those non-Jewish, Christian theologians who later sought to construe the Jewish construal in the light of traditions about Jesus become the Christ did so in terms of their new Christian subjectivity. What Christians call apostolic faith, the faith of the first apostles shared by each new generation of disciples, finds its normative witness in the church's scripture. The critical presence of this scripture from beginning to end in a theology in new socio-historical circumstances guarantees that apostolic faith a contemporary witness. It guarantees that the faith the church articulates today continues to be *Christian* faith.

Scripture, however, as we saw in the opening chapter, is not the only authority for Christian theology. There is another authority, the present situation of believers in every new age. The dynamic relationship of scripture and existential situation, so central to many contemporary theologies,[46] is suggested in my theory of the development of scripture, specifically in the relationship between foundational and secondary revelation. Foundational revelation is an immediate pre-reflexive human experience construed as the revelation of God. Secondary original revelation, or sacred scripture, is a reflexive expression of this foundational revelation mediated in language conditioned by socio-historical circumstance. The Second Vatican Council, as we have seen, expressed the dynamic of the theological construal of Christian scripture this way. "The sacred authors wrote the four gospels," selecting, synthesizing and explicating some things from the traditions "*in view of the situation of their churches.*" There is no reason to suggest any other dynamic for theological construal today. Paul's letters proclaimed what the churches of Paul's time believed about the God revealed in Jesus, and did not hide the dialectics that sometimes separated them; John's gospel proclaimed what John's church believed about the God revealed in Jesus, and did not hide the dialectic; *Christian* theology today asserts what the church believes about that same God in its situation at the beginning of a third Christian millennium, and ought not to hide the different interpretations that dialectically divide different theologies.

The socially constructed classic theology expressed in scripture resulted from a dialogue between an original pre-reflexive revelation and a socio-historically conditioned human experience. Postmodern theology also results from a similar dialogue, only now between that classic scriptural theology and socio-historically conditioned postmodern human experience. Christian theology in every age results from a dialogue between scriptural theology and human experience brought together by the theologian who participates in both. The postmodern theologian, as explained earlier in this book, seeks to mediate converted understanding of, truth about, and responsibility toward both the classic scriptural expression of God in terms of contemporary experience and contemporary experience in terms of the classic, scriptural rule of faith, much as the Pastoral Epistles can be said to have done for Pauline theology.[47] The Pontifical Biblical Commission explains why this method is necessary. "Although their message is of lasting value, the biblical texts have been composed with respect to circumstances of the past and in language conditioned by a variety of times and seasons. To reveal their significance for men and women of today, it is necessary to apply their message to contemporary circumstances and to express it in language adapted to the present time,"[48] a clear statement of the import of socio-historical context in the special theological language of the church.

Before Hans Georg Gadamer's hermeneutical circle underscored the mutuality of question and answer,[49] Tillich, claiming dependence on Calvin's *Institutes,*[50] named this theological dynamic *correlation.* He insisted on "mutual dependence between question and answer. In respect to content the Christian answers are dependent on the revelatory events in which they appear; in respect to form they are dependent on the structure of the questions which they answer."[51] I already expressed my dissatisfaction with Tillich's correlational approach, for I am persuaded that it is not truly correlational. As Tillich sees it, human experience raises *questions* to which Christian tradition provides *answers*. In this kind of correlation, the dialogue partners are far from equal, as I argued earlier they have to be for a genuine dialogue. I prefer a dialogue in which human experience enters as equal partner into dialogue with the Christian tradition, and I earlier named this dialogue mutual, critical, self-mediation. The first step in this self-mediation is the effort by the theologian to understand both past tradition and current experience in their socio-historical contexts. The first part of this task, as I explained in chapter 1, is theological, and it requires research, interpretation, history, and dialectic; the second part of the task is sociological, and it requires detailed description and analysis. The second step is the truly mediational step, the translation, interpretation, and articulation of the past tradition in present cultural categories, and it requires the exposition of foundations, the formulation of theological (not yet ecclesial) doctrines, their arrangement in systematics, and their effective communication. This two-step process truly mediates what needs to be mediated, not reflexive expressions of original revelation but original revelation itself and contemporary human experience. This mediation, and only this mediation, enables the translation and interpretation of what is believed to be original revelation in terms capable of bringing the present community of believers to understanding of, and faith in, the continuing self-revelation and presence of God in human experience. This method of mediation "is not *a* method of theology, but *the* method of a discipline that seeks to preserve the meaning of the past but understand it in a distinctly present-day manner."[52] Original revelation is not something that happened only in the distant past; God continues to reveal Godself in the "deeds and words" of today.

The standard metaphor for this dialogue, in both Protestant and Catholic theologies, is translation. In this metaphor, "doing theology is the last moment in a continuous movement in which the *same* 'meanings' are stated in different 'forms,' first in the translation (in the ordinary sense) of Hebrew and Greek texts into, say, English, then exegesis of their 'meanings,' and finally translation (in the special, metaphorical sense) of those same 'meanings' into a contemporary idiom."[53] I cannot accept this metaphor as it is usually applied, for two reasons.

First, translation in its ordinary sense, from Greek into English, for instance, is more than word-for-word equivalence. "The passage from one language to another necessarily involves a change of cultural context. Concepts are not identical and symbols have a different meaning,"[54] which makes possible different imaginative and emotional praxis. A harmless example is the Matthean parable: "You are the salt of the earth..." (5:13). Verbally accurate as this translation is, it does not come close to communicating the literal meaning of the Greek words in their first-century Palestinian context. That happens only when "earth" is fully elaborated as "earthen oven," and "salt" as a fire-catalyzing agent.[55] Secondly, the translation metaphor so presumes conceptual continuity and harmony, that it leaves no room for discontinuity and disharmony. Conceptual disharmony, however, is already a feature of the scripture itself, and conceptual discontinuity is what much Christian theology "authorized" by scripture evinces. The Nicene *homoousios* is in sharp conceptual discontinuity with the biblical "Son of God," and with John's "the Word was made flesh" (1:14); the Aristotelian-Thomistic *transubstantiatio* is in equally sharp discontinuity with Mark and Matthew's "This is my body" (Mark 14:22; Matt 26:26). With due respect to Tillich, *homoousios* and *transubstantiatio* encode conceptual, imaginative, and praxis contents not found in any scriptural symbol. If they are in any continuity with scripture, it is not continuity of the *same symbols* or the same content but continuity of the *same process* of symboling, mediating transcendence in symbols drawn from human experience. The subject matter of all religious and theological interpretation, as I noted in the beginning, is the original, immediate, experiential, pre-reflexive self-revelation of God, not the secondary, reflexive scriptural symbols in which this self revelation is mediate. As long as ecclesially approved symbols, however different from traditional symbols, mediate the same transcendence as traditional ones, they are authorized by the canonical scripture. The authority of scripture lies ultimately in its canonized mediation of the foundational revelation or presence of God. Scripture authorizes, in turn, only those symbols which continue to mediate that revelation in present history, and does not authorize any symbol which either does not or has ceased to mediate that revelation. There are two ways to be unfaithful to a traditional symbol, Rahner notes: one is to abandon it; the other is to preserve it in a petrified form which no longer mediates the presence of God.[56] The first leads to mere anthropology, the second to fundamentalism and idolatry. Scripture authorizes neither way as Christian.

## Conclusion

I align with Kelsey. "Scripture is authority for theological proposals, not by being the perfect source of the content that they fully preserve, but by providing a pattern by which the proposal's adequacy as [Christian] elaboration can be assessed."[57] To conclude and summarize this proposal, I offer three ways in which scripture acts as authority for the Christian appropriateness of theological construals. First, and negatively, scripture excludes certain theological construals as not genuinely Christian. It excludes, for instance, any theology which presents God as impersonal or uncaring, or which presents Paul or John, not Jesus, as the ultimate medium in human history of the revelation of God. Secondly, and positively, scripture offers, not one, but a plurality of imaginative models for shaping theologians and their theologies. Theologians who accept a Pauline model (Luther and Barth, for instance) will construe, and have scripturally authorized, a significantly different Christian theology from those who accept a Markan model (Johann Baptist Metz and every theology of the world), or a Matthean pattern (every radical communal sect), or a Lukan pattern (Pentecostalists with their insistence on the presence of the Spirit), or a Joannine pattern (Karl Rahner or any mystic). Käsemann's dismissal of the Pastoral Letters as "early Catholicism"[58] leaves no doubt about the themes of institution and tradition found in them. Thirdly, converted theologians who take scripture as canonical in its entirety, and not in its separate propositions, take one part of the whole in organic relationship with every other part of the whole. In that case, theological construal is authorized as appropriately Christian, not by one isolated sentence from the canon but by that one sentence in relationship to the whole. There is, consequently, in the Christian traditions, a moving away from what may be called a "biblical rules" approach. "Realizing the impossibility of transposing rules from biblical times to our own, interpreters look for larger themes, values or ideals which can inform moral reflection without determining specific practices in advance."[59]

I conclude my analysis of the correlation of scripture and theology by putting before you with approbation a creative proposal made by the English scholar, Frances Young. Young offers music as an analogy for scripture, and explores musical performance "to illuminate the process of appropriating the Bible in the modern world."[60] A musical score provides the foundation for many interpretive cadenzas, none of which is necessarily correct or incorrect. When the score is played by an orchestra, diverse instruments combine to create an overall performance. Of course, what Young presents is analogy; of course, analogy limps, especially when taken as literal fact. Imaginative, insightful, and critical Christian faith enable this one to soar. Karl Barth believed that Mozart's lifestyle was irremediably frivolous, and yet he began each day by listening to Mozart's music. Mozart, he enthused, was "the agent by which little bits of horn, metal and catgut could serve as the voices of creation."[61] Mozart's creative ear for music made him a mediator to other ears. Theologians, who would play theological music from a scriptural score, need both an ear for the score and attention to their own social contexts to compose variations upon it.

## Questions for Discussion

1. Explain the principle of third generation. What are its implications for the writings of the gospels and the later New Testament documents?

2. "The original revelation of the divine Mystery is a pre-reflexive experience construed as religious." Explain in your own words what this statement means. Given your explanation, what would it mean, then, to state that sacred scripture is secondary foundational revelation?

3. In official Catholic theology, the literal meaning of the text, which is the meaning intended by the author, has priority over all other meanings. What are the implications of this position for reading the scriptures? How would one go about isolating the meaning intended by the author?

4. What does it mean to you to say that scripture is itself theology? What implications does this theological fact have for theologians reading scripture and constructing their theologies on the basis of what they read?

5. Scripture is not the only source for Catholic theology; present human experience is also a source. Why is this (remember Lonergan's definition of theology)? What are the implications for theology, and for sociology, from this theological fact?

# FIVE

# The Church Emerging
# in the Human Community

Theology, I have argued following Lonergan, is the tutored reflection on two interrelated dimensions of reality, the self-communication of God to humankind and the existential relationships of humans to God, to one another in community, and to the created universe. It develops in two phases: a phase of research, interpretation, history and dialectic, which mediates the theological past to the present, and a phase of foundations, doctrines, systematics, and communications, which mediates the present theological situation to the future. In this chapter, I apply this tutored method of theology to establish an authentically Catholic theological doctrine of church, which emerged as social institutionalization of the Jesus movement, first, in a Jewish socio-historical context and, then, in a Greco-Roman context. Given everything we have said about the connection of social context and structure, it is predictable that the early Jewish form of church and the later Greco-Roman form would be different, for structures formed in different socio-historical contexts are inevitably different. These different forms or models of church have occasioned heated dialectic in the Catholic Church in the past century, and continue to occasion it since the upheaval created by the Second Vatican Council. Before we can proceed further, we must first consider the contemporary dialectic about church, satisfactorily resolve it, and agree on a theology of church which either sustains or negates my arguments in the final two chapters. As we proceed, we will also keep an eye on socio-theological influences.

## The Second Vatican Council and Church

Ecclesiology, the theology of church, assumed center stage in Christian theology in the twentieth century. For almost the entire century, Orthodox, Anglican, and Protestant Christians in the World Council of Churches, especially in its Faith and Order Commission, sought to elucidate the nature, the structure, and the mission of the church. The impetus for this work was doubly rooted. It was rooted, first, in the desire to discover and describe in contemporary terms what the one church established by Christ is in the plan of the God confessed as Father, Son, and Spirit. It was rooted, secondly, in the painful desire to embrace all the Christian churches that have arisen in history into that communion for which Christ so fervently prayed: "that they may all be one, even as you, Father, are in me and I in you; that they also may be in us" (John 17:21).

In the Roman Catholic Church, which initially remained aloof from this ecumenical movement, ecclesiology since the Council of Trent had been largely apologetic. Against the sixteenth-century reformers, it concentrated on maintaining the visible structure of the church, the primacy of the papacy for apostolic succession, and hence the presumption that only the Roman Catholic Church is to be identified with the church originated by Jesus Christ. Against the assaults of developing European states, the church was presented as a perfect society that is "complete and independent in itself and possesses all the means necessary to attain its proposed end."[1] A Preparatory Commission for the First Vatican Council in 1870 drew up a fifteen-chapter document on this church to be discussed at the council, but the outbreak of the Franco-Prussian War and the invasion of the Papal States by the armies of Piedmont permitted discussion of only four of the fifteen chapters, those that focused on the primacy of the pope within the church. The result was an unbalanced, undialectical ecclesiology which cast a Greco-Roman model of church in exclusively hierarchical terms, almost as an absolute monarchy. Though Pope Leo XIII in *Satis Cognitum* (1896) and Pope Pius XII in *Mystici Corporis* (1943) sought to emphasize the church's connection to the triune God, much remained to be done to right the ecclesiological imbalance.

It was no surprise, therefore, that, in preparation for the Second Vatican Council and for the *aggiornamento,* or updating, called for by Pope John XXIII, a Theological Commission prepared a draft document on the church. There was a surprise, however, at least for those wedded to the neo-scholastic theology in which the document was articulated, when it was discussed at the opening of the council. The draft was roundly rejected by the council fathers as an inadequate theological doctrine in the twentieth-century situation and was returned to the Theological Commission with Pope John's words ringing in its ears. "This deposit of faith, or truths which are contained in our time-honored teaching, is one thing; the manner in which these truths are set forth with an unchanged meaning is another."[2] I believe that the overwhelming rejection of this preparatory document, and of the equally inadequate one on the sources of revelation, was the rejection also of neo-scholasticism as the exclusive way to articulate Catholic ecclesiology.

There is almost unanimous agreement that the Dogmatic Constitution on the church, *Lumen Gentium,* is the principal achievement of the Second Vatican Council. That judgment is easily sustained for two reasons: first, because of the importance of its content for understanding church and the church's mission in the world; second, because of the foundational position *Lumen Gentium* holds in the entire council *corpus.* In one way or another, the work of the council and its documents focused on the church. As Pope Paul VI put it in his first encyclical *Ecclesiam Suam* (1964), the church was the principal object of attention of the Second Vatican Ecumenical Council.[3] The cornerstone of this central document, in again almost unanimous Catholic judgment, as we shall see, is the theological notion of *koinonia*-communion.

The fact that Pope John XXIII summoned a "pastoral" council has led to not a little confusion. Some theologians argue that, since it was a *pastoral* council, it made no *doctrinal* decisions. That argument misunderstands the nature of "pastoral" and its relationship to doctrine. There is no separation between doctrinal and pastoral. Pastoral *is* doctrinal expressing itself in practice; it *is* abstract doctrinal theory expressing itself in concrete actions. Doctrine is not some timeless, absolute reality to be gazed at or to be chanted as a mantra. Doctrine is to be lived (cf. Matt 7:21) in every here and now and, when doctrinal theology is lived, it is translated into and embodied in pastoral theology. There is no effective doctrinal theology without pastoral theology; there is no genuine pastoral theology unless it is firmly rooted in orthodox doctrine. Paraphrasing the council's opening Message to Humanity, I wish to suggest, *in oratione recta,* how the church may renew itself, so that it may be found "increasingly faithful to the gospel of Christ." I seek to present to the men and women of the present age God's truth for the church "that they may understand it and gladly assent to it,"[4] and be drawn to live it in not only the church but also the world where the church is raised up to be *Lumen Gentium,* a light to the nations, and "a universal sacrament of salvation."[5]

The terms of the modern Catholic debate over ecclesiology have been starkly delineated by Yves Congar, the leading Catholic ecclesiologist of the twentieth century. He points out two distinct attitudes which are required of Catholics on the basis of two quite distinct theological models of church. Obedience to church authorities is called for when the church is conceived on the model of a society subject to monarchical authority, and dialogue and consensus are called for when the church is conceived on the model of a communion. He adds the historical note that "it is certain that this second conception was the one that prevailed effectively during the first thousand years of Christianity, whereas the other one dominated in the West between the eleventh-century reformation and Vatican II."[6] Edward Kilmartin argues in similar vein, emphasizing that the patristic and medieval notion of reception, with which we shall deal at length in the next chapter, was "a tributary of the dominant ecclesiology of that age: a communion ecclesiology."[7] The Second Vatican Council sought to resolve the debate between the two models of church which Congar cites, church as hierarchical or monarchical institution and church as communion, and did resolve it in favor of church as communion, but the ecclesial reception of its resolution is still far from achieved.

The connection between structure and socio-historical context was luminously exemplified in Europe in the years that followed the two devastating world wars in the twentieth century. The postwar years were characterized by clamorous calls for renewed human community to replace impersonal institutions, and this desire for genuine interpersonal and social communion was a socio-historical precondition for the Vatican Council's preference of a model of church as communion. That this was the council's preferred ecclesiological model is the opinion of several notable commentators: the secretary of the council's Central Commission, Monsignor Philips,[8] of Pope John Paul II, who taught in his important letter on the laity that "communion is the very mystery of the Church,"[9] of the 1985 Roman Synod, which judged that its vision of church as *koinonia*-communion was the council's most important teaching,[10] and of Cardinal Joseph Ratzinger and the Congregation for the Doctrine of the Faith, who judged that "the concept of communion lies 'at the heart of the Church's self-understanding.' "[11] There should be today no theological doubt about the correctness of Jerome Hamer's judgment: *The Church is a Communion.*[12] But there is doubt, particularly among those who continue to take the hierarchical model for granted, and who still suspect and fear that there is something doubtfully new and non-traditional about the claim that the church is communion. There is still the effort, as in Ratzinger's letter, to sustain an overly hierarchical and juridical vision of church. A brief analysis of the genesis of Vatican II's Dogmatic Constitution on the church will clarify both the root of that suspicion and the fact that it is unfounded, and will show that the conception of church as communion is, in fact, not a *new,* but a *renewed,* vision in the Catholic traditions.

As we have already seen, in preparation for the council, a Central Theological Commission had prepared a traditional, post-Tridentine, neo-scholastic document on the church organized in four chapters: "Nature of the Church," "Hierarchy in the Church," "Laity in the Church," and "States of Perfection in the Church." In 1962, during the opening session, that document was overwhelmingly rejected by the bishops in council and returned to the Commission to be, not just cosmetically amended, but radically reworked to bring it in line with Pope John's call for the *aggiornamento* of doctrinal language. By the end of the Second Session in 1963, the document had been suggestively rearranged in eight chapters: "the Mystery of the Church," "the People of God," "the Hierarchical Structure of the Church," "the Laity," "the Call of the Whole Church to Holiness," "Religious," "the Eschatological Nature of the Church," "the Role of the Blessed Virgin Mary in the Mystery of Christ and the Church." This rearranged document became the Dogmatic Constitution on the Church, *Lumen Gentium,* approved overwhelmingly at the council's Third Session on November 21, 1964, on a vote of 2151 to 5. This overwhelming approval established *Lumen Gentium* as the *Magna Carta* for any subsequent reflection on church in the Roman Catholic tradition.

Congar describes the transition from the preparatory document to *Lumen Gentium* as a transition from the priority of "organizational structures and hierarchical positions" to "the priority and even the primacy of the ontology of grace."[13] Edward Schillebeeckx describes it as a twofold decentralization: a vertical decentralization from triumphalist church to glorified Christ and a horizontal decentralization from an exclusive focus on Roman primacy, hierarchical ministry, and Roman Catholic Church to an inclusive focus on universal episcopacy, people of God, and other Christian churches respectively.[14] I prefer to describe the transition differently. It is a transition from an exclusively juridical vision that sees church as institution and structure to a theological one that sees it as mystery and graced communion. It is a transition from an exclusive fixation on hierarchical office and power to an appreciation of co-responsibility and service, from an exclusive focus on Roman primacy to an inclusive ecclesial communion. It is a transition from exclusive focus on the external reality of institution to focus on the internal reality of grace. The rearrangement of the four neo-scholastic chapters of the preparatory document into the final eight, and especially the emphasis intended by placing the chapters on mystery and people of God before the one on hierarchy, provide ample evidence of the council's conviction that the church is primarily a mysterious communion between God and believers, and between believers one with the other, and only secondarily a hierarchical institution. Theologically, interpersonal communion precedes social institution.

*Lumen Gentium* affirms that the church *is* a mystery, *is* "a kind of sacrament or sign of intimate union with God,"[15] *is* "a communion of faith, hope and love,"[16] *is* a pilgrim people of God,[17] before it *has* external and hierarchical structure. It speaks at length of those structures, necessary to any social institution in the historical world, but it speaks of them only as the external sign and instrument of what really counts, namely, a pilgrim people of faith and hope and love called into communion-being by the God to whom it is on its way. However *renewed* that vision may be for post-Tridentine Catholics, it cannot be considered *new,* since its themes derive from the earliest apostolic church. Old or new, we need to consider it at some length.

## Church as Mystery

As already noted, an opening chapter on the Mystery of the Church was added to *Lumen Gentium* in the reworking that followed the rejection of the preparatory document in 1962. The word "mystery" is used in the first chapter of the document and four other times (LG, 5, 39, 44, 63), but nowhere is it defined. In 1964, however, after insistent questions, an official interpretation of the word was provided. The word "mystery" "points to a transcendent, divine reality that has to do with salvation and that is in some sensible way revealed and manifested. The term, therefore, which is found in the Bible, is very suitable as a designation for the Church."[18] To say that the church is mystery, therefore, is yet another theological way to say that God has communicated Godself to historically emergent humankind in Jesus of Nazareth, confessed as the Christ, and that this divine self-communication continues in the communion of the followers of Christ called in special theological categories the church, the body of Christ.

According to the council, therefore, to say that the church is a mystery is to say, first, that in and through it a divine, salvific reality is present and made visible in the world. It is to say, secondly, that because this mystery is a reality in the human world it conceals as much as reveals the God who is at its core. Paul VI underscored this dimension. "The Church is a mystery," he taught, "that is, a reality imbued with the presence of God and, therefore, of such a nature that there are ever-new and deeper explorations of it possible."[19] John Paul II echoes this position: "the Church is a great mystery, and how do we communicate mystery?"[20] The theocentric, transcendent, grace dimensions of the church, which we dealt with briefly in the opening chapter, are underscored in the word "mystery" and give ecclesiology an entirely different focus from the exclusively structural, juridical, and triumphalist focus of the post-Tridentine era. Post-Tridentine ecclesiology saw the church as a hierarchical structure, with hierarchical ministers to teach, govern, and sanctify the church, and whom the non-ministerial, lay members of the church were to obey. It was a church in which structures, doctrines, and laws were of prime importance. Though it is quite schizophrenic in its treatment of the hierarchical and communion models of church, as are most of the council's documents because of the dialectical way they were composed, *Lumen Gentium* predominantly demurs from this model, and declares that although structures, laws, doctrines, sacraments, or hierarchical ministers are not unimportant, they are not primary. The mysterious presence at its core of the God who is communion and uncreated, operative grace, and who calls men and women to communion with God and one another is primary. The human desire for communion noted at the outset is not satisfied ultimately by mere human communion. It is satisfied perfectly only by communion with God, the council teaches, echoing Augustine's ancient confession, "thou hast made us for thyself, and our hearts are restless until they rest in thee."[21]

The church and its structures are not ultimate, the council insinuates, but only a means to communion. If the church is to be faithful and thus survive the gates of death (Matt. 16:18), it will not be because of unchanging structure, infallible doctrine, precise laws, or magical sacraments. It will be because of the indefectible presence and saving action of the God confessed as Father, Son, and Holy Spirit. The novelty of *Lumen Gentium* is not that it teaches *new* doctrine, but that it recalls the church to a *renewed* contemplation of the presence of God within it and the created world, and asserts that it is communion with this Mystery-God that constitutes the church's very essence as a communion of salvation. The council's insistence on locating the church in the category of *mystery* rather than in the category of *nature* was intended to direct attention to the grace at the interior of the church rather than to its all-too-human exterior. "The Council's *aggiornamento* [updating]," Walter Kasper notes, "consisted in the fact that it again moved into the foreground the mystery of the Church, which can only be grasped in faith, over against the one-sided concentration on the visible and hierarchical form of the Church, which had held sway during the previous three centuries."[22] When we look more closely at that mystery, we shall discover that it is a mystery of communion.

## Church as Communion

Webster derives *communion* from the Latin *communis,* common, itself deriving from *cum munus,* common duty, common task, common undertaking. General etymological meaning, however, does not tell the whole story of special theological language and by itself is not an adequate guide to the church's faith. *Communion* translates the general Greek category *koinonia,* which connotes common possession, solidarity, and co-responsibility.[23] Its Latin, special-category equivalents are manifold: *congregatio, societas, coetus, adunatio, corpus, communio, populus, ecclesia,* each with a specification such as *fidelium* or *christianorum,* as in *communio fidelium,* the communion of the faithful. The fundamental Christian meaning of communion designates the communion of the faithful with God in Christ through the Spirit, and hence their common participation in Christian goods. In that each is in communion with God, all are also in communion with one another (see 1 John 1:3, 6). Communion in the church is, first, with the triune God: the Creator who created men and women for participation in the divine communion,[24] the Son who was sent "to establish peace or communion between sinful human beings" and the Creator,[25] the Holy Spirit who unites the church in "communion and service."[26] It is, secondly, and as the fruit of communion with God, a communion of historically emergent men and women with one another. The Orthodox have long honored this twofold communion as *sobornost,* communion animated by the Spirit of God.[27]

There is, therefore, ancient warrant for the official note from the Vatican Council in November 1964. "*Communion* is an idea which was held in high honor in the ancient Church.... It is understood, however, not of a certain feeling, but of an *organic reality* which demands a juridical form."[28] This explanation makes clear that communion is not only internal, invisible, sacramental communion with God but also external communion instituted by Christ and constituted by the Spirit of Christ, and "composed of all those who receive him in faith and in love."[29] It is a historical "communion of life, love and truth,"[30] the life, love, and truth of God in Christ through the Spirit actively discerned and shared in the communion of believers that confesses the three as one God. This *koinonia*-communion is already clearly exemplified in the earliest Jerusalem church, which devoted itself to "the apostles' teaching and communion (*koinonia*)" (Acts 2:42) and "had everything in common (*panta koina*)" (Acts 4:32). Paul lets us know that the sharing in communion is not limited to a local church but reaches out to all the churches. The churches in Macedonia and Achaia, he tells us in his original Greek, "have been pleased to make *koinonian*" for the church at Jerusalem (Rom 15:26; cf. 2 Cor 8:4). He indicates the personal cost of such sharing when he praises "the generosity of your *koinonias* for them and for all others" (2 Cor 9:13).

John Paul II characterizes this *kononia*-communion as "the incorporation of Christians into the life of Christ and the communication of that life of love to the entire body of the faithful."[31] Hamer characterizes it as external communion in the *means* of grace, word, faith, doctrine, sacrament, and

internal communion in the *life* of grace, loving union with the triune God.[32]
I differentiate three levels of ecclesial communion. On a first level, all confess
the same truth, participate in the same sacraments, worship the same God.
On a second level, all live the same Spirit-filled life, shepherded by the same
Spirit-gifted authority. On a third level, all love and act as members of one
people and one body in communion with one another and with the God who
called them into, and sustains them in, communion-being as the people of
God and the body of Christ. It is only this third level that gives to churches
as far apart as Ireland and Singapore more than an agreement in faith and
obedience, ultimately, to the same visible head. It is on this third level that
all are genuinely united in the one Spirit-constituted communion for it is
only in and through the love of the neighbor-in-communion that we can
genuinely love and be in communion with God (Matt 25:31–46; 1 John
3:15–18; James 2:14–18).

That is why I prefer the active word "communion" over the passive word
"community." Sad history teaches us that there are many human and ecclesial groups arrogating to themselves the name of community, while giving
no verifiable evidence of genuine human communication, communing, or
communion. There is no genuine community without active communion,
without the active and mutual sharing of life, love, and truth. "We give one
another life," Jürgen Moltmann comments, "and come alive from one another. In mutual participation in life, individuals become free beyond the
boundaries of their individuality."[33] Communion always produces a community of love, but community does not always produce communion. In
the people "made one with the unity of the Father, the Son and the Holy
Spirit"[34] there is no option to communion. A consideration of that people
will further illuminate the communion-church.

## People of God and Communion

The communion that is the church is a communion of individuals-in-
relation, that is, of persons, and *Lumen Gentium* selects an interpersonal,
people-image as its preferred image for church.[35] I note this fact because
it is theologically significant and, to some extent, unexpected, for prior to
the council the preferred image had been the image of the body of Christ,
highlighted in Pius XII's encyclical, *Mystici Corporis*. We must avoid an easy
error here. It is easy to deal with people of God and body of Christ as if
they presented us with an either-or situation, either people of God or body
of Christ is the best and even the only image for church.[36] Nothing could
be further from the truth. The two images are not in competition but are,

rather, complementary. "Both attempt to highlight certain dimensions of the disciples of Jesus Christ in their communion with the triune God, Jesus and one another."[37] I shall deal with each image in turn.

Since the council, there have been two misplaced emphases related to people of God. The first emphasis underscored *people,* an emphasis, I submit, that is misplaced because in this people the emphasis is always on *God.* The specific characteristic of the people that is church is not that it is a people but that it is *God's* people. Such was the Deuteronomist's message to Israel: "the Lord your God has chosen you to be a people for his own possession, out of all the peoples that are on the face of the earth" (Deut 7:6). Such also was Peter's message to the new people of God, the church: "you are a chosen race, a royal priesthood, a holy nation, God's own People" (1 Pet 2:9). Such too was Vatican II's message: "it has pleased God to make men [and women] holy and save them not merely as individuals without any mutual bonds, but by making them into a single People."[38] The specific characteristic of the people that is church is that it is *God's* people. God calls them into being and sustains them in being as people-in-communion, with God and with one another. The people have no meaning, not as people, not as church, apart from the God who is their origin and goal, their alpha and omega (Rev 1:8). I must note here and clarify a theological debate over the extension of the term "people of God."

Some theologians argue that the term "people of God" refers to the whole of humanity, others that it refers only to the Christian church. There are, I believe, valid arguments on both sides of this issue. Karl Rahner puts his position this way: "based on the two coinciding facts of the natural unity of the human race and of the real incarnation of the word of God," there is a people of God long before either Israel or the church.[39] The church, gathered by Christ and constituted by Christ's Spirit, is a sacrament, both a sign and an instrument, of the reality that the entire human race is the consecrated, graced, and saved people of God. Yves Congar, on the other hand, while admitting that "this people of God is *de iure* [that is, by right] coextensive with humanity," suggests that there is more to being this people than simply belonging to humankind. There is required a certain structure and that structure results from a second initiative of God beyond creation,[40] namely, God's election. God was pleased "to make men holy and save them not merely as individuals without any mutual bonds, but by making them into a single People."[41] God "gathered together as one all those who in faith look upon Jesus as the author of salvation and the source of unity and peace, and has established them as the Church."[42] This people-church is "the new people of God," "a messianic people" whose head is Christ, whose law is "the new commandment to love as Christ loved us," whose goal is "the kingdom of God."[43]

I agree with Congar. All of humanity, created and saved by God in Christ, is *de iure* the people of God in communion. The original Fall, however, detailed in Genesis, is a falling out of communion with God and with one another (Gen 3 and 11:1–9). *De facto,* in fact, the people of God is the Christian church. That people is in the world as a "wondrous sacrament,"[44] as both a sign and an instrument of the salvation, reconciliation, communion, and peace to which all of fractured humankind is called. When *Lumen Gentium* uses the term "people of God," and when I use it in this book, it is to be understood in the *de facto* sense as referring to church and not to humankind in general.

The second misplaced emphasis related to people of God also falls on *people,* this time as if it referred to lay people distinct from ordained people, laity distinct from hierarchy. This misinterpretation led to the further misunderstanding of the people of God in political categories, as a *democracy* rather than as a *communio,* and led to a call for the democratization of the church. Nothing could be further from the meaning of the biblical and conciliar image people of God. It is true that the English word "laity" derives ultimately from the Greek word *laos,* people. But, again, general etymology does not tell the whole story. In the special language that is theology, *laos tou theou,* people of God, distinguishes between the people of God and the people who are not God's people *de facto.* It does not distinguish between groups in the people, between ordinary people and hierarchical leaders, for instance, between laity and clergy. It denotes not parts but the whole, not distinction but communion, not isolated individuals but individuals-in-relation, Christian persons. It denotes the whole people of God in communion. The church is neither a political democracy, which emphasizes equal *individuals,* nor a political monarchy, which emphasizes unequal *individuals.* It is a *koinonia,* a communion of persons, individuals in relationship, sharing equally in the good things of the one people of God, "life, love and truth."[45]

## Body of Christ and Communion

I have already asserted that body of Christ and people of God are not competing but complementary images of the church. In his treatment of people of God, Neils Dahl asserts that the difference in the two images lies in the fact that "the Church in the Old Testament was exhaustively expressed by the term People of God, while the Church of the New Testament is the People of God only in that it is simultaneously the Body of Christ."[46] *Qahal,* the

Hebrew assembly brought together by God's call (Deut 4:10; 9:10; 10:4; 18:16; 23:2–9), becomes in the Septuagint *ekklesia*, the word used also for the assembly of Christians in the New Testament (Acts 5:11; 8:3; 1 Cor 4:17; Phil 4:15). In the Old Testament, the assembly of Israel is *God's* people; in the New Testament, the assembly of Christians, *ekklesia*-church, is *God's* people too, but only in Christ, only to the extent that they are also *Christ's* people. The church of Christ is also the church of God (cf. 1 Thess 1:1; Rom 16:16; 1 Cor 1:2; 10:32; 11:16, 22; 15:9; 2 Cor 1:1; Gal 1:13; 1 Thess 2:14; 2 Thess 1:4). People of God and body of Christ do not describe two entirely disparate realities, but one reality from two different perspectives, the one people that is simultaneously Christ's and God's.

There are two different, but complementary, themes in the development of the term "body of Christ" in the Pauline literature.[47] In the letters to the Romans and Corinthians, we find a first theme of the communion of believers in the body of Christ. "The chief interest," as Heinrich Schlier notes, "is that the local Church is one Body from many members, that is, it is a charismatic organism."[48] That communion of all in the ecclesial body of Christ is made visible in, and is nourished by, the communion of all in the eucharistic body of Christ. "Truly partaking of the Body of the Lord in the breaking of the eucharistic bread," *Lumen Gentium* explains, "we are taken up into communion with him and with one another."[49] In the theology of the Catholic traditions, sacraments do not merely manifest some reality, they also realize it and make it concretely real. Eucharist, therefore, does not merely manifest communion in the body of Christ, it also effects communion. In eucharist the Holy Spirit moves believers to communion, thus constituting the *koinonia*-communion that is the church of Christ and of God. Where eucharist is celebrated in communion, there is wholly church. When Catholic theologians say that the church of Christ is essentially eucharistic,[50] they mean that it is in the eucharistic meal, above all, that the Spirit of God makes believers-in-communion, thus constituting the church.

*Lumen Gentium* cites with approval the words of the Byzantine prayer of episcopal consecration: a bishop is "the steward of the grace of the supreme priesthood, especially in the eucharist...by which the church constantly lives and grows." It adds that "this Church of Christ is truly present in all local congregations of the faithful which, united with their pastors, are themselves called Churches in the New Testament."[51] What this means theologically, as the recent letter from the Congregation for the Doctrine of the Faith explains, is that the communion that is Church "is rooted not only in the same faith and in the common baptism, but above all in the eucharist and in the episcopate."[52] While acknowledging this teaching, however, along with the further conciliar teaching that this church is formed in and out of the churches, *ecclesia in et ex ecclesiis*,[53] the letter proceeds to read this formula in John Paul II's new and inverted version, the churches in and out of the church, *ecclesiae in et ex ecclesia*.[54] Since that teaching appears to qualify that of the council, we must consider it briefly.

The Congregation's letter confronts the question of unity and diversity in ecclesial communion, a question which, in reality, is the question of the relationship between the one catholic church of Christ and the diverse local churches. It develops this relationship along the lines of John Paul II's new formulation. The universal church has priority, both temporal and ontological, over all local churches, which develop in and from it, and the bishop of the universal church, who exercises the Petrine ministry, has ontological priority over all other bishops. This line of argument permits the conclusion that a church or ecclesial community not in full communion with the church of Rome and its bishop is "wounded." It would appear also to lead to the conclusion that local churches are merely "parts" of the universal church, which is then no more than a federation of local churches, a conclusion that the letter explicitly rejects.

It seems to me sounder, both theologically and ecumenically, to say with the Joint Working Group of the Roman Catholic Church and the World Council of Churches that "the universal Church is not the sum, federation, or juxtaposition of the local Churches, but all together are the same Church of God present and acting in this world."[55] The universal church and every local church exist simultaneously. There is no precedence of one over the other, as is demonstrated at Pentecost, the birth of the first local and universal church. The universal church is not the sum of all the local churches; but neither are the local churches simply parts of a pre-existing universal church. Each local church, as the ecumenical pioneer Jean Jacques von Allmen, expresses it, "is wholly Church, but it is not the whole Church."[56] That is, of course, what *Lumen Gentium* also taught, if in other words. "The Church of Christ is truly present in all legitimate congregations of the faithful. . . . Christ is present [in them]. By virtue of him, the one, holy, catholic and apostolic Church gathers." The council's clinching argument is the ancient Pauline one: "The partaking of the Body and Blood of Christ does nothing other than transform us into that which we consume."[57] A local church, gathered for eucharist with its bishop, and precisely because it is so gathered, is wholly the body of Christ and symbol of the universal church made concrete and visible in it.

A second theme touching the body of Christ emerges in the letters to the Ephesians and Colossians. While retaining the formula "we are members of his body" (Eph 5:30; Col 3:15), a new theme is introduced, namely, that the body which is the church has a "head," a leader, who is Christ (Eph

1:22–23; Col 1:18; 2:19). Since Christ is now risen, "the Body of Christ is more clearly the risen body become the fullness of divinity, that is, the bodily instrument through which divine blessings come to the world."[58] To grasp the import of the word "body" in these texts, however, a socio-cultural adjustment must be made. In Hebrew usage, "*basar* does not signify a principle or element of a human being, but rather the entire human being in its concrete individuality."[59] For Hebrews, like Jesus and Paul, the body is the person made visible and accessible, the person acting in the world. Augustine's articulation still expresses it best: "the whole Christ is head and body . . . the head the Savior himself . . . the body the Church throughout the whole world."[60]

To say, then, that the church is the body of Christ is to say that the people in communion with Christ incarnate him, make him visible, accessible, and active in every socio-historical world. After his resurrection, Christ in his body-church is active in the emergent human world as a "life-giving spirit" (1 Cor 15:45), showering the members of his body with gifts "as he (and his Spirit) wills" (1 Cor 12:11; Eph 4:11–16). "By these gifts he makes them fit and ready to undertake the tasks and offices advantageous for the renewal and upbuilding of both the Church"[61] and the world. The *charismata* of the Spirit fit the body of Christ for communional[62] ministry in the fallen world. They also ensure that the body's ministry is in continuity with the ministry of Christ, for there is no ministry in the body other than Christ's ministry.[63]

## Vatican II Ecclesiology

I have described the transition from the preparatory document on the church to *Lumen Gentium* as a transition from a vision of church as structure and hierarchical institution to a vision of it as communion and grace. In the post-Reformation period, despite everything in the church that was in obvious need of reformation, the structural emphasis was necessary to affirm, against Protestant claims, the historical visibility of Christ's church. It was not an incorrect affirmation, but it did become an overly exclusive one. Reading nineteenth-century Roman manuals on ecclesiology, one could be forgiven for assuming that Christ's church was *only* a visible, hierarchical institution and nothing more. *Lumen Gentium* eliminated that juridical emphasis, as an exclusive emphasis, and replaced it with a communional and sacramental emphasis. As Congar comments, "the first value is not organization, mediatorial functions or authority, but the Christian life itself and being a disciple." He adds, correctly, that "all this was evident to one who reads the holy scriptures, the fathers of the church, even the great medieval and scholastic theologians."[64] This return to the sources of theology, *ressource-ment*[65] as it came to be called, is an approach to constructive theology most closely associated with French theologians of the period between 1930 and 1950, among them most notably Henri de Lubac, Hans Urs von Balthasar, Jean Daniélou, Yves Congar, and Marie-Dominique Chenu. It was their more careful reading of the sources of the Scriptures, the fathers, and the subsequent theological tradition that made possible the transition achieved in *Lumen Gentium*.

The modern treatment of the church as the body of Christ emphasizes the presence of God within it, calling attention to the life of the Spirit and grace which is, therefore, available to all the members. The treatment of the church as people of God complements this treatment by focusing on the church as a reality composed of socio-historically emergent human beings who confess that Jesus is the Christ of God. The official theological instruction introducing the chapter on the people of God at Vatican II, indeed, indicated that one of the purposes of the chapter was to show the church as a reality being formed in history. Christ's church is a divine-human communion, composed of a divine head and a human body. As a communion embracing socio-historically emergent women and men, as well as the eternal God, the church is necessarily situated in social history, formed in history, and in need of being reformed in history. At each succeeding moment of that history, it behooves it to remember its origin and its goal in God. It behooves it also to heed the Vatican call: "embracing sinners in her bosom, [the church] is at the same time holy and always in need of being purified, and incessantly pursues the path of penance and renewal."[66] In terms of the meaning of theology espoused in this book, we can say that ecclesiology has two tasks, one theoretical, the other practical. It has, first, the task of remembering its past and of mediating that past to the socio-historical present situation, and it has the task of evaluating that past and allowing its evaluation to be the catalyst of a transition to a renewed present and future situation that more closely approximates the rule of God in human affairs preached by Jesus (Mark 1:15; Matt 3:2).

*Lumen Gentium* sketches the history of God's *de facto* people, from Israel's election to the church's election to be God's people. This notion of election highlights the graced character of the people. It is a priestly people, "participating in the one priesthood of Christ";[67] it is a prophetic people, sharing in "Christ's prophetic office";[68] it is a royal people, sharing in the royal office of Christ the King. It is a people made priest and prophet and king by the constituting action of the Holy Spirit. Since church leaders have not always known how to resist misreading and abusing their kingly office, it is necessary to state that it is a sharing, not in the autocratic power of Roman emperors and seventeenth-century European kings, but in the service of the servant-king Christ. It is *diakonia*-service, not *dominium*-rule. The church is constituted more to be of service to God's people and to nurture Christ's body emerging in social history than to rule over either as a divine-right monarch (cf. Acts 20:28). I conclude this chapter by considering how that service developed in the church as an essential part of its constitution.

## The Bible and the Demands of Love and Justice

"It has pleased God," the Second Vatican Council taught, "to reveal himself and to make known the mystery of his will." The pattern of this revelation "unfolds through deeds and words which are intrinsically connected: the works performed by God in the history of salvation show forth and confirm the doctrine and realities signified by the words; the words, for their part, proclaim the works, and bring to light the mystery they contain."[69] The God of both Israel and Christianity is a God who acts and speaks efficaciously, a God whose word is also event or happening. The Psalmist extols this God of action and pours ridicule on all other gods who cannot match Yahweh's activity. "Our God is in the heavens, God does what God pleases. Their idols . . . have mouths but do no speak, eyes but do not see. They have ears but do not hear, noses but do not smell. They have hands but do not feel, feet but do not walk." (Ps 115:3–7).

Since Yahweh is a God of action, every confession of belief in Yahweh, of necessity, is rooted in historical events or happenings. The most radical of historical and revelatory events was the great Exodus, the experience of Israelites in Egypt, in liberation from Egypt, in desert, and in settlement in the land where "milk and honey flow" (Deut 26:9).

> When your son asks you in time to come, "What is the meaning of the testimonies and the statutes and the ordinances which the Lord our God has commanded you?" then you shall say to your son. "We were Pharaoh's slaves in Egypt and the Lord brought us out of Egypt with a mighty hand; and the Lord showed signs and wonders, great and grievous, against Egypt and against Pharaoh and all his household before our eyes; and he brought us out from there that he might bring us in and give us the land which he swore to give to our fathers. The Lord commanded us to do all these statutes, to fear the Lord our God, for our good always, that he might preserve us alive as at this day. It will be righteousness for us if we are careful to do all this commandment before the Lord our God, as he has commanded us." (Deut 6:20–25)[70]

God frees Israel from oppression in Egypt in signs and wonders that reveal unmistakably that it is God who is acting. This liberation is made fully real by the fulfillment of God's promise to settle Israel in the "land where milk and honey flow" (Deut 26:9). It is in the interpretation of that liberation and settlement in the land that the revelation of Yahweh, the God of Israel, is discerned. The response of biblical faith to God's liberating action, Israel's right action or righteousness, is the putting into practice of God's commandments. When we ask in what actions that righteousness is to be concretized, the Bible universally leaves us in no doubt.

Yahweh, the God of Israel, intervenes in history in signs and wonders, not only to manifest power but also to manifest that power is to be used in defense of the defenseless poor and oppressed. Yahweh is "father of the fatherless and protector of widows...God gives the desolate a home to dwell in; God leads out the prisoners to prosperity; but the rebellious dwell in a parched land" (Ps 68:5–6). To know this God is not, as it is in Greece, to know *that* God is and *what* God is; it is, in Hebrew religion, to love God and act like God. In Gustavo Gutiérrez's formulation, "to know God as liberator *is* to liberate, *is* to do justice,"[71] always remembering how Yahweh intervened in history to create liberation and justice for Israelite slaves in Egypt. That memory returns again and again.

> You shall remember that you were a slave in Egypt and the Lord your God redeemed you from there; therefore, I command you to do this. When you reap your harvest in your field, and have forgotten a sheaf in the field, you shall not go back to get it; it shall be for the sojourner, the fatherless, the widow; that the Lord your God may bless you in all the works of your hands. When you beat your olive trees, you shall not go over the boughs again; it shall be for the sojourner, the fatherless, and the widow. When you gather the grapes of your vineyard, you shall not glean it afterwards; it shall be for the sojourner, the fatherless, and the widow. You shall remember that you were a slave in the land of Egypt; therefore, I command you to do this. (Deut 24:18–22)

What Jesus, the righteous Jew whom God raised from the dead (Acts 3:14–15), would later advance as a reciprocal relationship between God and "the least of these my brethren" (Matt 25:40) has always been embedded in his Jewish tradition as a reciprocal relationship between God and the poor. The prophets consistently link these two and proclaim that to know and love God requires action against the injustice and oppression perpetrated against God's people. Jeremiah, for instance, proclaims this prophetic message:

Hear the word of the Lord, all you men of Judah who enter these gates to worship the Lord. Thus says the Lord of hosts, the God of Israel. Amend your ways and your doings and I will let you dwell in this place. Do not trust in these deceptive words: "This is the temple of the Lord, the temple of the Lord, the temple of the Lord." For if you truly amend your ways and your doings, if you truly execute justice one with another, if you do not oppress the alien, the fatherless or the widow, or shed innocent blood in this place, and if you do not go after other gods to your own hurt, then I will let you dwell in this place, in the land that I gave of old to your fathers forever. (7:2–7)

The reciprocation could not be made clearer. Knowledge and love of God are proved in practice by action on behalf of justice for the poor and oppressed. Proverbs offers an axiom about this reciprocative preferential option for the poor: "He who mocks the poor insults his creator" (17:5).

Isaiah's messianic formulation of the connection between right living and justice for the poor leads us into the New testament, where Luke and Jesus select it for commentary in Jesus' home synagogue of Nazareth.

The Spirit of the Lord God is upon me, because the Lord has anointed me to bring good tidings to the afflicted; he has sent me to bind up the brokenhearted, to proclaim liberty to the captives, and the opening of the prison to those who are bound; to proclaim the year of the Lord's favor, and the day of vengeance of our God; to comfort all who mourn; to grant to those who mourn in Zion — to give them a garland instead of ashes, the oil of gladness instead of mourning, the mantle of praise instead of a faint spirit, that they may be called oaks of righteousness.... For I the Lord love justice, I hate robbery and wrong. I will faithfully give them their recompense and I will make an everlasting covenant with them. (61:1–8)

This predilection for the poor and the oppressed, Isaiah prophetically proclaims, will be characteristic of the coming Messiah, the ultimately righteous one of Israel. That the Messiah has come in Jesus is proclaimed in Luke's and Jesus' commentary on the text: "today this scripture has been fulfilled in your hearing" (Luke 4:21).

The confession of the followers of Jesus of Nazareth was and is that he is the promised Messiah, the Christ (Mark 1:1; Matt 1:1), the one anointed by God "to bring good tidings to the afflicted." The gospels symbolize his messianic anointing in his baptism, the descent of the Spirit of God upon him, and his designation as "beloved son" (Mark 1:9–11; Matt 3:13–17; Luke 3:21–22), and immediately after he is anointed he proclaims the advent of the kingdom or reign of God (Mark 1:15). The nature of this reign is the full import of Luke's use of the Isaiah text cited above, "today this scripture has been fulfilled in your hearing:" the reign of God is a reign of justice in favor of the poor, the oppressed, the marginalized. Jesus' proclamation of this reign, not only in words but more importantly in actions, is what led him, first, to his death and, then, to his resurrection by God (1 Cor 15:4; Rom 6:4; 8:4; Col 2:12; Acts 2:24, 32; 3:15). For the entire body of disciples, and not just for the two on the road to Emmaus, "their eyes were opened" (Luke 24:31) by his resurrection, in which God verified both that the words and actions of Jesus were right with God and that he was, indeed, the "holy and righteous one" (Acts 2:14).

The eyes of Jesus' followers were so thoroughly opened that, ultimately, they confessed not only that he was the Christ, the holy and righteous one sent by God, but that he was very God in human form, God made man full of grace and truth, God pitching his tent among men and women (John 1:14). The universal biblical reciprocation between God and the poor reaches an unsurpassable high point in Jesus, who "is precisely God become poor,"[72] and it is in precisely his life on behalf of his poor sisters and brothers that he is recognized as God's beloved Son. Like any good Jew socialized in his time and place, Jesus continued both to uphold the reciprocal relationship between God and the poor and to insist that to know and love God is to act against every injustice perpetrated against the poor. Matthew makes his position clearest in his Sermon on the Mount: "Not every one who *says* to me 'Lord, Lord,' shall enter the kingdom of heaven but the one who *does* the will of my Father who is in heaven" (7:21). The disciples who responded to Jesus' invitation to "follow me" (Mark 1:17; Matt 4:18) upheld the same relationship and equally insisted that it is to be lived not in words but in action. Again, Matthew makes it clearest, in his powerful final judgment scenario.

> Then he will say to those at his left hand, "depart from me you cursed into the eternal fire prepared for the devil and his angels; for I was hungry and you gave me no food, I was thirsty and you gave me no drink, I was a stranger and you did not welcome me, sick and in prison and you did not visit me." Then they also will answer, "Lord, when did we see thee hungry or thirsty or a stranger or naked or sick or in prison, and did not minister to thee?" Then he will answer them, "Truly, I say to you, as you did it not to one of the least of these, you did it not to me." (Matt 25:41–45)

Matthew's final comment is a chilling woe for those who do not recognize the reciprocation between God and the poor and a blessing for those who do: "And they will go away into eternal punishment, but the righteous into eternal life" (25:46)

James, as radically Jewish as either Jesus or Matthew, has his own formulation of the reciprocation between God and the poor. "What does it profit, my brethren, if a man says he has faith but has not works? Can his faith save him? If a brother or sister is ill-clad and in lack of daily food, and one of you says to them 'Go in peace, be warmed and filled' without giving them the things needed for the body, what does it profit? So faith by itself, if it has no works, is dead" (James 2:14–17). Luther sparked a long and false debate between Catholics and Lutherans about the respective values of faith and good works, as if Lutherans valued only faith and Catholics only good works. That debate has now been laid formally to rest by the agreement between Lutherans and Catholics articulated in their *Joint Declaration on the Doctrine of Justification.*[73] The theological reality is that Luther and the theologians who followed him never doubted that faith is proved in action, in other words that faith must work, and the Catholic Church never doubted that faith is necessary for salvation.[74]

The pattern of service to others, particularly to the poor and the oppressed, which Jesus exemplifies in his life and unceasingly seeks to inculcate in his disciples, is a Christ-ian[75] pattern highlighted throughout the New Testament and intimately related to the universal reciprocation between God, God's Christ, and God's least. The synoptic Christ articulates the pattern unequivocally: "The Son of Man came not be to be served but to serve, and to give his life as a ransom (redemption) for many" (Mark 10:45; Matt 20:28). Service, *diakonia,* is Christ's way of relating to others; service of others, especially of the least, is what he seeks to inculcate in his disciples. He instructs them that those who have authority over the Gentiles lord it over them. "But it shall not so among you; whoever would be great among you must be your servant, and whoever would be first among you must be slave of all" (Mark 10:42–44; Matt 20:25–27). There is abundant evidence that they never seemed to understand.

John's Supper narrative highlights this Christ-ian emphasis on service, which has been somewhat obscured by the Catholic emphasis on the transformation of bread and wine in eucharist. The narrative describes Jesus' washing of his disciples' feet, a prophetic action that reveals Jesus' will to be remembered as Servant, and challenges those who remember him to do the same. Lest this point be missed, as it has been regularly missed in Christian history, John's Jesus underlines the challenge in his final testament: "I have given you an example that you also should do as I have done to you" (13:15). Jesus, he of right action and righteousness, who lived a life of neighbor-love (Lev 19:18; Mark 12:31) as service to others, challenged his disciples to do the same. Xavier Léon-Dufour interprets this foot-washing service as integral to the paschal meal, to the Christian eucharist which derives from it, and to the character of both as memorial meals.[76] I am arguing here that it is integral also to the way Christ-ians, committed to the reciprocation between God and the least, are to live their lives apart from eucharist.

Pope John Paul II, in his important letter on the Lay Faithful, teaches that "communion is the very mystery of the church."[77] The Congregation for the Doctrine of the Faith cites the pope's words with approval: "the concept of communion lies at the heart of the church's self-understanding."[78] These opinions echo the judgment of the 1985 Roman Synod[79] and of the secretary of the Second Vatican Council's Central Theological Commission that its vision of church as *koinonia*-communion was the council's most important teaching.[80] The church *is* a communion;[81] communion *is* the church's very essence. Communion is a common word in the Catholic tradition but, in recent Catholic tradition, it has not been used of the church. Rather it has been used as an expression for receiving the body of Christ in eucharist.[82] The two uses of the term, however, are not unrelated, and Paul was the first to enunciate their connection. "The cup of blessing which we bless, is it not a communion in the blood of Christ? The bread which we break, is it not a communion in the body of Christ? Because there is one bread, we who are many are one body, for we all partake of the one bread" (1 Cor 10:16–17). The Second Vatican Council taught this same doctrine explicitly. "Truly partaking of the Body of the Lord in the breaking of the eucharistic bread, we are taken up into communion with *him* and with one another."[83] That statement is important for the argument of this essay and for the reciprocation between God and the poor.

Participation in eucharist leads to communion not only with God in Christ but also with the body of believers, the church. Communion in the church is an essentially eucharistic reality, in both a weak and a strong sense. The weak sense is the sense of holy communion in the body of Christ in and through bread and wine. The more important strong sense is that the eucharistic meal is the sacrament, that is, both the sign and the instrument,[84] of the communion of believers not only with their Lord but also with one another. It was and is because believers share food and drink in the name of Christ that they were and are made one in communion.[85] Clement, professor at the catechetical school in Alexandria at the beginning of the second century, roots this *koinonia*-communion in God. "It is God Himself who has brought our race to *koinonia* by sharing Himself... by sending his Word to all alike... and by making all things for all." This God-created *koinonia*, he explains, is intimately related to our question of justice for the least. "Everything is common, and the rich should not grasp a greater share. The expression 'I own something and I have more than enough, why should I not enjoy it?' is not worthy of a human nor does it indicate any *koinonia*. The other expression, however, does: 'I have something, "Thou shalt love thy neighbor as thyself." ' "[86]

Clement was not the first to relate *koinonia*-communion in Christ's church to reciprocation between God and the least. That relationship is already exemplified in the earliest Jerusalem church, which devoted itself to "the apostles' teaching and communion *(koinonia)*" (Acts 2:42) and "had everything in common *(panta koina)*" (Acts 4:32). Paul makes clear that communion is not just between the members of a local community but reaches out to embrace all the churches, telling us in his original Greek that the poor churches in Macedonia and Achaia "have been pleased to make *koinonian*" for the church at Jerusalem (Rom 15:26; cf. 2 Cor 8:4) and praising "the generosity of your *koinonias*" (2 Cor 9:13). Such genuine communion among believers sharing the eucharistic meal, Paul argues, is a necessary precondition for truly celebrating the Lord's Supper. When there is no such communion among believers, as there is not at Corinth, neither is there communion with the Christ they confess as Lord. In such circumstance, Paul judges, "it is not the Lord's Supper that you eat" (1 Cor 11:20). That judgment ought not to come as a surprise, given the final Judge's pronouncement that "as you did it not to one of the least of these you did it not to me" (Matt 25:45). When there is no communion in real time with the least in the body of believers, neither is there communion with the Christ and Christ's God.

The theologians who have most clearly interpreted and asserted the connection between ritual sacraments, ecclesial communion, and communional Christ-ian life in the present age are liberation theologians. They correctly interpreted the biblical data we have considered as a preferential option for the poor and enunciated this option first as a theological doctrine which then became established as an ecclesial doctrine of the Catholic Church. This doctrine gained its preeminence as a result of two conferences of Latin American bishops, the first at Medellín in Colombia in 1968, the second at Puebla in Mexico in 1979. Medellín adumbrated the phrase, "preferential option for the poor," Puebla explicitly adopted it. Among the signs of authentic Christianity, the bishops taught, are "preferential love and concern for the poor"; they pledged themselves "to make clear through our lives and attitudes that our preference is to evangelize and serve the poor"; "a preferential option for the poor," they taught, "represents the most noticeable tendency of religious life in Latin America."[87] Explaining how this doctrine relates to eucharist, an Asian representative, Tissa Balasuriya, writes: "The eucharist is spiritual food insofar as it leads to love, unity and communion among persons and groups. Today this requires love among persons and effective action for justice. The eucharist must also lead us to a response to the suffering of the masses, *often caused by people who take a prominent part in the eucharist.* Unless there is this twofold dimension of personal love and societal action, the eucharist can be a sacrilege."[88] Balasuriya"s judgment concretely illustrates the ethical demand of reciprocation which flows from the celebration of eucharistic communion in the church. The phrase I have chosen to underscore, which is demonstrably correct beyond debate, illustrates the Vatican Council's confession that the church embraces sinners in her membership and is, therefore, "at the same time holy and always in need of being purified" and renewed in its commitment to Christ and to the God he reveals.[89]

The connection between the celebration of Christian sacraments and the ethical demand to go forth and live like Christ in one's socio-historical circumstances is a firm theological position in the church, and it is not a new position. Already in the third century, Cyprian of Carthage argued that putting on Christ in baptism is quite meaningless unless it is followed by a Christlike life. "To put on the name of Christ and not continue along the way of Christ, what is that but a lie?"[90] If we have put him on, "we ought to go forward according to the example of Christ."[91] In the twentieth century, John Paul II agrees: initiation into communion in the church is initiation also into the mission of the church. "Communion gives rise to mission, and mission is accomplished in communion."[92] The communion that is the mission of the church, I have already argued, is twofold: it is the communion of believers one with the other and the communion of believers with Christ and Christ's God. Those two communions are reciprocal, the one depending on the other, and they are celebrated, proclaimed, and made real in eucharist, and are intended to be lived apart from eucharist in actual Christ-ian lives. It is not difficult to see how this sharing in the church, the body of Christ, shares also in the ancient reciprocation between God and, especially, God's least, the easily ignored poor and oppressed.

## The Historically Emerging Church

If the foregoing theological analyses are correct, then we are in a position to make several conclusions about the church emerging in the socio-historical human community of our time. First, the church is a communion of believers in the God made known in Christ, as that communion has been described by the Second Vatican Council and elaborated theologically in the years since the council. The primary concern of this church is not organization and structure, and the monarchical authority traditionally associated with hierarchical organization, but ongoing discernment of and fidelity to the Mystery-God at the heart of the church, the Christ who is the mediator of this God to women and men, and an active Christ-ian life of discipleship. The church is a communion of believers with God and one another, the people of God and the body of Christ, with the important proviso that these terms are all understood as active terms, describing primarily not any ecclesial structure, but the active life that believers live.

Second, in imitation of the God and the Christ in whom they believe, the life of believers in the world is a life not only of words but above all of deeds. The God of Israel is a God of action, and the Christ of God is a Christ of action. The Lord God brought Israel "out of Egypt with a mighty hand; and the Lord showed signs and wonders, great and grievous, against Egypt and against Pharaoh and all his household before our eyes; and he brought us out from there that he might bring us in and give us the land which he swore to give to our fathers" (Deut 6:21–23). Isaiah described the Christ whom the Lord would send. "The Lord has anointed me to bring good tidings to the afflicted; he has sent me to bind up the broken hearted, to proclaim liberty to the captives, and the opening of the prison to those who are bound; to proclaim the year of the Lord's favor and the day of vengeance of our God; to comfort all who mourn" (61:1–2). Jesus, the Christ God sent, made that description his own. Christ's church in the world cannot but do otherwise. The reciprocal relationship between God and the poor evident in the First Covenant is replicated by Jesus in the Second Covenant, and has to be progressively replicated in our day by Christ's church. The preferential option for the poor is not to be understood as an option the church can either take or leave. It is an option it has to take to support any claim of fidelity to the God it believes in and the Christ whom this God sent to be the salvation of the world.

Third, in the present world situation in which division, hatred, racism, classism, sexism, and social sins rampantly abound, a genuine communion, servant church, with a preferential option for the underside poor and oppressed,[93] is necessarily an injustice-resistant and transformative community.[94] Its first task will be to transform itself into a resistant communion, which consciously and steadfastly stands for the reign of God in the world, as described and exemplified by Jesus, and stands against every human distortion of that reign to be a transformative agent of its universal coming. Theology will have an important role to play in this task, as theologians become more and more religiously, morally, intellectually, and psychically converted, and summon the church to the mission given it by Christ, to be his active body in the world. The church's second task, having transformed itself, is to transform the world. This task will be fulfilled more and more in direct relation to the degree to which the church itself has become a transformed and resistant communion. The religiously converted and transformed church, the sacrament of Christ in the world[95] and the sacrament of salvation,[96] is to be a genuine *Lumen Gentium,* a light to the nations, mediating a transformation of the world into a world communion that embraces peoples far beyond its own boundaries. Israel's choice was once "between suffering servanthood as a light for the nations and a self-enclosed parochialism that would literalize the symbols of deliverance by reifying them in institutions." Theology's choice today "is between accepting its foundational role in generating the superstructure of a world-cultural community or closing in on itself in promoting new forms of revelational positivism." The church has a choice too, between "dialogical participation in a community that transcends its boundaries and either anxious withdrawal into sectarian self-protection or non-dialogical authoritarianism masking itself as proclamation."[97] There is no doubt about the direction in which modern popes are nudging a reluctant church.

In 1946, Pius XII described the essential mission of the church as including the building up the human community according to Christian principles. The lay faithful, he insisted, "are in the front line of the church's life; through them, the church is the vital principle of human society. Consequently, they must have an ever more clear consciousness, not only of belonging to the church, but of *being* the church."[98] The Second Vatican Council articulated Pius's thought more directly, teaching that "a secular quality is proper and special to laymen,"[99] a teaching that Pope Paul VI repeated a decade later. The church, he taught, "has an authentic secular dimension, inherent to her inner nature and mission, which is deeply rooted in the mystery of the Word incarnate and which is realized in different forms through her members."[100] Both the nature and the mission of the church are rooted in the incarnation, that central Christian doctrine which confesses that God became human in Jesus, after and in the light of which nothing on earth is ever exclusively profane or secular, not even laity and their life in the world.

Pope John Paul II continued that line of thought. The lay faithful, he teaches, are "disciples and followers of Christ, members of the church who are present and active in the world's heart so as to administer temporal realities and order them toward God's Reign." The secular character at the core of this definition is to be read, he insists, with a *theological* and not just with a sociological meaning. "The term *secular* must be understood in the light of the act of God...who has handed over the world to women and men so that they may participate in the work of creation, free creation from the influence of sin and sanctify themselves."[101] Communional service in and for the world, no matter what service it is, is not just *secular* service, in the sense that it falls outside of God's plan of salvation. It is also *salvation* service, in the sense that it is also for the consecration and the salvation of the world. John Paul returns to this theme again and again.[102] I add only that the secular character of the laity is to be understood also in the light of the incarnation. A theological characteristic of laity is that they live in the world, know the world, value the world, and seek to permeate it with the Spirit of Christ and of the gospel.

The theological secularity which is a distinctive mark of laity is never to be confused with that godless secularization of which John Paul II frequently complains.[103] Secularization, on the one hand, names a process in which the material world becomes so exclusively "real," that the life of Christian faith is diminished. When that process goes so far as to extinguish faith, then a person has become *secularized,* a baptized non-believer. Such non-believers cannot incarnate for the world the communion-church which is in the world as a sacrament of communion, of peace, of service, of salvation. Nor can they incarnate the Spirit who calls the world to communion and peace, the Christ who seeks to serve the world by proclaiming to it the liberating word of God, or the God whose word is reconciliation and peace. For they no longer believe any of this. Secular, on the other hand, as it is used of the lay faithful, identifies a twofold theological quality of Christian believers. They are, first, firmly situated in the secular world where they can, therefore, secondly, incarnate the church, the Christ and the Spirit of the God in whom they passionately believe and with whom they intimately commune. For a Christian to be secular in this sense is a double badge of honor, for it bespeaks commitment both to the world and to the triune God who wills to save it. Such secularity is the distinctive character of the distinctive ministry of lay Christians. It demands deep faith, without which it easily becomes secularization. But until and unless that sad moment of transformation occurs, Christian secularity should never be confused with godless secularization.

Karl Rahner asserts of the Chalcedonian dogma of the mystery of Jesus as true God and true man that it is both an end and a beginning. "We shall never stop trying to release ourselves from it," he said, "not so as to abandon it but to understand it... so that through it we might draw near to the ineffable, unapproachable, nameless God, whose will it was that we should find him in Jesus Christ."[104] So we say also of the Second Vatican Council's categorization of the church as mystery and communion. It is an end of past theological and ecclesial debate, but it is also a new beginning of the emergent search for the reality it articulates, communion with God in Christ through the Holy Spirit whose desire it is to be found in the human communion that is the church, the body of Christ and the people of God. When he promulgated *Lumen Gentium,* Pope Paul VI stated that "henceforth it will be possible to have a fuller understanding of the thought of God in relation to the Mystical Body of Christ, and we shall be able to draw therefrom clearer and surer norms for the life of the Church, greater strength to lead men [and women] to salvation, better hopes for the reign of Christ in the world."[105] I hope we can fairly appropriate this statement as our own at the end of this chapter. We shall see in the chapters that follow what difference this approach to church makes to other ecclesial doctrines.

## Conclusion

This chapter examined and underscored a crucial transformation in the theology of church effected by the Second Vatican Council in the socio-historical context of the late twentieth century. That transformation is from a focus on church as hierarchical institution to a focus on church as communion, a theological model which Monsignor Philips, secretary of the council's Central Commission, declared to be the council's preferred model of church.[106] This judgment was later embraced by Pope John Paul II, who taught that "communion is the very mystery of the Church,"[107] and Cardinal Ratzinger of the Congregation for the Doctrine of the Faith, who taught that "the concept of communion lies at the heart of the Church's self understanding."[108] There is no theological doubt today that the church is to be attended to, imaged, understood, and judged to be a communion. This model of church gives primary attention to the God who is uncreated, operative Grace dwelling with and in the church, rather than to hierarchical structure and authority. It is this indwelling Grace who is the life-source of the church as communion, as body of Christ, and as people of God. Communion in the church is twofold: the people are in communion with God and, because they are in communion with God, they are also in communion with one another, in faith, in love, in mutual service, in discipleship of Jesus of Nazareth whom they confess as the Christ. The council specifies the task of the communion-church in the plural socio-historical contexts of the world to be "a kind of sacrament or sign of intimate communion with God,"[109] "a universal sacrament of salvation,"[110] that is, in the special theological categories of the Catholic tradition, both a sign and an instrument of the forgiveness, reconciliation, communion, and peace between all human beings and the God who created them for Godself.

As always for the followers of Jesus, faith in and love of this communion-church is proved in communional *praxis,* by mutually faithful and loving actions. "Not everyone who *says* to me, 'Lord, Lord,'" Jesus teaches, "shall enter the kingdom of heaven, but the one who *does* the will of my father" (Matt 7:21). Both Cyprian, third-century bishop of Carthage, and John Paul II, twentieth-century bishop of Rome, continue this ancient tradition. Cyprian teaches that putting on Christ in baptism is meaningless and useless unless baptism is followed by Christlike action. "To put on the name of Christ and not continue along the way of Christ, what is that but a lie?"[111] John Paul teaches the same thing, though in contemporary theological language. "Communion and mission," he teaches, "are profoundly connected with one another, they interpenetrate and mutually imply each other. Communion gives rise to mission and mission is accomplished in communion."[112] One cannot be genuinely in communion with God or with fellow believers without actively responding to the Jesus' invitation, "Follow me" (Mark 1:17). Everything that follows in this book is built on the foundation of a church that is the communion of the whole people of God.

## Questions for Discussion

1. What are the implications that result from the Second Vatican Council's rejection of its prepared document on church and its replacement with *Lumen Gentium?* Do these implications have any effect on your life as a member of the church?

2. Reflect on the theological and social differences that follow if the church is dealt with as essentially a hierarchical institution or essentially a communion.

3. What do you understand by the word "mystery," and what are the implications of that understanding for your life as a member of the church?

4. What implications for your Christian life does the biblical and Catholic teaching on preferential option for the poor have? How could this teaching ever be verified by sociologists?

5. "Communion and mission are profoundly connected with one another, they interpenetrate and mutually imply each other. Communion gives rise to mission and mission is accomplished in communion." Reflect on the meaning of this teaching of Pope John Paul II and on its implications for your Christian life.

# Reception and *Sensus Fidei*

In chapter 2, following Robin Gill, I suggested that sociology can illuminate the *social structure* of theology, the concrete *is* of the ecclesial and
theological situation rather than the abstract *ought to be*. Sociology, I argued, can provide empirical description of the actual situation which the
theologian can take, distill through ecclesial and theological filters, and
proceed to prescription of what ought to be. This chapter reflects on that
suggestion and attempts to concretize it theologically. It examines two theological realities, *sensus fidei* and *reception,* explores their relationship to the
data of sociological research, and concretizes the exploration in a consideration of the sociological data and theology around two Catholic moral
doctrines, divorce and remarriage without prior annulment and artificial
contraception. A *theological* reflection on the actual situation of both doctrines and a *sociological* consideration of the data suggest that a dramatic
development and re-reception[1] of both doctrines is under way and that the
development is in line with previous dramatic developments of doctrine in
the church.

## Faith and Praxis

This chapter might be described as an exercise in Don Browning's descriptive
theology or Rahner's practical theology, the "theological discipline which is
concerned with the church's self-actualization here and now — both that
which *is* and that which *ought to be*."[2] Practical theology is *theological*
reflection in and conditioned by the church's actual situation. It does not
explain that situation in the classicist way from deductive theological principles but reflects inductively and critically on the empirical description
of the actual situation, to test it for ongoing meaningfulness in light of
both the received tradition and the actual socio-historical situation. Practical theology grows out of the relationship between *theoria* and *praxis*
which, for the church, is the relationship between *faith* and *praxis*. To recognize scientifically the church's actual situation and to perform the required

theological reflection, Rahner argues, "practical theology certainly requires sociology."[3]

The development in the two moral doctrines under discussion, as I have already explained in the Prologue, can be detected in both the high tradition, comprised of believers whose grasp of the philosophical precision of the language in which Catholic doctrine is articulated enables them to understand the meanings embedded in doctrine, and the low tradition, comprised of believers who do not understand the language and, therefore, as often as not, misunderstand doctrine. The theologian's task is to speak *from* the actual faith situation of the church, not only to hand on the traditional doctrine which comes from the past but also to evaluate it for meaningfulness in the present situation and to hand it on, unchanged or changed as required by critical judgment, to shape the future theological and ecclesial situation. Charles Péguy, whose thought Congar claims as the root of the *ressourcement* theology which flourished in the middle of the twentieth century and provided the foundation for the theological developments in the Second Vatican Council, expresses the theologian's task well. It is "a call from a less perfect tradition to a more perfect tradition, a call from a shallower tradition to a deeper tradition, an overtaking of depth, an investigation into deeper sources; in the literal sense of the word a 're-source.'"[4] If that is the task, then sociology, which explores and manifests the present doctrinal situation, can be as much a handmaid for contemporary theological reflection as philosophy was for medieval Aquinas and his followers.

No Catholic theologian would deny that ecclesial faith is the primary source for theological reflection,[5] but that faith always includes *praxis* or action. That is the pattern, as we saw, that stretches from second-generation Paul, who speaks of the *fruits* of the Spirit (Gal 5:22–23), to third-generation Matthew, "you will know them by their *fruits*" (7:16), and James, who insists that "faith by itself, if it has not works, is dead" (2:14–17). As I insisted in the Prologue, these biblical texts are advanced not to prove the connection between faith and practice but to reveal a pattern that pervades the New Testament and establishes the connection between faith and practice as a long-standing Catholic position. In the Catholic tradition, one has always been able to argue from the presence of genuine faith to appropriate *praxis* and, conversely, from actual *praxis* to the faith that underpins it. Sociology, again, can play an important part in that argument by illuminating present action, making it possible for theologians to conclude to the faith behind the *praxis*. That is probably why the Second Vatican Council taught that "in pastoral care sufficient use should be made, not only of theological principles, but also of the findings of secular sciences, especially psychology and sociology." By making use of these sciences, the council goes on to assert, "the faithful will be brought to a purer and more mature living of the faith."[6] My claim in this book is a similar claim, namely, that sociology has an important part to play in manifesting and interpreting what the church actually believes and ought to believe and what it does and ought to do in response to what it believes.

## Reception

Reception is an ecclesial process by which virtually[7] all the members of the church assent to a teaching presented to them as apostolic truth and ecclesial faith, thereby assimilating the doctrine into the life of the whole church.[8] The teaching may come to them internally from their own church, for instance, from an ecumenical council or a decision of the magisterium, or it may come to them externally from another religious community, as ecumenism came to the Catholic Church from the Protestant traditions. In either case, though it is not what makes the teaching true or false, reception flows from a critical judgment of the data and a responsible decision that the teaching is good for the whole church and is in agreement with the apostolic tradition on which the church is built. It is important to be clear from the outset that reception is not a judgment about the truth or validity of a teaching, but a decision about its efficacy in the life of the church. A non-received teaching is not *eo ipso* false or invalid; it is simply judged by a large majority of believers to be irrelevant to the life of the church. As culture, time, and place necessarily inculturated the gospel, the good news of what God has done in Jesus the Christ, so too do they also inculturate every doctrine and every reception of doctrine.[9] The act of reception, therefore, cannot and does not receive the tradition of the past unchanged; the past is always re-appropriated or re-received in the present.[10] In Catholic history, there are many examples of both reception and non-reception.

Already in the New Testament, Jesus and those he sends are to be received (Matt 10:40–41; Mark 6:11; Luke 9:5). There is a theological truth embedded here that should never be forgotten, namely, reception in the Christian church is primarily the reception of a *person,* Jesus the Christ, never only the reception of words or doctrines about the Christ or the God he reveals. The word of God is also to be received (Mark 4:20), as is the message of Jesus (Matt 19:11–12; John 3:11; Rev 2:41) and the gospel (1 Cor 15:1; Gal 1:9–12), leading Giuseppe Alberigo to define the church as "the communion of those who receive the gospel."[11] The implication is always that without reception the person, and the word the person speaks, is ineffective (see Luke 4:16–29).

In the pre-Nicene and pre-Constantinian church, reception was connected more with personal *koinonia*-communion than with doctrinal teachings. The pre-Nicene church was not highly organized and was essentially more local than universal. Unity was achieved in this loosely organized collection of churches more by the sharing of *koinonia*-communion among local churches than by legislation or teaching that bound all of them. All local churches had received the apostolic tradition that they should be, and should be seen to be, one, and they knew themselves to be one in virtue of their shared *koinonia*-communion.[12] This *koinonia*-communion, the community of the faithful, the union of all who believe in Christ, is twofold. It designates fundamentally the communion of all the faithful with God in Christ and through Christ's Spirit and, consequently, the communion of all with one another. Its synonym is *eirene*-peace, not simply the absence of conflict nor uniformity of teaching, but true personal and social identity with the community of believers. Burial sarcophogi frequently testify that a Christian *vixit in pace* and *obiit in pace,* she lived and died in the peace and communion of the church.

There is, therefore, ancient warrant for the official note from the Second Vatican Council in November 1964. "*Communion* is an idea which was held in high honor in the ancient Church.... It is understood, however, not of a certain feeling but of an *organic reality* which demands a juridical form."[13] This explanation makes clear that communion is not only internal, invisible communion with God in Christ but also external, verifiable communion constituted by the Spirit of Christ and composed of "all those who receive him in faith and in love."[14] This *koinonia*-communion is already exemplified in the earliest local church in Jerusalem, which devoted itself to "the apostles' teaching and communion (*koinonia*)" (Acts 2:42) and "had everything in common (*panta koina*)" (Acts 4:32). Paul shows that this communion reaches out to all the churches. The churches in Macedonia and Achaia "have been pleased to make *koinonian*" for the church at Jerusalem (Rom 15:26; cp 2 Cor 8:4). He indicates the personal cost of such sharing when he praises "the generosity of your *koinonias* for them and for all others" (2 Cor 9:13).

Churches maintained communion in a variety of ways, especially through letters, of which there were two kinds. First, travelers were provided with a letter from their local church, a sort of Christian identity card, that would indicate to the churches through which they passed that they could be received in communion. Second, letters were sent from one bishop to another to testify to and promote their communion. Notice of the death of a bishop and the election of a new bishop was required to be sent so that the churches could maintain up-to-date lists of all those churches and bishops with whom they were in communion. In 268, the Synod of Antioch sent a long letter to other local churches, explaining the excommunication of Bishop Paul of Samosata because of his views about Jesus, and the election of Domnus as his replacement. "We are informing you of his appointment," the letter explained, "that you may write to him and receive from him a letter establishing communion."[15] In 325, the Council of Antioch wrote to Bishop Alexander of Thessalonica warning him of the false doctrines of Bishops Theodotus of Laodicea, Narcissus of Neronias, and Eusebius of Caesarea, and requesting that he pass on this message to other bishops. "We are writing to you," they explained, "to let you know that you should be on your guard against communicating with them, against writing to them, and against receiving letters of communion from them."[16] Loosely bound local churches were clearly conscious of both their communion with one another and their responsibility to maintain it. The sending of letters to one another was a concrete acknowledgment of this communion and their reception cemented it.

Communion was signified in a second important way, through the role of the elected leader of the community, the *episkopos* or overseer, who would develop into bishop in the later church. For the early followers of Jesus, the *ekklesia* or gathering of believers was a central reality of their faith, and the role of the bishop as pastoral and ritual leader of the gathering was a central facet of the *ekklesia*. In the deutero-Pauline Letters to Timothy and Titus, there is detectable a new ecclesial arrangement of *presbyteroi* and *episkopoi*, with little distinction between them,[17] commissioned by the laying on of hands to pastor the community in the apostolic faith. In Ignatius, *episkopos* of Antioch (d. ca. 117), we begin to detect for the first time a clearly delineated different picture, in which *episkopos* is not just a member of the presbyteral college but also its head. His letters to the Magnesians and Smyrneans indicate similar ministerial arrangements in those cities, with Damas presiding over the Magnesians and Polycarp over the Smyrneans.[18] The bishop presides in the church and at eucharist surrounded by his presbyters, who form an apostolic council to sustain him.[19] "No one is to do anything in the church without the bishop. A valid eucharist is one which is either under his presidency or the presidency of a representative appointed by him. . . . It is not right to baptize without the bishop, nor to celebrate the *agape* without him. Whatever he approves is approved also by God."[20] For Ignatius, the bishop is an important minister indeed, but he is not a priest.

Ignatius and Irenaeus, bishop of Lyons, who followed him, maintained a clear distinction between apostles and bishops; Cyprian, bishop of Carthage in the middle of the third century, did not. He saw the biblical apostles as the first *episcopi* and the *episcopi* of his day as their successors, holding the very same position the apostles held in the church. This theological perspective allowed him to argue for the superiority of bishops over all other ministries, since "the Lord elected apostles, that is, Bishops and leaders, whereas deacons were constituted ministers by the apostles."[21] Construed on this strong foundation, Cyprian's position on the exalted nature of the bishop is not difficult to understand. "You should know that the Bishop is in the Church and the Church is in the Bishop, and whoever is not with the Bishop is not with the Church."[22] Cyprian's exalted notion of bishop became the position of the Western church and remains its position today, and it had important implications for *koinonia*-communion. The bishop, who presided over the local church, also represented his church in the communion of churches. It was in this latter role that he and the bishops of other local churches forged a communion of bishops, signifying mutual reception of their local churches in the communion of those who believe in Christ and the God he reveals.

The mutual reception of and communion between bishops and their churches was frequently made visible in the celebration of eucharist, a third important way for expressing reception. Two or more bishops might concelebrate eucharist, and at Easter, Eusebius tells us, they might send the eucharist to one another. The celebration of eucharist and the sharing in communion, as John D. Zizioulas insists, "express the 'ecclesia of God' and her unity *par excellence*."[23] The Catholic Church has always been in reality, as the Second Vatican Council defined it to be, "an altar society" where "the faithful are gathered together through the preaching of the gospel of Christ and the mystery of the Lord's Supper is celebrated."[24]

The first-century church has an important lesson for every contemporary church: difference of opinion did not necessarily imply the negation of the right to share communion. In the dispute over the date of Easter, the bishop of Rome, Victor, threatened to cut off from communion the Quartodeciman bishops of Asia Minor. Irenaeus wrote to Victor, begging him not to do anything that would rupture communion, pointing out the behavior of his predecessor, Anicetus, toward Polycarp, the bishop of Smyrna. Though neither could convert the other to his opinion about Easter, they "remained in communion with each other, and in church Anicetus made way for Polycarp to celebrate the eucharist, out of respect obviously. They parted company in peace [*eirene*], and the whole Church was at peace, both those who kept the day and those who did not."[25] The importance of both ecclesial communion and eucharistic communion as its sign are heavily underscored in another, negative way. In cases of heresy and schism, which caused the rupture of communion, both orthodox and heretic carried eucharist with them when they traveled, precisely to avoid any intercommunion with the other and all that would be implied by it.

What we have been describing might be called "direct reception," the direct, mutual reception of one local church and another. As local churches multiplied in the Roman empire, however, and as Constantine positioned himself centrally both politically and religiously, the socio-historical context of the churches so changed that direct, church-to-church reception ceased to be adequate to both the political and the religious situation. Both empire and church began to see themselves as more and more universal and centralized and more and more in need of unity for the sake of the universal. Two great interpretive variations of Christian theology, Arianism in the East and Donatism in North Africa, demonstrated how the universal unity of the church could be challenged and how that ecclesial challenge, in its turn, could imperil the unity of the empire. After he defeated Licinius at the Milvian Bridge, Constantine was not prepared to accept such peril, and he initiated the practice of the Synod of the *universal* church, also called the Ecumenical Council.

Two things made these synods *ecumenical*. The first was that the bishops of all the local churches of Christendom gathered to debate and decide in the name, not just of some local church, like the Council of Antioch in 268, but of the universal church. The second was that their teachings were to be received universally. These councils, of course, did not arise out of nothing. They were occasioned by the "fault lines" and the "volcanic soil" of the established socio-ecclesiological context of communion, in which mutual reception and communion among local churches for the sake of the communion of a loosely knit universal church was regarded as essential. In the ecumenical council, in which they gathered as representatives and, indeed, personifications of their local churches, bishops came to be regarded as *collegium episcoporum,* a college of bishops, endeavoring to meet the needs of the whole church. The ecumenicity or universality of these councils changed the mode of reception. When the local church was in the foreground, reception could be direct; when the universal church emerged into the foreground, the collegial teaching of its bishops called for universal reception throughout the Christian world. It is not difficult to predict that such universal reception might not happen quickly, or that it might be hastened by a "reception by obedience" to an external authority, either the emperor seeking peace in his empire, or the bishop of Rome seeking peace in the universal church in which his role as prime receiver of conciliar teaching was being ever more clarified with the passage of time. The example cited above of Victor and the Quartodeciman bishops of Asia is a classic example of the growing authority of the bishop of Rome in the universal church.

The reception that ultimately made a synod ecumenical was, more often than not, a long, tense, and controverted process. Indeed, Giuseppe Alberigo points out that, when the process of reception of a council teaching was not long and controverted, the impact of that teaching on the church was not very profound.[26] Extraordinary reverence and authority are given in the church to the early ecumenical councils, especially to the first ecumenical council of Nicea (325) and its Christological confession, but it was not always so. A few months after the council, a number of bishops under Arian influence withdrew their reception of its doctrine about the divine sonship of the Word and returned to the teaching of Arius rather than the teaching of Nicea. This was the controverted situation which led to Jerome's famous dictum: "the whole world woke from a deep slumber and discovered that it had become Arian."[27] It was not until the Nicene creed was officially received by, first, the Council of Constantinople (381) and, then, the Council of Chalcedon (452) that it became the foundational confession of the Christian church.[28] Nicea, that is, had to wait fifty-six years for full reception.

The same long, controverted process of reception took place with the teaching of the Council of Chalcedon (452) on the two natures in Christ. Alois Grillmeier demonstrates how the continuous efforts of succeeding bishops of Rome, from Leo the Great, whose clarifying *Tome* was so crucial for establishing the teaching of the council, to Gregory (590–604), were required to ensure the reception of this teaching in the face of continuing theological vacillation and political interference. He highlights three populations in which the reception of Chalcedon, and any other council, had to take place for it to be effective, and that reception took centuries to be complete. The first reception, by the bishops of the church, and especially by the bishop of Rome, Grillmeier calls "kerygmatic reception," for it involves not only reception but also official proclamation of the council's teaching. The second reception, in the minds and hearts of the faithful, is the result of that proclamation in liturgy and instruction. The third, theological reception is the result of the critical, interpretive efforts of theologians, reflecting on the teaching and seeking to explain it to believers.[29] Richard Hanson's comment is entirely apposite. The process of reception is not so much a process of "majestic pondering" as a journey from preliminary uncertainty to final solution through trial and error.[30] All of this makes Zizioulas's comment on the importance of reception in the church exactly right: "the Church was born out of a process of reception and has grown and existed through reception."[31]

Grillmeier's kerygmatic reception by the bishops of the Catholic Church, especially the bishop of Rome, focuses attention on what became an essential for reception by the universal church, namely, reception by the bishop of Rome. By the second century, as we have seen, it was widely accepted within the Catholic Church that the bishop represented his church. In the next three centuries, it also became widely accepted that the bishop of Rome represented not only the church of Rome but also the universal, ecumenical church,[32] so that it could be said that "no council can be ecumenical if the see of Rome does not receive it."[33] The growth in importance of this papal reception is already well documented and need not be detailed here. What concerns us here is a change, yet again, in socio-theological context which provoked a critical change in the process of reception in the Catholic Church.

The emergence of a strong papal power, particularly in the second millennium,[34] led to the decline of reception as it was practiced in the first millennium and the emergence of reception by obedience. What the bishop of Rome received as the doctrine of the Catholic Church was then received and taught by his fellow bishops and received unquestioningly by the body of the faithful. Reception, which had been a long and controverted process in the first millennium, was now, or at least appeared to be, instantaneous obedience. The classical notion of reception in which the whole body of believers received truth and rejected falsity continued as the theological underpinning of reception by obedience, but it was not in the forefront as it had been in the first millennium. That was the socio-theological context until the decades just prior to the Second Vatican Council when, thanks to the leadership of Pius XII,[35] the historical efforts of the theologians of *la nouvelle theologie,* and growing lay movements within the church, the classical notion saw a re-awakening, which would be confirmed by the council as the perspective on reception of the ecumenical, catholic church.

There are many classic examples of non-reception in history. The Councils of Lyons (1274) and Constance (1439) both produced decrees of union to heal the rift between the churches of the East and West, but both came to nothing when the people and clergy of the Eastern churches refused to received them. Closer to modern times there are four classic examples of non-reception leading to dramatic development of Catholic teaching. The first of these is the doctrine on usury. Between 1150 and 1550 the church taught that "seeking, receiving, or hoping for anything beyond one's principal — in other words looking for profit — on a loan constituted the mortal sin of usury."[36] The Council of Vienne (1311–12) condemned the taking of interest in the most severe terms. "If anyone should fall into that error of pertinaciously persisting to affirm that interest taking is not a sin, we declare he should be punished as a heretic."[37] This doctrine, which forbade usury as contrary to the natural law, church law, and the gospel, was taught by the ecumenical councils, Lateran II (1139)[38] and Lateran III (1179),[39] and by popes and theologians unanimously. Its reception was altered by the historic rise of capitalist economies and the approval of interest by lay and clerical believers alike.

The second example is slavery. As late as 1860, the church "taught that it was no sin for a Catholic to own a human being; to command the labor of that other human being without paying compensation...to sell him or her for cash."[40] In 1866, the Holy Office, formerly the Holy Inquisition and now the Congregation for the Doctrine of the Faith, issued an instruction about slavery. "Slavery itself, considered as such in its essential nature, is not at all contrary to the natural and divine law, and there can be several just titles of slavery."[41] Gradually, however, as modern European cultures came to value the uniqueness of the human person, this teaching's status became non-received and it was abandoned in the final quarter of the nineteenth century.

The third example has to do with the teaching on religious freedom. From the middle of the fourth to the middle of the twentieth century, a sixteen-hundred year-tradition, the Catholic Church taught that only Christian faith had the right to freedom of expression and worship, and that those who did not share that faith could be punished, even by death, for their false belief. In 1864, Pius IX condemned "that erroneous opinion, most fatal in its effects on the Catholic Church and the salvation of souls, called by our predecessor Gregory XVI *insanity*, namely, that freedom of conscience and worship is each man's personal right which ought to be proclaimed and asserted in every rightly constituted society."[42] Against the loud objections of a vocal Vatican minority, this tradition was un-received by the Second Vatican Council and re-received in a way that affirmed as a sacred religious right the freedom to believe as one freely chooses. Brian Tierney comments that to argue that this shift in church teaching is not a correction of a past error but a simple development of what was already implicit in the tradition is "to strain human credulity too far," and that anyone "who believes that will believe anything."[43]

The fourth example is a crucial doctrinal example. From the Council of Trent in the sixteenth century to the Second Vatican Council in the twentieth, non-Catholic Christians were held to be excluded from the body of Christ. The council, again over the objections of a vocal Vatican minority that held such a traditional doctrine could not be abandoned, un-received this teaching and re-received it as "all who have been justified by faith in baptism are incorporated into Christ; they therefore have a right to be called Christians, and with good reason are accepted as brothers by the children of the Catholic Church."[44] All four of these examples illustrate what theologians call *non-reception* of a traditional teaching that leads to dramatic development and re-reception. These cases will be exemplary when we consider what the church might learn from the sociological data about divorce and remarriage and contraception.[45]

Ladislas Orsy's description of the process of the reception of law is paradigmatic of all reception. He distinguishes two stages in the life of a law. In the first stage, the actor is the legislator, who conceives, formulates, and promulgates the law. In the second stage, the actors are the subjects of the law, who must understand the meaning and value of the law, decide to implement it, and then affirm it by observing it or, by not observing it, bring to the attention of the legislator the difficulty of the law. "When this process is completed and the law is observed throughout the community, its reception is achieved; it has become a vital force that shapes the life of the church."[46] Orsy points out that all this must be done under the umbrella of communion. Margaret Farley asserts, correctly, that this two-stage process is not only useful but actually *needed* in the case of moral norms. "This is because understanding of moral choices cannot come merely from receiving laws or rules. It entails at the very least a discernment of the meaning of laws and rules in concrete situations."[47] Such discernment and understanding require reflection on human experience, personal, social, and religious, and the social sciences throw revealing light on that experience. I agree wholeheartedly with Farley's further assertion that "it is inconceivable that moral norms can be formulated without consulting the experience of those whose lives are at stake."[48] It is equally inconceivable that doctrines can be formulated without consulting the faith of the whole church which is articulated in them. As has been already explained, before he defined the dogma of the Assumption of Mary, Pope Pius XII surveyed the bishops of the world to find out whether or not their various churches received the doctrine. It never occurred to him to define the dogma without consulting "the church." All of which leads us into the consideration of another ecclesiological concept related to reception, namely, *sensus fidei*.

## Sensus Fidei

*Sensus fidei,* and its historical cognates, *sensus* or *consensus fidelium, sensus ecclesiae, sensus catholicus, communis ecclesiae fides,* is a theological concept which denotes "the instinctive capacity of the whole Church to recognize the infallibility of the Spirit's truth."[49] It is a spiritual charism of discernment, possessed by the whole church, which recognizes and receives a teaching as apostolic truth and, therefore, to be believed. *Sensus fidei* was sharply focused for moderns by John Henry Newman's *Rambler* essay *On Consulting the Faithful in Matters of Doctrine.* Newman suggested that *sensus fidei* was "a sort of instinct, or *phronema,* deep in the bosom of the Mystical Body of Christ," and cited with approval Moehler's opinion that the Spirit of God arouses in the faithful "an instinct, an eminently Christian tact, which leads it to all true doctrine."[50] Newman's careful effort to explain that *consult* meant simply establishing the fact of the laity's belief and not their enthronement as judges of orthodoxy did not forestall a storm of protest from those whose perspective was that faith was gifted to the apostles, transmitted by them to their bishop-successors, and transmitted by them in turn to an obedient faithful. In a letter to the soon-to-be Cardinal Manning, Bishop Talbot went so far as to describe Newman as "the most dangerous man in England."[51] It is of both theological and sociological interest to note, in the categories being developed in this book, that the theological storm arose only among those theologians whose taken-for-granted perspective or province of meaning led them to understand reception as obedience to an unquestioned magisterium.

The root of the theological concept *phronema* is in scripture. Paul exhorts the Philippians to "have this [common] mind (*phroneite*) among yourselves, which is yours in Christ Jesus" (Phil 2:5). The theological use of the concept is constructed upon this scriptural foundation. For Newman, with his great reverence for Christian tradition, the great teacher was Athanasius, who insisted that scripture should be interpreted according to tradition and cited "the *phronema* of Catholics"[52] as a central component of the tradition. This *phronema,* Femiano explains, is understood by him as "a type of prudential judgment by which the faithful sense the truths of faith" and is externalized as "the voice of the Christian people."[53] Truth is always achieved only in judgment; Catholic truth is achieved only in the judgment of all Catholic people.

*Sensus fidei,* therefore, intends a gift of the Holy Spirit related to the traditional objective and subjective realities of faith, *fides quae creditur* and *fides qua creditur,* objective faith which is believed and subjective faith by which the believer believes. It relates to objective faith, the concepts, words, and the realities they intend, which are handed on to the church from the past and which the church, in turn, hands on to contemporary believers to be believed. It relates also to subjective faith, the personal act of faith by which the individual believer actually believes and embraces the object proposed by the church to be believed. Both objective and subjective faith are necessarily influenced by and created in the socio-historical contexts of their times. At this stage of this book, we now know that different socio-historical contexts might yield different experiences, understandings, and judgments of meaningfulness. Congar insists that the content embedded in *sensus fidei,* and its historical variations, is a universal belief of the fathers of the church, the thirteenth-century Scholastics, and the theologians of the sixteenth century. All acknowledged both the objective-abstract and subjective-practical side of faith and listed *sensus fidelium* "among the *loci theologici,* that is, among the criteria of Christian thought."[54]

The theological concept of *sensus fidei,* therefore, is much older than Newman and the nineteenth century. Vincent of Lerins formulated the ancient rule of faith in the fifth century: *quod ubique, quod semper, quod ab omnibus creditum est,* what is believed everywhere, always, and by all.[55] Aquinas explained *sensus fidei* in scholastic language. The faithful understand a teaching *per modum connaturalitatis,* that is, they incline naturally in faith to adhere to what is in harmony with the true meaning of the word of God.[56] Christian apostolic faith connaturally recognizes a truth that belongs to it. Robert Bellarmine added his opinion that "what all the faithful hold as a matter of faith is necessarily true and of faith."[57] In every development of doctrine that has taken place in the church, and there have been many, Lerins's rule was the essential factor in the reception or non-reception of a doctrine as the faith of the universal church. Though one could complain that Pius XII surveyed only the bishops of the world, and not the whole church, before he defined as Catholic dogma the Assumption of Mary, it still never occurred to him to define the dogma on his own authority without somehow consulting "the church."

One of the subtexts at the Second Vatican Council, and in the theological developments that followed it, was a debate over who precisely were the *all* in Lerins's rule of faith, always, everywhere, and *by all.* Vatican theologians argued that it was only the magisterium who determined doctrine and that they, therefore, were the *all,* a claim that had become common only since the definition of papal infallibility by the First Vatican Council in 1870. Conciliar bishops and theologians responded with the more historically accurate claim that the church's faith was preserved in the faith of *all* the faithful, lay and clerical together. They argued that, although the magisterium ultimately spoke *for* the church, it was also obliged to speak *from* the church and that, when it structured doctrine along only magisterial lines, ignoring a clear *sensus fidei* in the whole church, it was being unfaithful to the church's primary rule of faith. The Vatican I Constitution *Pastor Aeternus* made it clear that, even on those rare occasions when he speaks infallibly, the pope does not create faith *ex nihilo* but judges and declares what already is the faith of the church, and only when he does so does he enjoy "that infallibility the Redeemer willed his Church to have in defining doctrine on faith and morals."[58] At Vatican II, the position of conciliar bishops and theologians prevailed.

The council taught that the doctrine of the Catholic Church is preserved by the Holy Spirit in all the faithful, laity and hierarchy together. "The body of the faithful *as a whole,* anointed as they are by the Holy One (cf. 1 John 2:20; 2:27), cannot err in matters of belief [they are infallible]. Thanks to a supernatural sense of the faith (*sensus fidei*) which characterizes the people *as a whole,* it manifests this unerring quality when, 'from the bishops to the last of the faithful,'[59] it manifests universal agreement in matters of faith and morals."[60] John Paul II adds his authority, teaching that the discernment of the full dignity of marriage "is accomplished through the *sensus fidei,* and is therefore the work of the *whole Church* according to the diversity of the various gifts and charisms."[61] He cites the above text from *Lumen Gentium* and 1 John 2:20 in support of this teaching. John could not be clearer: "You, no less than they, are among the initiated; this is the gift of the Holy One and by it you *all* have knowledge" (1 John 2:20). He is even clearer a few verses further on: "The anointing which you have received from him abides in you, and you have no need that anyone should teach you, as his anointing teaches you about everything, and is true, and is no lie" (1 John 2:27). Catholic tradition enshrines this belief in the doctrine that the Spirit of God is gifted to the whole church.

These texts make two things clear. First, *sensus fidei* of virtually the whole church is a gift of grace; its source is the Spirit of God. Second, this gift of grace is given to the *whole church,* laity and clergy alike; it is not a gift given only to a hierarchical few. "The entire People of God is the subject that receives."[62] The church has always been convinced that authentic *sensus fidei* and reception require *universalis ecclesiae consensione* (consent of the whole church),[63] *totius mundi reverentia* (the reverence of the whole world),[64] *universalis ecclesiae assensus* (the assent of the whole church),[65] and that this reverence and assent is a sign of the presence of the Spirit in the whole church.[66]

The continuation of the above-cited passage from *Lumen Gentium,* in Austin Flannery's translation, introduces another consideration. "By this sense of the faith...the People of God, guided by the sacred *magisterium* which it faithfully obeys (*cui fideliter obsequiens*), receives...truly the word of God."[67] The Latin word *magister,* the root of *magisterium,* literally means *master,* schoolmaster, ship's master, master of a trade; in the medieval church, it came to mean one who has authority deriving from mastery of a subject. Thomas Aquinas, for whom the symbol of genuine authority was the *cathedra* or chair, distinguished two kinds of *magisterium:* that of a bishop, *magisterium cathedrae pastoralis,* and that of a theologian, *magisterium cathedrae magistralis.* The former derives from ordination as a bishop, the latter from mastery of the theological tradition. In the Catholic

Church of the past two hundred years, *magisterium* has come to be restricted exclusively to the teaching authority of bishops.[68]

Flannery's translation of the sentence from *Lumen Gentium* cited above underscores the current attitude Vatican theologians demand of believers toward the ecclesial magisterium: the people of God are to be guided by the magisterium and are to *obey* it.[69] The translation of the Latin *obsequium* by the English *obedience,* however, is seriously doubtful. In the official English translation of the *Code of Canon Law, debitum obsequium* is translated as *due respect* (Can 218), and *religiosum obsequium* as *religious respect* (Can 752 and Can 753). There is a wide gulf between obedience and respect, and Flannery's translation tendentiously and falsely bridges the gulf in favor of passive obedience rather than respectful dialogue. Francis Sullivan's reading of *obsequium* appears more accurate theologically. "As I understand it, then, to give the required *obsequium religiosum* to the teaching of the ordinary magisterium means to make an honest and sustained effort to overcome any contrary opinion I might have, and to achieve a sincere assent of my mind to this teaching."[70] In a church which is communion, any effort to evaluate a magisterial teaching will include open dialogue, uncoerced judgment, and free consensus. That is the way genuine reception happens and authentic *sensus fidei* is formed.

There is an active dialectic in the church, then, over the interpretation of reception; reception is a matter of either fiat or dialogue. Vatican theologians seek to reduce it to magisterial fiat and believers' obedience, in keeping with the hierarchical model of church still favored by them, "a wholly pyramidal conception of the Church as a mass totally determined by its summit."[71] In the communion model of church re-introduced into the Catholic world by the Second Vatican Council[72] and examined in the preceding chapter, reception requires active dialogue, judgment, and consensus among the virtually whole body of the communion's faithful. Reception "is not a matter of blind obedience to formal authority, but of the divinely assisted recognition of the truth of what is taught."[73] Congar points out that obedience is called for "if the church is conceived as a society subject to monarchical authority," and dialogue and consensus are required "when the universal church is seen as a communion of churches." "It is certain," he continues, "that this second conception was the one that prevailed effectively during the first thousand years of Christianity, whereas the other one dominated in the West between the eleventh-century reformation and Vatican II."[74] Edward Kilmartin agrees, emphasizing that the patristic and medieval notion of reception was "a tributary of the dominant ecclesiology of that age: a communion ecclesiology."[75]

Reception of doctrine is not the task of the magisterium alone but "of the *whole* people ... from the Bishops to the last of the faithful."[76] In the case of infallible statements, "the assent of the Church can never be lacking to such definitions on account of the same Spirit's influence, through which Christ's *whole* flock is maintained in the unity of the faith and makes progress in it."[77] If "Christ's whole flock" is involved in receiving *infallible* teaching, it is a safe theological conclusion that the whole flock is involved also in the process of receiving non-infallible teaching. The instances of dramatic development noted in the previous section suggest one obvious reason why this must be so: authoritarian pronouncements do not necessarily assure correct understanding or freedom from error.

## Sociology

The two most influential theologians in the Latin church used Greek philosophy as a tool to construct their theologies. Augustine used Plato and Aquinas used Aristotle. Aquinas's Aristotelianism was initially condemned by the church but eventually developed into the Scholastic theology that dominated Catholic thought in the early twentieth century. "The outstanding event in the Catholic theology of [the twentieth] century is the surmounting of [this] Scholasticism."[78] Scholasticism sought to construct a systematic theology that provided a timeless norm for a timeless church. The twentieth century, steeped in historicity, judged that norm to be just too timeless; it could not stand as the theology of a church which, far from being timeless, is inescapably time-conditioned.[79] Vatican II demanded that Christians scrutinize "the signs of the times" and interpret them "in the light of the gospel,"[80] and scholastic theology, with its ahistorical conceptual system, could not stand up to such scrutiny and gave way. The question continues to be "gave way to what?" The partial answer of this essay, founded in the teaching of Vatican II noted earlier that "in pastoral care sufficient use should be made, not only of theological principles, but also of the findings of secular sciences, especially psychology and sociology,"[81] is that, when contemporary theologians seek to understand *what* is actually received and believed, sociological research is as indispensable a tool as Greek philosophy was for Augustine and Aquinas.

The Catholic Church praises sociological research, teaching that "methodical research in all branches of knowledge ... can never conflict with the faith, because the things of the world and the things of faith derive from the same God."[82] It asks its theologians "to seek out more efficient ways ... of presenting their teaching to modern man: for the deposit and the truths of faith are one thing, the manner of expressing them is quite another."[83] John Paul II teaches that "the church values sociological and statistical research," but immediately adds the proviso that "such research alone is not to be considered in itself an expression of the *sensus fidei*.[84] The pope is correct. Empirical research neither creates nor expresses *sensus fidei*, but it does manifest *what* is actually believed and not believed. As noted earlier, only when he received a virtually unanimous affirmative response to his quasi-sociological survey about whether the local churches believed that Mary was assumed into heaven did Pius XII define in infallible judgment that Mary's Assumption was a universal belief, and therefore a dogma, of the Catholic Church. Though he did not consult *all* the faithful, from the bishops to the last of the faithful, it still never occurred to him, with all his papal authority, to define the dogma on his own without somehow seeking to determine the universal *sensus fidei*.

How could Lerins's rule of faith, everywhere, always, and by all, ever be determined without sociological survey? Of course, such survey does not create either subjective or objective faith, *fides qua creditur* or *fides quae creditur*, which is a gift of God; neither does it express faith; but it does manifest *fides quae creditur*, what is actually believed. "Doctrines," Martin reminds us, "do not land like meteorites from outer space but grow organically where they have a supporting, fertile niche or cranny."[85] Sociological surveys illumine the niches and crannies and the doctrines that grow in them and without such empirical illumination the work of theologians tends to appear, at best, no more than interesting speculation or, at worst, abstract anachronism. Gill offers a judgment which theologians of all stripes should heed. Christian ethicists, he complains, have been "reluctant to admit that sociology has any constructive role to play in their discipline. It is rare to find a Christian ethicist prepared to examine data about the moral effects of church-going. Instead Christian communities have become far *too idealized*."[86] What Gill asserts about ethicists I assert here about the magisterium, which tends to talk about faith and beliefs as they *ought* to be, rather than as they *are*. If "the body of the faithful as a whole cannot err in matters of belief,"[87] then they must be infallible in the beliefs they actually believe. It is that actual belief that can be illuminated by sociological survey.

John Paul's words cited above are intended to suggest that the *theological* reality, *sensus fidei*, is not reached solely by demonstrating sociologically majority reception or non-reception of a teaching or decision. The church, as has so often been pointed out, is not a political democracy in which majority head count controls reality. Neither, however, is it a monarchy. The church is, rather, a communion of faithful who accept the apostolic faith handed down to them in the rule of faith recorded in their scriptures. Those very scriptures or, more precisely, Christian interpretations of them illustrate

why majority rule can never be the sole rule of faith. The authentic Catholic
approach to reading the scriptures today is a historical-critical approach:
the literal meaning of the texts is the meaning intended by the writers at
a particular time, place, and culture.[88] The approach of a large majority
of Christians, Catholic and Protestant alike, is different; the literal meaning of the text is the meaning they find in and through modern language
translations, ignoring the time, culture, and place of the writer. Interpreting
documents written in another time and another culture is always a difficult
task, requiring competence in languages, cultures, social rules, and histories
that are not one's own. It would be disastrous to permit anyone unskilled
in these specialties to judge what the gospel writers did and did not mean.
Only those believers who understand the specialties involved are qualified
to be judges. A majority opinion that results from a lack of education, in-
competence, and ignorance can never be permitted to be the exclusive rule
of faith.

The same argument applies to church doctrines. Such doctrines, which are
not only ends but also beginnings of theological developments,[89] are articulated in concise, technical language: *homoousios, hypostasis* (incorrectly
equated with the English *person*), substance, accident, transubstantiation.
They are best understood by believers who grasp the philosophical and theological precision of the language of the ecclesial high tradition, and are as
often as not misunderstood by believers of the popular low tradition who
do not understand either the language or its precision. Theological doctrines
and their meanings can be properly evaluated only by believers who understand the historical, philosophical, and theological competencies involved.
Dulles argues that, to determine *sensus fidei,* "we must look not so much
at the statistics, as at the quality of the witnesses and the motivation for
their assent."[90] I agree. *Sensus fidei,* the connatural capacity to discern the
truth into which God as Spirit is leading the church, must itself be carefully discerned by all who are competent. John Paul II is correct: a simple
head count does not necessarily express the faith of the church. A count,
however, which includes virtually *all* the faithful, especially virtually *all* the
theologically competent faithful, most certainly manifests the actual faith of
the whole church. What sociology can and does show is that, in the case
of the moral doctrines related to divorce and remarriage without annulment, and birth control, the contemporary *sensus fidei* of both competent
and non-competent faithful shows a dramatic development and is virtually
at one.

I turn now to what I promised earlier, the distinction between *faith* and
*belief.* It is impossible to read the New Testament and not be impressed

by its insistence on faith as a means of salvation. Jesus complained frequently and insistently of the absence of faith. Paul passionately defended the necessity of faith against the legalism of the Judaizers. The Council of Trent, while rejecting Luther's claim that *faith alone* was required for salvation, still underscored the importance of faith in the process of salvation. It taught that "we may be said to be justified through faith, in the sense that faith is the beginning of man's salvation...without [faith] it is impossible to please God (Heb 11:6) and to be counted as his sons."[91] The faith that is at stake here is what I have called subjective faith, *fides qua creditur*. It "includes knowledge of a saving event, confidence in the word of God, man's humble submission and personal self-surrender to God, fellowship in life with Christ.... Faith is man's comprehensive 'Yes' to God's revealing himself as man's savior in Christ."[92] *Fides qua creditur*, subjective faith, is a personal *process*, a personal 'I believe" to God revealed in Christ. *Fides quae creditur*, objective faith, is a *product* of reflection on that process which results in propositional formulae, or doctrines, about God that I judge to be true and assent to unconditionally. These propositional or doctrinal products are also called beliefs. Catholics and Lutherans now agree that genuine faith yields good fruits in the social world, having laid to rest the polemical and false debate between them about faith and good works. "We confess together," they declared, "that good works — a Christian life lived in faith, hope, and love — follow justification and are its fruits. When the justified live in Christ and act in the grace they receive, they bring forth, in biblical terms, good fruit."[93] Genuine Christian faith, subjective or objective, as I explained earlier, always includes action in accord with faith.

## The Second Vatican Council, Communion, and Reception

The church's understanding of reception is historically correlated with its understanding of itself. Reception is most visible and effective when the church understands itself to be a communion of churches; it is least visible and effective when the church understands itself to be one, universal church, a sort of super-diocese. Both these understandings of church were in evidence at the Second Vatican Council, and a task for the council was to discriminate between them. There is no doubt that the prevailing Catholic ecclesiology of the time was the understanding of a universal church under hierarchical leadership. Ecclesiology, in Congar's judgment, was "practically reduced to a hierarchology."[94] The schema presented to the council by Cardinal Alfredo Ottaviani on November 13, 1962, was a summary of this ecclesiology: the church is a perfect but unequal society, within which clergy, not laity, are the recipients of God-gifted powers of sanctifying, teaching, and governing. Bishop Emil de Smedt spoke for the majority of the fathers when he judged that schema to be overly legalistic, clericalist, and triumphalist,[95] and it was overwhelmingly rejected and returned to the Preparatory Committee with a request for a new schema that would balance the institutional, juridical elements of the church with its mystical, spiritual elements.

An important voice in the debate over a new schema was that of Cardinal Giovanni Battista Montini of Milan, soon to be Pope Paul VI. A few weeks after the rejection of the Ottaviani schema, he spoke in his local church in Milan of the ongoing debate about the church. "Yesterday, the theme of the Church seemed to be confined to the power of the Pope. Today, it is extended to the episcopate, the religious, the laity, and the whole body of the Church. Yesterday, we spoke of the rights of the Church by transferring the constitutive elements of civil society to the definition of the perfect society. Today, we have discovered other realities in the Church, the charisms of grace and holiness, for example, which cannot be defined by purely juridical ideas. Yesterday, we were above all interested in the external history of the Church. Today, we are equally concerned with its inner life, brought to life by the hidden presence of Christ in it."[96] There could not have been a more concise distillation of the salient points of the debate, and the cardinal's judgment is confirmed by a consideration of the titles of the opening chapters of the Ottaviani schema and the revised one presented to the council on November 1, 1963. The first chapter of the rejected schema was "The Nature of the Church," assumed to be already known and, therefore, specifiable; the first chapter of the revised schema was "The Mystery of the Church," assumed to be hidden and, ultimately, not completely specifiable. Pope Paul VI's definition of the mystery involved explains why: "a reality imbued with the presence of God and therefore, of such a nature that there are ever-new and deeper explorations of it possible."[97] His successor, John Paul II, agrees, teaching that "the Church is a great mystery, and how do we communicate mystery?"[98]

The acknowledgment of the church as mystery, rather than perfect society, initiated a search for a recognition of its essence rather than for ways and means to perfect it institutionally. The finally approved Dogmatic Constitution on the Church, *Lumen Gentium,* taught that the functions of sanctifying, teaching, and governing in the church are conferred on bishops by episcopal ordination and that they are to exercise these functions in communion with the bishop of Rome. Local churches, in which the church of Christ "is really present ... in so far as they are united to their pastors [bishops],"[99] and universal church are in intimate relationship, as are bishops of local churches in the College of Bishops under the leadership of the bishop of Rome. There was also clear pronouncement on the status of laity, which was ultimately appropriate recognition of their baptism and all that flows from it. In virtue of their baptism, laity are commissioned, not to shun the world, but to honor it as part of creation and to sanctify and redeem it by incarnating the presence of God in it in their life and work. Baptism also creates a relationship with all who are baptized and "who are honored with the name of Christian."[100]

All the essential relationships in church, that of all the baptized among themselves, that of the baptized with their local bishops, that of the bishops in the College of Bishops, that of the bishops with the leader of the College, the bishop of Rome, and that of all the local churches in the universal church, were summed up in *Lumen Gentium* in three organic images: mystical body of Christ, following Pius XII's encyclical letter of that title; people of God, an important image in both Testaments; and *koinonia*-communion, "the term that most aptly expresses the mystery underlying the various New Testament images of the Church."[101] In *Lumen Gentium,* neither of the images, mystical body or people of God, was given a clear preference over the other, and in the post–Vatican II church the image that is slowly and painfully being preferentially received is that of communion. I conclude this chapter with a summary of that development already fully considered in the previous chapter.

There is no doubt that the reception of the council's teaching on communion as the essence of the church, like the reception of the Christological doctrine of Chalcedon, was and continues to be greatly facilitated by the pronouncements of successive bishops of Rome. In a 1971 audience, Paul VI explained that at the council the church rethought itself and offered an essential and accessible definition: "the Church is a communion."[102] In a 1976 audience, he explained that communion means "unity with God...[and]...brotherly love in sharing the same faith, the same hope, and the same charity." On that same occasion, he added the telling comment that "ecumenism has reawakened the necessity of [communion] for everyone."[103] Later that same year he repeated and further explicated the definition. To say the church is a communion "is to say it is a community *sui generis,* at once spiritual and visible; human but animated by a super-human action of the Holy Spirit.... The Church, which is communion with Christ and with God in the Holy Spirit, aims at being communion with men." In that same audience, he repeated his openness and predilection for ecumenism when he explained that Christianity "is a company of local communities, all of which are conscious of being a communion."[104] John

Paul II agrees. In his important Apostolic Exhortation on the Lay Faithful, he teaches that "communion is the very mystery of the Church"[105] and, in an address to the bishops of the United States, he explains that "the concept of communion lies at the heart of the Church's self-understanding."[106] Papal reception of the doctrine of the church as communion could not be clearer. That reception of the doctrine is widespread also among the bishops of the universal church is evident from the judgment of the 1985 Synod of Bishops that its vision of church as *koinonia*-communion was the council's most important teaching.[107] All these receptive judgments confirm the judgment, immediately after the council, of Monsignor Gerard Philips, secretary of the council's Central Theological Commission, that the guiding vision of the council's vision of church was its notion of church as communion.[108]

The council definitively challenged the long-standing Catholic view of church as a perfect but unequal society. Congar argues that the transition from the preparatory schema to *Lumen Gentium* was a transition from the priority of "organizational structures and hierarchical positions" to "the priority and even primacy of the ontology of grace."[109] Schillebeeckx argues that it was a double decentralization: first, from militant and triumphalist church to glorified Christ and, second, from an exclusive focus on Roman primacy, hierarchical ministry, and Roman Catholic Church to an inclusive focus on universal episcopacy, the people of God, and other Christian churches respectively.[110] I offer a different characterization of the transition. It is a transition from a juridical vision that views the church as institution and structure to a theological vision that views it as mystery and graced communion. It is a transition from juridical fixation on hierarchical office and power to a theological appreciation of ecclesial communion, co-responsibility, and Christian service. It is a transition from focus on juridical externals to focus on the theological reality and implications of internal grace. *Lumen Gentium* offers ample evidence of the council's conviction in the middle of the twentieth century that church is a mysterious vertical communion between God and believers and a horizontal communion between believers before it is a juridical, hierarchically controlled institution. Reception of that teaching is now well under way, and is already deeply rooted. The journey to full, irenic reception, as always, has been and will continue to be long, controverted, and dialectical; but so it was for Nicea and for Chalcedon, fifty-eight years for the former, one hundred and fifty years for the latter. The Second Vatican Council ended in 1965. Those for whom mathematics is less obscure than constructive theology can easily do the projections. They will also be at home in the next chapter, where statistical numbers will be the fore.

## Conclusion

In the forefront, this chapter has been about two ecclesial realities, *sensus fidei* and reception. The former is an instinctive or connatural capacity of believers to recognize infallibly the truth to which the Spirit of God is leading the church, the latter an ecclesial process by which virtually all the members of the church judge a teaching presented to them to be Spirit-revealed apostolic truth and assent to it as ecclesial faith. At root, however, the chapter has been a continuation of reflection on the church as communion begun in the preceding chapter. Both *sensus fidei* and reception are essentially communional realities; and, though there is an ongoing dialectic about the interpretation of church as hierarchical institution or communion, and a consequent dialectic about reception as obedience to the hierarchical magisterium or as the *consensus fidei* of the whole church, there is no doubt that the Second Vatican Council's major and primary teaching is its teaching on the church as communion. This teaching is further fortified by the council's teaching on *sensus fidei* and reception as a matter for the whole communion-church, laity and hierarchical clerics alike. "The body of the faithful *as a whole,* anointed as they are by the Holy One [in Christian initiation]...cannot err in matters of belief. Thanks to a supernatural *sensus fidei* which characterizes the people *as a whole,* it manifests this unerring quality when, 'from the bishops to the last of the faithful,' it manifests universal agreement in matters of faith and morals."[111]

The dialectic will persist for many years to come, as it always does after an ecumenical council, especially when the controverted matter is of great import for the church, as was the case, for instance, with the Council of Nicea's teaching on the Word as God and the Council of Chalcedon's teaching on the two natures in Christ. As happened historically, however, for both Nicea and Chalcedon, the teachings of recent bishops of Rome leave no doubt about the direction the reception of the Second Vatican Council is headed. The pope who pastored the council to completion through a thicket of dialectical controversies, Paul VI, had no doubt about the definition of church offered by the council: "the Church is a communion."[112] His present successor, John Paul II, is just as strong: "the concept of communion lies at the heart of the Church's self-understanding."[113] The *sensus fidei* of Catholic bishops gathered in Synod in 1995 agreed with that of their leader: its vision of church as *koinonia*-communion, they taught, was the council's most important teaching.[114] What we have learned so far about the mediation of sociology on theology leads us to understand that a change in the ecclesial understanding of church will necessarily lead to a change in the ecclesial understanding of theological realities related to church, such as *sensus fidei* and reception. In the next chapter, we consider the possible outcomes of that converted understanding on two Catholic moral teachings, divorce and remarriage with annulment, and contraception.

## Questions for Discussion

1. How do you understand the relationship between faith and practice? Can you give instances of this relationship in your life?

2. How do you understand reception? Who is to be involved in the reception of doctrine?

3. How do you understand *sensus fidei?* Who is to be counted when the *sensus fidei* of the church is judged?

4. What is the relationship between the theological concepts of church as communion, *sensus fidei,* and reception? What dialectic surrounds this relationship?

5. Do you know of any instances of re-reception and transformation of Catholic teaching other than the four listed in this chapter?

# SEVEN

# Sociology, Divorce and Remarriage, Contraception

## Sociology

I argued in the opening chapter that sociology can be of great help in the inductive clarification of the actual *is* of a theological situation rather than the deductive, prescribed *ought to be*. I further argued that the sociological clarification of the actual *is* does not by itself prescribe the theological *ought to be*. The theologian relies on the sociologist for description of what *is;* for prescription of what *ought to be,* this sociological description is distilled through the theologian's own theological and ecclesial filters. This chapter carries that argument a step further by arguing that, when the empirically clarified theological situation is either the reception of, or the *sensus fidei* with respect to, a theological doctrine, then sociological and practical theological description coincide and the theologian's prescription of what *ought to be* must necessarily take account of this sociological description and proceed from it. I am arguing here, not that sociological description is the sole factor for theological prescription but that theological prescription should take full account of any demonstrated *sensus fidei* or reception or non-reception of a doctrine.

There are many sociological descriptions that inform us about the received and non-received faith-praxis of Catholics in the United States.[1] I cite only three, and for better focus and illustration I restrict my analysis to their description of the situation with respect to the doctrines related to divorce and remarriage without annulment, and artificial contraception. William V. D'Antonio and his colleagues conducted three surveys among American Catholics, in 1987, 1993, and 1997. They report increasing agreement with the following two statements: "a person can be a good Catholic without obeying the church hierarchy's teaching on divorce and remarriage" and a "person can be a good Catholic without obeying the Church hierarchy's teaching on birth control." For the three studies, the level of agreement with

143

the first statement increased from 57 percent to 62 percent to 64 percent; the level of agreement with the second statement increased from 66 percent to 73 percent and then declined slightly to 71 percent.[2] The authors comment that the majority of American Catholics saw these two items as neither "defining a good Catholic today" nor "definitive of a good Catholic." A 1996 Gallup study replicated these data: 61 percent of Catholics believed that those who remarry without annulment are still good Catholics, and 89 percent believed that Catholics who use some form of artificial birth control are still good Catholics.[3]

D'Antonio and his colleagues note a "shift from 1987 to 1999 [that] depicts a trend from conformity to autonomy."[4] This trend is confirmed by the responses to a question about the locus of moral authority. In 1999, only 19 percent of respondents assigned the moral authority for getting remarried without an annulment to church leaders, while 45 percent assigned it to the individual; and only 10 percent assigned the authority for practicing contraceptive birth control to church leaders, while 62 percent assigned it to the individual.[5] Dean Hoge and his colleagues also document this trend from conformity to authority. In their study, 73 percent of Latinos and 71 percent of non-Latinos agreed that, in the realm of morality, the final authority about good and bad is the individual's informed conscience. They comment that "this reliance on the individual authority is the same found in past research on Catholic young people."[6] It is also found in other sectors of the church besides America.[7] Though such data are not expressions of the beliefs of Catholics, they do two important things: they manifest what the beliefs of Catholics actually are and how they are at serious variance with the beliefs proposed by the magisterium. This data cannot be ignored by theologians who wish to be taken seriously in the public arena, where claims about "what the Church believes" are so easily contradicted by the data of sociological research. I propose now, as concrete examples of *sensus fidei* and reception in the contemporary church, to examine the data of sociological research with respect to divorce and remarriage without annulment, and artificial birth control, and to ask what impact that concrete, empirical data might have on theological prescription.

## Divorce and Remarriage

Sociological research today demonstrates three things about divorce and remarriage: first, the national divorce rate remains high, about 40 percent; second, divorce has serious negative effects on American families and, therefore, American society; third, Americans now live in a culture of divorce in which many young adults despair of the possibility of achieving a happy, stable marriage.[8] Catholics are not immune. Though research in earlier periods found Catholic marriages to be generally more stable than Protestant marriages,[9] studies using more recent data suggest a growing convergence between Catholic and Protestant rates of instability.[10] Another recently published study reports that Catholics are now more likely than Protestants to both cohabit and divorce,[11] while yet another reports that the Catholic divorce rate is now 15 percent lower than the rate among Protestants. This last study also reports that about 50 percent of divorced Catholics remarry, only about 5 percent of them in the church, having received a declaration of annulment.[12] Almost two out of every three (65 percent) American Catholics believe that one can be a good Catholic without obeying the church's teaching on divorce and remarriage,[13] and this issue of remarriage is a major reason for Catholics to sever connection to the church. Only 60 percent of divorced and remarried Catholics, compared to 80 percent of first-marriage Catholics, remain attached to the church.[14] At the very least, these sociological data cry out for, first, theological attention, understanding, judgment, and decision and, then, pastoral action. Reflection on these data was prominent at the Synod of Bishops in 1980.

Archbishop Derek Worlock of Liverpool, for example, pointed out the significantly changed context of marriage in the modern world: the changed role of women and the movement away from patriarchal marriage to companionate or peer marriage in which the spouses are equal; the desire of men and, especially, women for a more satisfying personal fulfillment in their sexual relationships and marriages; women's greater economic independence with the concomitant diminished need to remain in loveless and sometimes brutal marriages; and the increased availability of reliable means to regulate fertility. He pleaded directly with the Synod and indirectly with the pope for a nuanced re-reception of the traditional teaching about divorce and remarriage that would take account of changed circumstances and yield a more compassionate approach to remarried Catholics in second marriages.[15] Such re-reception in the *sensus fidei* of both the low tradition and the majority of theologians in the high tradition is well documented by the statistics that opened this section, but no movement toward re-reception has yet been evidenced in the magisterium of the high tradition.

In 1994, the Congregation for the Doctrine of the Faith sent a letter to the world's bishops purporting to articulate Catholic doctrine about divorce and remarriage and claiming, citing Mark 10:11–12, "fidelity to the words of Jesus Christ."[16] The implication is clear: since the church's doctrine on divorce and remarriage is based on fidelity to the words of Jesus, it is irreformable. The competent exegete-theologian might accept that argument if the words of Jesus cited from Mark were the only teaching in the New

Testament on divorce and remarriage and the only one which the church followed. Neither, however, is the case. Already in the early New Testament period, a mere twenty years after the death of Jesus, Paul establishes an interpretive re-reception of Jesus' remembered command.

In his first Letter to the Corinthians, written as early as the year 52, Paul responds to questions posed to him by the Corinthian community, including one about divorce and remarriage. Paul responds with a command from the Lord: "To the married I give charge, *not I but the Lord,* that a wife is not to be separated from her husband. And, if she is separated, she is to remain unmarried or is to be reconciled to her husband. And a husband is not to dismiss his wife" (1 Cor 7:10–11). The custom of easy divorce was deeply rooted in the Greek social context, as it is now deeply rooted in the modern Western context, and it is not difficult to imagine Corinthians wanting to know what they were supposed to do now that they were Christians. Paul leaves them in no doubt: the wife is not to be separated from her husband and the husband is not to dismiss his wife, for such is the charge of the Lord.

Having responded to the question of divorce and remarriage in the case of two believers, Paul proceeds to the discussion of a case that must have been prevalent in the varied social contexts of the early Christian communities, as it is still prevalent in mission territories today, the case of the marriage in which one spouse has become a believer and the other remains a non-believer. Paul has two pieces of advice for the spouses in such marriages, each of them hinging on the attitude of the non-believer. The first advice relates to the case in which the non-believer is willing to continue to live with the believer: in this case, the non-believing spouse is not to be dismissed. In the case in which the non-believer is unwilling to live with the believer, Paul's advice is completely different. "But if the unbelieving spouse desires to separate, let it be so; in such a case the brother or sister is not bound. For God has called us to peace" (7:15). There is no suggestion that the marriage between a believer and a non-believer is not valid; there is no suggestion that Jesus' charge does not apply. There is only the suggestion that Paul is making an exception: "*I say,* not the Lord" (7:12). The preservation of peace, Paul suggests, is a greater value than the preservation of an unpeaceful marriage. The Roman church sanctioned this approach to dissolving a valid marriage in the twelfth century, continues to enshrine it in its law today, and calls the process the Pauline Privilege (Can 1143).

Matthew also nuances and re-receives Jesus' words with his own Jewish exception for the context of his Jewish-Christian community (5:32; 19:9). Again, there is Jesus' remembered logion, "What, therefore, God has joined together let not man put asunder" (19:6), and again there is an interpretive nuance, "Whoever divorces his wife, *except for porneia,* and marries another, commits adultery" (19:9). The interpretation of the exceptive phrase, "except for *porneia,*" predictably, has been endlessly debated in Christian history. I will not enter into that debate here, since I agree with Raymond Collins that "its meaning is not self-evident to modern interpreters."[17] I raise here a different question: does the exceptive clause originate in the teaching of Jesus or of Matthew? Is it rooted in that stratum of the gospel which faithfully records the words of Jesus, or is it from that stratum which derives from the author in light of the needs of his particular first-century Jewish community? I accept the majority scholarly opinion that the latter is the case, given Matthew's acknowledged penchant for adding to the words of Jesus for his own purposes, and given the absence of the phrase in Paul, Mark, and Luke. I wish to underscore only one conclusion from that. Matthew did not hesitate to interpret the words of Jesus in light of the needs of his own Jewish-Christian church, that is, a church composed of Jews who had been "converted" to Christianity but who still adhered to the Jewish law, including the law of divorce for *erwat dabar* or *porneia* (Deut 24:1–4). That interpretation, which became canonical, is already a re-reception of Jesus' words.

The sociologist could point out that there are divergent accounts in the New Testament of Jesus' saying about divorce and remarriage because it was re-received by divergent Christian communities who had different concerns about marriage and divorce that needed to be addressed, and that sociological fact is now taken for granted also by Catholic theologians. The reception of the words of Jesus shaped by contextual need, and validated by the early church, was continued in the later church by Gratian in respect to what consummates a marriage as indissoluble (1140), and by the sixteenth-century popes Paul III (1537), Pius V (1561), and Gregory XIII (1585) with respect to the circumstances of polygamy and slavery, the so-called Petrine Privilege.[18] This consistent interpretive re-reception of the words of Jesus in the church makes any argument based exclusively on the words of Jesus at best incomplete and at worst dishonest. There is a long Catholic tradition of re-reception of the words of Jesus about divorce and remarriage conditioned by changed socio-historical contexts. There is no sound theological reason why re-reception should not continue when socio-historical contexts change.

This brief consideration of the traditional data on divorce and remarriage leads to several important conclusions. First, it is incorrect to speak of New Testament *teaching* on divorce and remarriage, as if there was only one. There are several *teachings* and they do not all agree. Second, not all these teachings derive from Jesus, as the Congregation for the Doctrine of the Faith ahistorically insinuates. Thirdly, diverging accounts of divorce and remarriage, and of other matters as well, are an integral part of the New Testament and later Christian traditions because the diverse cultural followers of Jesus sought to translate the meaning of his life, death, and resurrection into the socio-historical contexts of their concrete lives. Fourthly, though one element in those diverging accounts, namely, the demand for indissoluble marriage, was later singled out and allowed to override all the others, that fact should not be allowed to obscure either the original or ongoing divergence.

The Catholic Church accords great veneration to ecumenical councils, most especially to the first of them, the Council of Nicea (325), whose Creed established the doctrinal basis of the Christian faith. The solemn teaching of Nicea is intimately related to the church's teaching on divorce and remarriage, and has much to say to its pastoral practice today. The council's Canon 8 goes to the very heart of the question of divorce and remarriage.

> As regards those who define themselves as the Pure and who want to join the Catholic and Apostolic Church, the holy and great Council decrees that they may remain among the clergy once hands have been imposed upon them. But beforehand they will have to promise in writing to comply with the teachings of the Catholic and Apostolic Church and to make them the rule of their conduct. That is to say, they will have to communicate both with *those who married a second time* (*digamoi*) and with those who failed under persecution but whose time has been established and whose moment of reconciliation has arrived. They will, therefore, be bound to follow the teaching of the Catholic and Apostolic Church completely.[19]

According to this Canon, the "Pure," those who belonged to the rigorous sect called Novatians,[20] had to promise in writing to accept the teaching of the Catholic Church before they could be reconciled with it. Specifically, they had to accept to live in communion with those who had been married twice (*digamoi*) and those who had apostatized during persecution but who had completed their penance and had been reconciled to the church. We are concerned here only with those *digamoi* who have done penance and have been reconciled to the church.

Novatian teaching excluded from penance and reconciliation those who were guilty of certain sins "leading to death," among them *digamia* which refers to remarriage either after the death of a spouse or after a divorce. Since, however, remarriage after the death of a spouse was not considered a sin leading to death until long after the Council of Nicea, the council's *digamoi* must be those who have remarried after a divorce or repudiation. That "sin," according to the council, can be forgiven and reconciliation with the church can be achieved after a period of suitable penance. Acutely relevant is the fact that neither the church before Nicea nor the council itself, in keeping with the proscriptions of Deut 24:1–4, which were binding in the church before Nicea and which forbade a husband to take back his repudiated wife after she had married another,[21] required the repudiation of the new spouse as a pre-requisite for forgiveness and reconciliation. One of the great fathers of the Eastern church, Basil, bishop of Caesarea, explicitly reports the treatment of a man who had abandoned his wife and remarried, who had "done penance with tears," and who, after seven years, had been accepted back "among the faithful."[22] The man's second marriage is accepted and neither the repudiation of his second wife nor his taking back of the first is demanded as a pre-requisite for full communion. This teaching of Basil is the foundation for the teaching and practice of the Orthodox Church known as *oikonomia,* to which I will return later.

The Catholic Church has never actually practiced in history what is enshrined in its law, namely, that "the essential properties of *marriage* are unity and indissolubility" (1983 Can 1056). The actual number of marriages the church holds to be canonically indissoluble is, in reality, very limited. If the church truly believed that indissolubility was an essential property of *marriage,* and not just of *Christian marriage,* and that by the will of God "from the beginning" (Mark 10:6; Matt 19:4), then it would treat all marriages as indissoluble. It does not and never has. The church accepts the marriages of the non-baptized as valid when they have been performed according to the laws which govern them, and yet, utilizing the Pauline Privilege, it regularly dissolves them "in favor of the faith of the party who received baptism" (Can 1143). It has further extended the Pauline Privilege, as already noted, to embrace the dissolution of valid marriages utilizing the misnamed and misleading Petrine Privilege, exercised by popes Paul III, Pius V, and Gregory XIII. An official commentary from the Canon Law Society of America apparently recognizes, but does not identify, the problem. It explains the obvious discrepancies between Canon 1056 and Catholic practice by declaring that "the essential properties of marriage, unity and indissolubility, must be understood in the context of sacramental marriage defined as the intimate community of the whole of life."[23] Canon 1056, however, does not say that the essential properties of *sacramental marriage* are unity and indissolubility but that the properties of *marriage* without qualification are unity and indissolubility. If *marriage* is indissoluble, then every marriage is indissoluble. That is never what the Catholic Church has practiced, and it is not what it practices today.

In Christian marriage, Canon 1056 adds, indissolubility is said to acquire "a distinctive firmness by reason of the sacrament" (Can 1056). We can presume that it is on this statement that the Canon Law Society's commentary cited above is based. Yet, in historical practice, this is no more true than the preceding statement. Valid sacramental marriages which have not been consummated are dissolved "by the Roman Pontiff for a just reason, at the request of both parties or of either party" (Can 1142). Long-standing church practice with respect to the dissolution of valid, sacramental marriages demonstrates anything but a belief that indissolubility is an essential property of marriage in general or of sacramental marriage in particular.

The official doctrine of the church on the indissolubility of marriage further demonstrates that fidelity to the words of Jesus is not the only criterion for ecclesiastical judgments about divorce and remarriage. Only that marriage "which is ratified (as sacrament) and consummated cannot be dissolved by any human power other than death" (Can 1141). The two conditions which make a marriage indissoluble in the eyes of the church, that it be both sacramental *and* consummated, are not conditions ever mentioned by Jesus or any of the New Testament writers. They are both the result of re-reception of the words of Jesus in socio-historical contexts long after his death, despite the ahistorical and egregiously incorrect teaching of the recent *Catechism of the Catholic Church* that "the marriage bond has been established by God himself in such a way that a marriage concluded *and consummated* between baptized persons can never be dissolved."[24] No Catholic theologian would debate that marriage was created by God. That the marriage bond becomes indissoluble, even in a sacramental marriage, only when the marriage is consummated is not a teaching of Jesus but a nuance added by Gratian in the twelfth century to resolve the contentious debate between the Roman and Northern European interpretations about what makes a marriage. It is nowhere even remotely suggested by Jesus.

Another nuancing of Jesus' logion about marriage is demonstrable in Catholic history. The gospels declare "what God has joined together *let not man put asunder*" (Mark 10:9; Matt 19:6). For the first thousand years of Catholic history, the church interpreted the subjunctive of this logion (Greek: *chōrizetō*; Latin: *separet*) as a *moral* demand; man *should not* put asunder what God has joined. In the twelfth century, again under the influence of Gratian, the *moral* demand was transformed into an *ontological* reality. The *should not* gave way to *cannot*, as in "a ratified and consummated marriage *cannot* be dissolved by any human power or for any reason other than death" (Can 1141). That progression from the words of Jesus, from the moral demand, to the philosophical words of the church, to the ontological reality, is clearly another nuance the church added to the words of Jesus. Notice that it is not *marriage*, but *sacramental and consummated* marriage, that cannot be dissolved. We consider that particular question in the following.

The Catholic Church, which teaches that the only marriage which is indissoluble is the sacramental and consummated marriage, today has a particular problem with respect to consummation: it has no criterion for judging when a marriage has been consummated and therefore made indissoluble. A theological question is consistently raised about the Catholic teaching on the effect of consummation: what is it that consummation adds to sacrament that makes the consummated sacramental marriage immune to dissolution while the unconsummated sacramental marriage is dissoluble? Pius XI suggested the answer lies in "the mystical meaning of Christian marriage," namely, its reference to that "most perfect union which exists between Christ and the church."[25] Loving sexual intercourse, the pope intends, is the most perfect union between a man and a woman and, therefore, the most perfect image of the steadfast, indissoluble union between Christ and the church. Since the one union is indissoluble, so must be the other. Though it does not specify as precisely as Pius that it is the *consummated* sacramental marriage that is indissoluble, the International Theological Commission offers the same reason for the indissolubility of Christian marriage. The ultimate basis for the indissolubility of Christian marriage lies in the fact that it is the sacrament, the image, of the indissoluble union between Christ and the church.

But questions remain. When Pius XI wrote in 1930, he took for granted the 1917 Code of Canon Law that dealt with marriage as a contract (Can 1012), that declared the object of the contract to be the exclusive and perpetual right to the body of the other for acts suitable for the generation of offspring (Can 1081, 2), and that declared the ends of marriage to be primarily procreation and secondarily mutual help and the remedy of concupiscence (Can 1013). In such a juridico-physicalist context, a single act of sexual intercourse might be judged to be the consummation of a marriage. In the changed theologico-personalist climate in which the Second Vatican Council rooted its doctrine on marriage, such a simplistic vision of consummation is problematic. The council teaches that marriage "is rooted in the conjugal covenant of irrevocable personal consent."[26] Despite insistent demands to retain the legal word "contract" as a precise way to speak of marriage, the council demurred and chose instead the biblical, theological, and personal word "covenant." Though the legal effects of contract and covenant are identical, this choice locates marriage as a primarily *interpersonal* rather than *legal* reality, and brings it into line with the rich biblical tradition of covenant between God and God's people and Christ and Christ's church. The revised Code also preferred *covenant* to *contract* (Can 1055, 1), though it relapses into contractual language some thirty times.

The council made another change to Catholic teaching about marriage, which is central to any modern theological discussion of consummation and which was later also incorporated into the revised Code. The traditional teaching on the ends of marriage was the primary end–secondary end hierarchy between procreation and spousal love (1917 Can 1013). Despite insistent demands to reaffirm this hierarchical terminology, the council refused to do so. It taught explicitly that procreation "does not make the other ends of marriage of less account," and that marriage "is not instituted solely for procreation."[27] That this refusal to speak of a hierarchy of ends in marriage was not the result of oversight but a deliberate choice was confirmed when the council's teaching on ends was incorporated into the revised Code (Can 1055, 1).

This change of perspective raises questions about the claim that the spouses' first sexual intercourse is the consummation or culmination of their mutual self-gifting and marriage. If the procreation of human life *and* the *consortium*-communion between the spouses are equal ends of marriage, why should an act of sexual intercourse alone be the symbol of the union of Christ and Christ's church? Why should the diachronic interpersonal union between the spouses, the traditional marital *consortium*, itself symbolized in sexual communion among other things, not be the symbol? This question has been exacerbated by the change in the way consummation is specified in both the council and the revised Code. A marriage is now said to be "ratified and consummated if the spouses have in a *human manner* (*humano modo*) engaged together in a conjugal act in itself apt for the generation of offspring" (1983 Can 1061, 1). The phrase I have emphasized has placed Catholic teaching on consummation and indissolubility on hold theologically and canonically, for as yet a theology of sexuality elucidating what sexual intercourse *humano modo* means has not been elaborated. Since marital intercourse *humano modo* cannot be precisely defined, neither can the marital consummation it is said to effect. And since the consummation of a marriage cannot be precisely defined, neither can the radical indissolubility of the marriage which hinges on it. Many more valid marriages than heretofore ever imagined are, therefore, now open to official Catholic dissolution.

The theological point here is clear. Despite its constant reference to the words of Jesus, the church's practice with respect to divorce and remarriage is not founded exclusively on the words of Jesus. Much of it is founded on the re-reception of the words of Jesus nuanced in the socio-historical contexts through which the church has passed in its journey to the modern world. Since that has been true so often and for so long in Catholic history, there is no theological reason why, in response to what sociology shows to be the virtually universal contemporary *sensus fidei* of both theologically and maritally competent faithful with respect to divorce and remarriage, it could not be yet again.

The Orthodox Church has a received approach to this question, known as *oikonomia*. While holding as firmly as the Catholic Church to the belief that the Jesus of the gospel presents Christians with a demand for indissoluble marriage, the Orthodox also acknowledge that men and women sometimes do not measure up to the gospel. They acknowledge that marriages, including Christian marriages, sometimes die, and that, when they die, it makes no sense to claim that they are still binding. A dead marriage, they explain, is as dead as a dead spouse. When a marriage is dead, *oikonomia* impels the church to be sad, but also to be compassionate and forgiving, even to the point of permitting a remarriage. The Council of Trent in the sixteenth century was asked to condemn this Orthodox practice, but it refused to do so on the basis that it could not be proved that it was contrary to the gospel.[28] On a vote of 179–20, the 1980 Synod of Bishops asked Pope John Paul II to consider this Orthodox approach for any light it might cast on Catholic practice. Twenty years later, despite insistent suggestions by bishops and theologians of the high tradition that this might be a fruitful line to pursue, and a documented *sensus fidei* in the low tradition, whose marital experience John Paul II asserts is among the diversity of gifts and charisms to be brought to bear to discern the *sensus fidei* of the whole church on the dignity of marriage,[29] nothing has happened.

## Procreation, Interpersonalism, and Contraception

In this section, I examine the socio-historical *contexts* of the Catholic Church's teaching on artificial contraception. I use *contexts* here in the plural, because there have been, at least, three different socially rooted theoretical contexts in which the church's teaching has been construed, and different consequences for *praxis* may be drawn from each of these different contexts. In the 1960s, the Second Vatican Council sought to discern the "signs of the times" with respect to marriage and family, following Pope John XXIII's instruction on the difference between the substance of Catholic faith, which remains stable always, and the forms in which that faith is expressed, which have changed many times before and could change again in new socio-historical contexts. One outcome of the council, achieved largely by diocesan bishops and theologians over the loud objections of Vatican functionaries,[30] was a re-reception of the Catholic theology of marriage which altered its teachings as surely as the reception of capitalist theories altered its teaching on usury and the reception of personalist theories altered its teaching on slavery. The socio-historical path to that re-reception will be illuminating.

One model of marriage dominated the Catholic theological tradition from the second to the twentieth century. That model presented marriage as a *pro-creative institution,* a socio-religious, stable structure of meanings in which a man and a woman become husband and wife in order to become mother and father; in order, that is, to procreate children. That model has its origin in the Genesis command to "be fruitful and multiply," (Gen 1:22), but it was greatly solidified in the Christian church's struggle to legitimate marriage as something good against Greek dualist theories. At the opening of the second century, echoing the biblical "God saw everything that he had made, and behold it was very good" (Gen 1:31), Clement of Alexandria combated the Gnostics, who argued that sexuality and marriage were evil, by asserting that they were necessarily good because they were created by the good God. They are good, however, only when used for procreation and for no other purpose.[31] Lactantius agrees: "We have received the genital part of the body for no other purpose than the begetting of offspring, as the very name itself teaches."[32] In his fourth-century debate with the Manichees, Augustine also presented marriage and sexuality as good because they were created by a good God.[33] Procreation is the primary purpose of both sexuality and mar-riage because "from this derives the propagation of the human race in which a living community is a great good."[34] Earlier in the same book, however, he had suggested another good of marriage, which "does not seem to me to be good *only* because of the procreation of children, but also because of the natural companionship of the sexes. Otherwise, we could not speak of marriage in the case of old people, especially if they had either lost their chil-dren or had begotten none at all."[35] This is a clear linking of marriage and sexual intercourse, not to procreation, but to the relationship of the spouses. Consideration of this relationship in the different socio-historical context of the twentieth century will yield a quite different model of marriage.

In the thirteenth century, Aquinas gave this priority of procreation its most reasoned argument. "Marriage has its principal end in the procreation and education of offspring." It has also "a secondary end in man alone, the sharing of tasks which are necessary in life, and from this point of view husband and wife owe each other faithfulness." There is a third end in believers, "the meaning of Christ and church, and so a good of marriage is called sacrament." For Aquinas, marriage has three ends: a primary end, procreation; a secondary end, faithful love; and a tertiary end, sacrament. "The first end is found in marriage in so far as man is animal, the second in so far as he is man, the third in so far as he is believer."[36] This is a tightly reasoned argument, as is customary in Aquinas, and its *primary end–secondary end* terminology dominated Catholic marriage manuals for the next seven hundred years. The validity of a model is determined, however, not by its intelligibility, the authority of its author, or its age, but only by the fact that it explains all that it purports to explain. Aquinas's authority cannot obscure the fact that his argument is a curious one, since the primary end of specifically *human* marriage is dictated by the human's generically *animal* nature. It was on that basis that his argument was challenged in the twentieth century. Before that challenge, however, it had been enshrined for the first time in an official Catholic document in the Code of Canon Law in 1917.[37] "The primary end of marriage is the procreation and nurture of children; its secondary end is mutual help and the remedying of concupiscence" (Can 1013, 1). There is something to be noted here that is not often adverted to, namely, that in Aquinas and the 1917 Code procreation is the primary end of *marriage,* not of *sexual intercourse,* as it would later become in Catholic history. This theologico-canonical fact needs to be remembered, for it will be important in a later context.

   The procreative institution is the result of a contract in which, according to the 1917 Code of Canon Law, "each party gives and accepts a perpetual and exclusive right over the body for acts which are of themselves suitable for the generation of children" (Can 1081, 2). Notice that the procreative marital contract was about *bodies* and their *acts;* the procreative institution was never about persons and their mutual love. Couples who hated one another could consent to the procreative institution as long as they exchanged legal rights to each another's bodies for the purpose of the procreation of children. In the Western world at the beginning of the third millennium, sociological research shows sexual intercourse is no longer viewed exclusively as being for biological procreation: 82 percent of young adult Americans now see it as for *making love,* not necessarily for making babies.[38] That meaning is replicated in the contemporary American Catholic scene via another research datum: 75–85 percent of Catholics, who consider themselves good Catholics, approve a form of contraception forbidden by the church.[39] The situation is the same elsewhere. Speaking of the situation in England, for example, sociologist Michael Hornsby-Smith notes that "the evidence we have reviewed suggests . . . that lay people . . . have largely made up their own minds on this matter, and now regard it as none of the business of the clerical leadership of the Church."[40] The theologian seeking factual judgment founded in empirical data has to ask whether or not such sociological data tell us anything about the truth of things.

   The model of marriage as procreative institution was thrust into center stage in the 1960s in the great debate over artificial contraception. I cannot provide here a detailed analysis of that debate, but neither can I pass over it in silence, for it is inextricably connected to any discussion of Catholic models of marriage.[41] The question of artificial contraception became a major moral question in the Catholic Church with the appearance of female cycle-regulating pills, still referred to today as "The Pill," as if there was only one. It became clearly focused in 1968 with the publication of Paul VI's encyclical *Humanae Vitae*, which emerged from the traditional biologically procreative model of marriage and prescribed that "each and every marriage act (*quilibet matrimonii actus*) must remain open to the transmission of life."[42] Paul VI took this statement from the Minority Report of the Commission John XXIII had set up, and he himself had expanded, to research and discuss the question. The Majority Report from that Commission, following what had been traditional between Aquinas and Pius XI re-received in a new interpersonal procreative model of marriage, argued that it is marriage itself (*matrimonium ipsum*), not "each and every marriage act," that is to be open to the transmission of life. It asserted that "human intervention in the process of the marriage act *for reasons drawn from the end of marriage itself* should not always be excluded, provided that the criteria of morality are always safeguarded."[43] The differential in the two positions was precisely the differential created by adherence to two different models of sexuality and marriage. The Minority Report followed the traditional biologically procreative model, the majority report followed the re-received interpersonal procreative model that emerged from the Second Vatican Council.

Norbert J. Rigali offers a useful category in which to consider that debate. He asks not what was the *outcome* of the debate in Pope Paul VI's controverted *Humanae Vitae*, that is well-known, but what was the *process* by which that outcome was reached.[44] That process can be quickly summarized. At the instigation of Cardinal Leo Josef Suenens, archbishop of Malines, whose ultimate intent was that an adequate document on Christian marriage be brought before the Second Vatican Council for debate, Pope John XXIII established a commission to study the issue of birth control. The commission was confirmed and enlarged by Pope Paul VI until it ultimately had seventy-one members, not all of whom attended its meetings or voted.[45] The final voting took place in two separate groups: the theologians on the commission voted 15–4 in favor of a change in the Catholic teaching on artificial contraception; the bishops and cardinals on the commission voted 9–2 in favor of a change. Both a majority report and a minority report were then submitted to Paul VI who, professing himself unconvinced by the arguments of the majority, and sharing the concern of the minority report that the church could not repudiate its long-standing teaching on contraception without undergoing a serious blow to its overall moral authority, approved the minority report in his encyclical letter *Humanae Vitae*.[46]

The question of contraception had been preempted from council debate and reserved to the pope and the Commission he had set up to study it. It was exempted, therefore, from the discussion of the meaning and ends of marriage from which the interpersonal model of marriage emerged as an established Catholic model. Richard McCormick commented in 1968 that "the documents of the Papal Commission represent a rather full summary of two points of view...the majority report, particularly the analysis of its rebuttal, strikes this reader as much the more satisfactory statement."[47] That judgment continues to be the judgment of the majority of Catholic theologians and the vast majority of Catholic couples, because they adhere to the same interpersonal model on which the majority report was based. Thirty-five years later, despite a concerted minority effort to make adherence to *Humanae Vitae* a test case of authentic Catholicity, the debate between the biological-procreative and interpersonal-procreative models perdures as a source of serious division in the church which is called to communion.

The unprecedented horrors of the first World War transformed the context of human affairs in Europe where the major horrors were localized. In philosophical circles, that transformation gave birth to a new movement known as personalism, which gradually impacted also theological circles. That personalism made its first, tentative Catholic appearance in December 1930, in Pope Pius XI's *Casti Connubii*, his response to the Anglican Lambeth Conference's approval of the morality of artificial contraception. That encyclical did two things which would haunt the Catholic theology of sexuality and marriage throughout the twentieth century. First, under the influence of "natural law thinking...so overwhelmed by modern scientific rationalism that it could now pronounce about the 'ends' or 'purposes' of sexual behavior,"[48] it introduced for the first time in theological history a new ecclesial doctrine, namely, procreation as the end of *sexual intercourse* rather than the end of *marriage*. Second, it initiated the expansion of the procreative model of marriage into a more personal model of conjugal love and intimacy. In *Casti Connubii*, the *procreative-institution* model underwent two significant and ultimately important changes: the model which traditionally presented procreation as the primary end of *marriage* was transposed to present procreation as the primary end of *sexual intercourse* and, at the same time, it began timidly to give way to a *procreative-union* model, in which procreation remained an important facet of marriage but did not encompass all that marriage is. Pius insisted that sexual intercourse had as its primary end procreation and also that it was an important element in the mutual love and life of the spouses.

This mutual love, proved as always by loving deeds, has "as its primary purpose that husband and wife help each other day by day in forming and perfecting themselves in the interior life ... and above all that they may grow in true love toward God and their neighbor." So important is the mutual love and life of the spouses, Pius argued, that "it can, in a very real sense, be said to be *the chief reason and purpose of marriage,* if marriage be looked at not in the restricted sense as instituted for the proper conception and educating of the child but more widely as the blending of life as a whole and the mutual interchange and sharing thereof."[49] If we do not focus in a limited way on procreation, Pius taught, but broaden the scope of the model to embrace also the marital love and life of the spouses, then that love and life is the primary reason for marriage. With this authoritative teaching, Pius introduced a new, transitional model of marriage, a procreative-union model, which, after thirty-five years of growing pains, blossomed into an entirely new and previously unheard of Catholic model of marriage, a model of *interpersonal union.*

Pius XI suggested there is more to marriage than the biologically rooted, act-focused, procreative-institution model can explain. He suggested a personal procreative-union model, a suggestion which was taken up by European thinkers, most influentially two Germans, Dietrich Von Hildebrand and Heribert Doms. In the opening paragraph of his work *Marriage,* Von Hildebrand highlights the problem with the procreative model. The modern age, he suggests, and remember he is talking of Europe in the 1930s, still reeling from the horrors of World War I, is guilty of anti-personalism, "a progressive blindness toward the nature and dignity of the spiritual person." This anti-personalism expresses itself in various forms of materialism, the most dangerous of which is biological materialism, which considers humans *only* more highly developed animals. "Human life is considered exclusively from a biological point of view and biological principles are the measure by which all human activities are judged."[50] The procreative-institution model of marriage, with its insistent emphasis on bodies and their biological functions, is wide open to the charge of, and was in fact charged with, biological materialism. It ignores the higher, personal, and spiritual characteristics of the human animal. So, too, is the centuries old Stoic-cum-Christian doctrine that argues from physical structure to human "nature" and "natural" ends. So, too, is Aquinas's position which founds the primary end of *human* marriage in the physical *animality* of men and women. To correct this biological, materialistic approach, Von Hildebrand offers a new model of marriage, claiming support from *Casti Connubii* for his central thesis that marriage is for the building up of loving communion between the spouses. Conjugal love, he argues, is the primary meaning and end of marriage.

In marriage, spouses enter an interpersonal relationship in which they confront one another as "I" and "Thou" and initiate a mysterious fusion of their very beings. This fusion of their personal beings, and not merely the physical fusion of their bodies, is what the oft-quoted "one body" of Genesis 2:24 intends. It is this interpersonal fusion which the bodily fusion of sexual intercourse both signifies and causes, and intercourse achieves its primary end when it actually does signify and cause interpersonal union. "Every marriage in which conjugal love is thus realized bears spiritual fruit, becomes *fruitful* — even though there are no children."[51] The parentage of this interpersonal model of marriage in modern personalist philosophy is as clear as the parentage of the traditional procreative model in Greek Stoic philosophy. I underscore again, however, that a demonstration of parentage is not *eo ipso* a demonstration of either truth or falsity. We must always be on guard against the generic fallacy. More important, and clearer, is the resonance of an interpersonal description of marriage and marital lovemaking with the lived experience of modern married couples.

Doms agreed with Von Hildebrand that what is natural or unnatural for human animals is not to be decided exclusively on the basis of what is natural or unnatural for non-human animals. Humans are specifically spiritual animals, vitalized by a human soul, and their sexuality is not to be judged, as the Stoics and Aquinas judged it, on the exclusive basis of animal biology. Human sexuality is essentially the reasoned drive to fuse, not only one's body, but also and primarily one's very self with another human being. Sexuality drives a man and a woman to make a gift of himself and herself (not just of his or her body) to another person, to create a communion of persons which complements and fulfills the lives of both. In this perspective marital intercourse, which should never be reduced to only genital intercourse, is an interpersonal activity in which a woman gives herself to a man and a man gives himself to a woman, and in which each accepts the gift of the other, to both signify and create interpersonal communion.

The primary end of sexual intercourse in marriage, then, is the marital union between the spouses, and this primary end is achieved in every act of intercourse in and through which the spouses actually enter into intimate communion. Even in childless marriages, which sociological data shows to be increasingly common today, marriage and sexual intercourse achieve their primary end in the marital union of the spouses, their *two-in-oneness* in Doms's language. "The immediate purpose of marriage is the realization of its meaning, the conjugal two-in-oneness.... This two-in-oneness of husband and wife is a living reality, and the immediate object of the marriage ceremony and their legal union." The union and love of the spouses tends

naturally to the creation of a new person, their child, who fulfills both parents individually and as a two-in-oneness. "Society is more interested in the
child than in the natural fulfillment of the parents, and it is this which gives
the child primacy among the natural results of marriage."[52] Contemporary
sociological data, however, demonstrates the fallacy in assigning primacy
to the child, for the relational well-being of the parents is the key to the
well-being of their child.[53]

The Catholic Church's reaction to these new ideas was, as so often in
theological history, a blanket condemnation which made no effort to sift
truth from error. In 1944, the Holy Office (now the Congregation for the
Doctrine of the Faith) condemned "the opinion of some more recent authors, who either deny that the primary end of marriage is the generation
and nurture of children, or teach that the secondary ends are not essentially
subordinate to the primary end, but are equally primary and independent."[54]
In 1951, after yet another world war of even greater horror, as the ideas of
Von Hildebrand and Doms persisted and gained more adherents, Pius XII
felt obliged to intervene again. "Marriage," he taught, "as a natural institution in virtue of the will of the creator, does not have as a primary and
intimate end the personal perfection of the spouses, but the procreation and
nurture of new life. The other ends, in as much as they are intended by
nature, are not on the same level as the primary end, and still less are they
superior to it, but they are essentially subordinate to it."[55] The terms of the
question of the ends of marriage could not have been made more precise.
Another question, however, was seriously clouded.

For twenty years after *Casti Connubii*, the Catholic Church struggled
with a paradox. Since, on the basis of natural law whose unquestioned author is God, the primary end of sexual intercourse in marriage is procreation,
every act of intercourse should be open to procreation. But a moral question arose. Is it moral for a couple to practice periodic continence with the
explicit intention of avoiding conception, that is, is it moral for a couple
intentionally to limit their sexual intercourse to the wife's monthly period of
infertility? This question raged for twenty years until Pius XII, in a speech
to Italian obstetricians in 1951, ruled that such action was moral as long
as there are "serious reasons" of a "medical, eugenic, economic, or social
kind,"[56] with no specification of what such serious reasons might be. Notice I said that Pius "ruled" that periodic continence is moral given serious
reason. The word "ruled" is chosen deliberately, for the pope offered no
theological or moral arguments in support of his opinion. The obligation to
procreate, he argued, rests not on individual couples but on the entire human
race. An individual couple can be excused from adhering to this obligation,
even for the lifetime of a marriage, if they have sufficient reason. This ruling,

later validated by Paul VI in *Humanae Vitae*, introduced a strange paradox into Catholic teaching about sexuality and marriage. On the one hand, God, the author of natural law, determined that the end of each and every act of sexual intercourse is procreation; on the other hand, the church of God determined that a couple may be sexually active and intentionally avoid this end if they have sufficient reason. Joseph Selling's comment is apposite. "Although it has never been admitted by the Magisterium, with the teaching on periodic continence the natural law approach to sexual morality had reached a cul-de-sac."[57] The Second Vatican Council would attempt to resolve this and other paradoxes in ecclesial doctrine about marriage by rejecting the model in which this papal argument is based.

Though the council did not deal in detail with marriage and the sacrament of marriage, *Gaudium et Spes* did provide material intimately related to our present discussion. Marriage, it taught, is a "communion of love...an intimate partnership of life and love."[58] In spite of insistent demands from a small minority to repeat the centuries-old tradition of marriage as procreative institution, thus consigning spousal love to its traditional secondary place, the council declared the mutual love of the spouses and their passionate desire to be best friends for life to be of the very essence of marriage. It underscored its preference for an interpersonal-union model by making another important change in the received tradition. When faced with demands to describe the consent that initiates marriage in the traditional way as legal *contract,* the council demurred and chose to describe it as interpersonal *covenant,* explaining its choice of "covenant" in only one terse explanation in the commentary given to the fathers along with the revised text in September 1965. "There is no mention of 'matrimonial contract' but, in clearer words, of 'irrevocable personal consent.' The biblical term 'covenant' (*foedus*) is added at the intuition of the Eastern Churches for whom 'contract' raises some difficulties."[59] The understanding of *covenant* as used by the council is dependent upon the intuition of the Eastern Churches and to that intuition, therefore, we must briefly turn.

The Orthodox intuition of marriage as covenant is located within the *oikonomia* or plan of the biblical covenants of God with Israel and the church. Covenantal election involves both God and people in a steadfast commitment, and in the church the fullest expression of that commitment takes place in the sacrament of marriage. "The covenantal bond within which God works out our salvation is in essence a nuptial bond. And, conversely, the nuptial relationship achieves its true purpose and attains its true fullness only insofar as it is based upon an eternal covenantal commitment."[60] The purpose of marriage between a man and woman is to create between them "a bond of covenant responsibility and faithfulness that represents and reactualizes the eternal bond established by God with his chosen people,"[61] and so it is that marriage is "a great mystery" which refers to Christ and the church (Eph 5:32). In such an expansive vision of marriage, it is little wonder that the narrow juridical vision of "contract" would create "some difficulties." The use of *covenant* rather than *contract* deliberately takes marriage out of its narrow, traditional, juridical sphere and situates it in the sphere of interpersonal, religious, steadfast commitment and responsibility. Its identification as a "biblical term" insinuates its connection to the sempiternal covenants between God and Israel and Christ and church.

Marriage is founded in "a conjugal covenant of irrevocable personal consent."[62] Though in truth "contract" and "covenant" share many of the same meanings, there is one major difference: contracts have people as witnesses, covenants have God as witness. Covenant is ineluctably related to God in a way that contract is not. "Covenant" is also a biblical word, saturated with overtones of divine, personal, mutual, steadfast love, characteristics which are now applied to the marriage between a man and a woman. The description of the object of the marital covenant places the interpersonal character of marriage beyond doubt. The spouses, the council teaches, "mutually *gift and accept one another;*"[63] the focus on animal bodies and acts is replaced by a focus on persons. In their marital covenant, spouses create, not a procreative institution, but a loving interpersonal union which, since covenanted love is steadfast, is to last as long as life lasts, and may or may not be procreative.

The council devotes an entire section to the love which founds marriage and sacrament. It interprets the *Song of Songs* as a canticle to human, genital rather than to divine, mystical love, the reading which had long been prudishly traditional in Jewish and Christian hermeneutics.[64] This marital love is "eminently human," "involves the good of the whole person," and is "steadfastly true." It is singularly expressed and perfected in genital intercourse, which signifies and promotes "that mutual self-giving by which the spouses enrich one another."[65] Marriage and the marital love of the spouses are still said to be "ordained for the procreation of children,"[66] but that "does not make the other ends of marriage of less account," and "*[marriage] is not instituted solely for procreation.*"[67] The intense and well-documented debate which took place in the council makes it impossible to claim that the refusal to sustain the received marital tradition was the result of an oversight. It was the result of deliberate and hotly deliberated choice, a choice replicated and given canonical formulation twenty years later in the revised Code of Canon Law in 1983. Marriage "is ordered to the well-being of the spouses and to the procreation and upbringing of children" (Can 1055, 1), with no suggestion that either end is superior to the other. It is "brought into being by the lawfully manifested consent of persons who are legally capable" (Can 1057, 1), and that consent "is an act of the will by which a man and a woman by irrevocable covenant mutually give and accept *one another* for the purpose of establishing a marriage" (Can 1057, 2). The Catholic Church revised its laws about marriage in the twentieth century to bring its laws about marriage into line with a newly received and developing theology of marriage, moving beyond the model of marriage as exclusively procreative institution to embrace a model of procreative interpersonal union in which the mutual love and communion of the spouses is as important as procreation.

Archbishop Joseph Bernardin of Cincinnati spoke at the 1980 Synod for the interpersonal procreative model of marriage and sexuality, arguing that the church needed a more positive theology of sexuality, situated not in bodily organs and their acts, but in the human person and the meanings persons find in those acts. Archbishop Angelo Fernandes of New Delhi made a plea for the millions of families in his diocese living in ignorance and destitution who have no realistic hope of ever exercising responsible parenthood or achieving the dignity of a true marriage. Bishop Jacques Jullien of Beauvais, France, presented the theological argument. The essentials of human, and therefore of marital, life and love are of the spirit, not of the body which is but an organ of the spirit, and the quality of a couple's Catholic commitment is of their spirit, not of their body and its acts. Cardinal Hume of Westminster added that if the Christian family was to exercise the "prophetic mission" assigned to it by the synodal working paper, the church's pastors had better pay attention to the *sensus fidei* expressed in the results of pastoral, or social scientific, consultations around the world. That mind, he continued, was a theological source for doctrinal awareness.[68]

The judgment of the majority of the competent, high-tradition faithful on the papal commission continues to be the judgment of the majority of Catholic theologians of the high tradition and the vast majority of Catholic couples in the low tradition. They do not receive the prescription that every act of sexual intercourse must be open to new life, because they do not receive the biologically procreative model of sexuality and marriage on which it is based. Rather, they re-receive the procreative model as an interpersonally procreative model on which the majority report was based. Their non-reception, remember, does not make the traditional teaching necessarily false; it does, however, make it irrelevant to the life of the whole church, a theological fact that has been abundantly documented by sociological research. Thirty-five years after the publication of *Humanae Vitae,* despite a

concerted and powerful minority effort to make adherence to the biologically procreative model a litmus test of authentic Catholicity, the dialectic
between the biologically procreative and interpersonally procreative models
persists tenaciously in the church. Magisterial efforts to silence key voices
in the theological debate, efforts which totally ignore the documented majority *sensus fidei* in both the theological high and popular low traditions,
have not succeeded in ending the debate. They have, however, succeeded,
as sociology again shows, in creating a loss of respect for church law about
sexuality in general.[69] Authority can dictate truth, but it cannot impose it.
In the constant authentic Catholic tradition, dictated or ruled truth becomes
effective only when it is received by those under authority.

The clear, sociologically documented non-reception of *Humanae Vitae*
and the nuanced re-reception of the procreative model in its interpersonal
form, among both those expert in theology and those expert in marriage,
suggest a contemporary example of re-reception and dramatic development
of doctrine in the church, in line with the developments that took place in the
doctrines on usury, slavery, religious freedom, and membership in the body
of Christ. Sociological research further suggests that dramatic development
is now well under way. It shows that the assertion, "the Church believes that
each and every marriage act must be open to the transmission of new life,"
is not true today for the vast majority of Catholics who make up the people
of God that is the church. Theologians can never be comfortable with any
statement of belief which can be shown empirically to be untrue. At the
very least, the social scientific data suggest a development that the whole
church, of both high and low traditions, "from the Bishops to the last of
the faithful,"[70] is called to faithfully discern in order to judge whether it is
or is not an authentic example of re-reception of the apostolic truth toward
which the Spirit of truth is constantly impelling the church.

## Conclusion

This chapter continues the project of this book as an exercise in practical
theology, "the theological discipline which is concerned with the Church's
self-actualisation here and now — both that which *is* and that which *ought
to be*."[71] That exercise includes exploration of the theological realities of
reception and *sensus fidei* and of their connection to the data of sociological
research. It demonstrates that both reception, a process by which virtually
all the members of the church assent to as apostolic truth and ecclesial faith
a teaching or decision offered to them, and *sensus fidei,* a charism of discernment, possessed by the whole church, which recognizes and receives
a teaching or decision as apostolic truth and, therefore, to be believed by

ecclesial faith, are matters for the whole church and not just for a hierar-chical few. The exploration focuses the questions of reception and *sensus fidei* on the Catholic doctrines of divorce and remarriage, and contracep-tion, and demonstrates that contemporary sociological research documents a re-interpretation and re-reception of both doctrines in a way that illumi-nates a dramatic development of doctrine in the church akin to others that have happened in the past.

The exclusive model of sexuality and marriage in Catholic thinking from the third century onward was a biologically procreative model, which focused on bodily organs and their functions and bodily acts and their pur-poses: the purpose of male and female sex organs and of the acts associated with them was procreation. Any use of the organs which was not biologi-cally procreative was held to be sinful. In the twentieth century, as Western social contexts changed and the human person came to be valued more, this biologically procreative model was re-received in a new, interpersonal form which focused on human persons, not their bodies and organs, and in which the mutual love and communion of the spouses was acknowledged as a purpose of marriage, at least, equal to biological procreation.

In the biologically procreative model, procreation was held to be the *pri-mary* purpose of marriage, and all other purposes were held to be *secondary*. Despite insistent demands by the Vatican theological minority at the council to continue to receive exclusively that model because it was the tradition of the church, the council refused to do so. It taught that marriage and conjugal love "are by their very nature ordained to the generation and edu-cation of children" but that "does not make the other ends of marriage of less account."[72] To underscore the change and so that its words would not be misunderstood, the Preparatory Theological Commission, which submit-ted documents to the full council for debate and vote, appended a note to this text which explained that it did not "suggest [a hierarchy of ends] in any way." Any doubt about this was removed by the publication of the new Code of Canon Law in 1983 which prescribed that marriage "is by its nature ordered toward the good of the spouses and the procreation and education of offspring" (Can 1055), with no suggestion of any hierarchy of ends.

Though both reception and *sensus fidei* can appear as highly abstract theological realities, of concern only to professional theologians, the doc-trines related to contraception and divorce and remarriage belong to the most practical and intimate daily lives of the vast majority of believers. Twenty years ago, Pope John Paul II, remember, in his letter on the family, asserted that the marital experience of those believers is among the diver-sity of gifts and charisms to be brought to bear to discern the *sensus fidei* of the church about marriage.[73] I conclude this chapter by suggesting that the sociological evidence is clear: what *is* in virtually the whole church is a re-reception of the doctrines of divorce and remarriage, and contraception. I further suggest it is past time to acknowledge theologically and to teach magisterially that re-reception as not only what *is* but also what *ought to be* the belief of the future church. That there is a problem, however, is made clear by a consideration of two pronouncements made by churchmen.

In a 1992 response to the exemplary process of consultation carried out by the American bishops in preparation for their pastoral letter on the concerns of women in the church, Bishop Francis Murphy reported, that "the most serious concern raised by Vatican officials was the consultation process.... They asserted that the Bishops are teachers, not learners; truth cannot emerge through consultation."[74] Four years later, in 1996, Cardinal Bernardin's Common Ground document asserted the contrary: "an essential element of Catholic leadership must be wide and serious consultation, especially of those most affected by church policies under examination. The church's ancient concept of reception reminds us that *all* the faithful are called to a role in grasping truth or incorporating a decision or practice into the Church's life."[75] The *Tablet* of London had abundant evidence in 1993 to opine that "there is danger of a division between the institutional Church and a popular Church going its own way.... The Mystical Body is rent."[76] In 2004, the judgment must be stronger: no longer is there danger of division; division is already widespread and growing. It is time, yet again, for faithful and loving dialogue, consensus, and the ancient rule of faith: *quod ubique, quod semper, quod ab omnibus creditum est,* inhibiting dicasterial statements to the contrary notwithstanding.

## Questions for Discussion

1. How do you understand the mediation of sociology in theology? Are the data of empirical studies in any way a source for theological reflection?

2. What fidelity to the words of Jesus do Paul and Matthew practice? What fidelity to the words of Jesus does the Catholic Church practice when it dissolves valid marriages on the basis of the Pauline and the Petrine Privileges?

3. The Catholic Church teaches that the only marriage that is indissoluble is the marriage that is sacramental *and* consummated. When did Jesus teach this? If Jesus did not teach it, why does the Catholic Church follow it?

4. What is the difference between the following two statements: every *marriage* must be open to procreation; every act of *genital intercourse* must be open to procreation? To which of them, if either, do you personally subscribe?

5. In your judgment, what is the relative importance of the love of the spouses and procreation in a marriage? In your judgment, what should the Catholic Church do about the documented *sensus fidei* of Catholic believers with respect to contraception?

# Epilogue

I described this book in the Prologue as an exercise in practical theology, the "theological discipline which is concerned with the Church's self-actualization here and now — both that which *is* and that which *ought to be*."[1] Since that which *is* requires uncovering and elaboration before that which *ought to be* can be rationally evaluated, and since the social science of sociology is fully equipped for uncovering and elaborating concrete reality, sociological theories, questions, data, and answers have been to the fore throughout the book. The reader might be led to conclude from this that the book is an exercise in sociology. That would be a mistake. Though the short-term project of the book is clearly *sociological,* to make known and elaborate for theologians the discipline of sociology, the long-term project is strictly *theological,* to show how sociological themes and data necessarily apply to both theologians and the theologies they elaborate. In this book, sociology is in focus only as a handmaiden of theology.

As sociologists are likely to be as indignant and irate as philosophers to hear their discipline described as a handmaiden of theology, I hasten to explain. It was Aquinas who bequeathed to the Catholic tradition the notion of philosophy as a handmaiden to theology, and he uses "handmaiden" with its normal connotation. A handmaiden is related to the one for whom she is handmaiden as inferior to superior, and for Aquinas that described the relation of philosophy and theology. Theology, he argues, "does not draw upon the other sciences as upon its superiors, but uses them as its inferiors and handmaidens; even so the master sciences make use of subordinate sciences, as political science and military science."[2] I do not agree with Aquinas on the ranking of the sciences. Though the formal object of theology, God, by definition, is infinitely superior to that of any of the social or physical sciences, and though, as Aquinas argues, theology draws its principles "immediately from God by revelation,"[3] the sociology advanced in this book quickly points out that the special theological categories of revelation, inspiration, and faith inevitably draw their meanings from a human perspective or province of meaning. That means that however much its object lies

168

beyond the human sphere, theology itself and the theologians who practice
it lie entirely within that sphere.

From a sociological perspective, specifically from the perspective of the
sociology of knowledge, theology is a human activity and a human construction. To that degree it is neither superior nor inferior to any other human
science. When I say, therefore, that sociology is a handmaiden of theology,
I do not intend to insinuate a superior-inferior relationship. I intend only
that sociology has important social facts to teach theologians who would be
psychically and intellectually, and perhaps also morally, converted. Readers
who have followed the argument of the book carefully, will know that I believe theology has equally important theological facts to teach sociologists
about the presence of God in the concrete human situation which they analyze. The relationship between the two disciplines is not one of superior to
inferior, but one of equals who have important human meanings to mediate
to one another.

Because theologians are first and essentially human beings acculturated
into a variety of human perspectives and provinces of meanings, only one of
which is theology, this book is also an interwoven twofold dialogue. There
is, first, an internal theological dialogue, which asks what the Bible and a
two-thousand-year ecclesial tradition has said theologically *in oratione obli-*
*qua*, and how that is to be mediated to, appropriated by, and transmitted
onward by the contemporary church and its theologians *in oratione directa*.
Three matters critical to that internal dialogue were considered: the definition of Christian theology, the origin of sacred scripture, and the nature of
the church which claims its origin in the scriptures and seeks to mediate
the meanings of the scriptures to each new Christian generation. The nature
of the church is, perhaps, the most pressing of these three, because how
one conceives church will determine how one conceives the functioning of
the other two theological facts presented in the book, namely, *sensus fidei*
and reception. Church was presented as a *koinonia*-communion instituted
by Christ, constituted by the Spirit of Christ, and "composed of all those
who receive him in faith and in love,"[4] a socio-historical communion "of
life, love, and truth."[5] Scripture was presented as the written theology of
the early generations of that communion, which resulted from reflection on
their immediate experience of Jesus and was canonized by a later generation
as the classic ecclesial rule of faith. Theology was presented as disciplined
reflection on two intimately interrelated dimensions of reality: first, the self-
communication of God to humankind; second, the socio-historical matrix in
which Christians live and relate to God, to God's created universe, to themselves as creatures within that universe, and to the socio-historical forces

which generate both progress and decline within that universe. All these presentations point to a second dialogue, external to theology.

This second dialogue is a dialogue of theology with sociology and the data it provides about theological doctrines. I repeat again that sociology is not theology, no more than theology is sociology or any other social science, *pace* Milbank, but that does not mean that the two disciplines are completely unrelated. Sociology is eminently equipped for the empirical scientific elucidation of the socio-historical situation of what *is,* including what theologically *is,* a fact that I exemplified in the two moral teachings about artificial contraception and divorce and remarriage without annulment. The question can be put baldly here: how can anyone say that *the church believes* that artificial contraception and remarriage after civil divorce and without annulment are morally wrong when some 89 percent of the communion-church does not believe the former and some 64 percent does not believe the latter. Congar provides an easy and incontrovertible answer. Obedience to authentic ecclesial authority is called for "if the Church is conceived as a society subject to monarchical authority," and dialogue and consensus are called for "when the universal Church is seen as a communion."[6] The theological fact that the church, after the Second Vatican Council, is now predominantly seen as a communion demands critical dialogue and consensus about the *sensus fidei* of the church rather than uncritical obedience.

The simple social fact that 89 percent of Catholics in the communion-church believe that they can practice prohibited methods of contraception and still be good Catholics proves nothing theologically. It does, however, raise questions that converted theologians cannot ignore without fulfilling contemporary scientific prophecies that theologians and their theologies have nothing to do with the real questions of the real world in which women and men who are members of the communion-church dwell. Another moral question presses the church in our day as much as does contraception and divorce and remarriage without annulment, namely, cohabitation prior to marriage. I did not introduce that question in this book because it has a different theological profile from the other, and I have also considered it elsewhere,[7] but, if for some 75–80 percent of Western women the first union is cohabitation and not marriage, again a social fact raises questions for theologians about what the communion-church believes. The socio-historical and theological fact of the non-reception and nuanced re-reception of long-held Catholic doctrines about usury, slavery, religious freedom, and membership in the body of Christ points to, and ecclesially legitimates, the direction in which the doctrines prohibiting contraception, remarriage without annulment, and premarital cohabitation will develop.

A word here about responsible behavior in the church. The Catechism teaches that "the Church's social teaching proposes *principles for reflection;* it provides *criteria for judgment;* it gives *guidelines for action.*"[8] This trinity, principles for reflection, criteria for judgment, and guidelines for action, came into Catholic social teaching via Pope Paul VI's *Octogesima Adveniens* in 1971.[9] It was repeated in the Congregation for the Doctrine of the Faith's *Instruction on Freedom and Liberation* in 1986,[10] and underscored again a year later in John Paul II's *Sollicitudo Rei Socialis.*[11] This approach to social morality, an authentically established part of the Catholic moral tradition in modern times, introduces a model of converted personal responsibility which underscores the responsibility of each person in the communion-church. John Paul II accentuates this Catholic perspective by teaching that, in its social teachings, the church seeks "to *guide* people to *respond,* with the support of rational reflection and of the human sciences, to their vocation as *responsible* builders of earthly society."[12] The relationship between the church teaching and the individual believer learning, which this approach advances, merits close attention in a church that is communion. Church teaching *guides;* responsible believers learning, drawing on church guidance, their own attentiveness, intelligence, rationality, and decisiveness, and the findings of the human sciences, *respond.*

The notion of responsibility introduces an important dimension of individual and communional freedom to the unnuanced notion of uncritical obedience. In social reality, the magisterium does not pretend to pronounce on every last detail or to impose final decisions; it understands itself as informing and guiding believers while leaving judgment, decision, and application to their faithful and responsible conscience.[13] Socio-moral principles are humanly constructed guidelines for attention, intelligence, judgment, decision, and action, not moral imperatives drawn from divine, natural, or ecclesiastical law, and demanding uncritical obedience to God, nature, or church. John Paul adds what the Catholic tradition has always taken for granted. On the one hand, the church's social teaching is "constant." On the other hand, "it is ever new, because it is subject to the necessary and opportune adaptations suggested by the changes in historical conditions and by the unceasing flow of the events which are the setting of the life of people and society."[14] Principles remain constant. Judgments and actions, as history amply demonstrates, can change after responsible reflection on changed socio-historical contexts and the ongoing flow of human events illuminated by the data of the social sciences. Since this approach is authoritatively advanced in social morality, and since social and sexual morality pertain to the same human person, it would appear that the same approach would apply to sexual morality. Indeed, since the whole person is more intimately involved in the sexual domain than in the social, should the sexual domain not "be *more than any other* the place where all is referred to the informed conscience?"[15] Part of the proposal of this book has been, under the guidance of ecclesial principles and the illumination of sociology, to refer the questions about contraception and divorce and remarriage to the psychically, intellectually, and morally converted, informed conscience.

Christians in general and Christian theologians in specific do not live in a comfortable theological cocoon; they live in the created world along with other human beings who appear to have decided that Christians have nothing to tell them about that world, about themselves in the world, or about the forces at work for good and evil in the world. Many of these others have perspectives on the world and answers for the world's questions that are different from Christian theological perspectives and answers. That raises the inevitable question of which perspective is right and true, a question that, in its turn, raises another question about necessary dialogue between theology and other human perspectives external to it. Individuals and the human world they inhabit are not two independent realities; they are realities which work in an ongoing dialectical and symbiotic interdependence. Human society, culture, perspective, province of meaning are human products and nothing but human products, and yet these products act back upon their producers to conform and control them. The temptation of psychically and intellectually unconverted individuals, be they theologians or sociologists, is always to assume that *our* way is the *right* way and *our* truth is the *real* truth. The sociology of knowledge scotches that unconverted approach.

Human truth, I argued with Mannheim and the sociology of knowledge, is relative to a given perspective or province of meaning and is supported by a plausibility structure that derives from that province of meaning. Each province of meaning has its own accent of reality, its own cognitive style, its own consistency and compatibility; and outside of a given province there is no possibility of grasping the truth held within that province. That raises the specter of relativism, so disconcerting to many. Relativism acknowledges that all human truth is inseparably bound to the socio-historical perspective of the thinker and concludes that, therefore, all human truth is *relative* and unreliable. I do not accept that judgment. All human truth is, indeed, inseparably bound to the socio-historical perspective of the thinker and is, therefore, *relational,* but that does not make it unreliable. It suggests only that truth-within-perspective is but partial truth in need of dialectical complementation by truths held in other perspectives. That suggestion is even truer, the Christian traditions universally teach, when it comes to human truth about God whom "no one has ever seen" (John 1:18; cp. Ex 33:20–24).

Augustine expresses the basic Christian, apophatic perspective when he argues, *"si comprehendis, non est Deus"*; if you have understood, then what you have understood is not God.[16] Aquinas expresses it in his mature doctrine of analogy: "now we cannot know what God is but only what God is not; we must, therefore, consider the ways in which God does not exist rather than the ways in which God does exist."[17] Rahner expresses the same perspective in modern special theological language when he writes that "revelation does not mean that the mystery is overcome by gnosis bestowed by God ... on the contrary, it is the history of the deepening perception of God *as* the mystery."[18] The God whom the communion-church believes in is always wholly other, *deus absconditus*, a hidden God, a transcendent Mystery, "blessedly present but conceptually inapprehensible, and so God."[19] Recognizing this Christian theme, the magisterium of the church teaches that "the fullness of truth received in Jesus Christ does not give individual Christians the guarantee that they have grasped that truth fully.... Christians must be prepared to learn and to receive from and through others the positive values of their traditions. Through dialogue they may be moved to give up ingrained prejudices [psychic conversion], to revise preconceived ideas [intellectual conversion], and even sometimes to allow the understanding of their faith to be purified."[20] Pope John Paul II approves.

John Paul teaches, in his personalist mode, that dialogue is rooted in the nature and dignity of the human person. "Dialogue is an indispensable step along the path toward *human self-realization,* the self-realization of *each individual* and of *every human community....* It involves the human subject in his or her entirety; dialogue between communities involves in a particular way the subjectivity of each."[21] I agree that every dialogue, even what appears to be a dialogue between communions, at root involves the subjectivity of each individual in the dialogue. Each must, therefore, in the language of this book, be attentive, be intelligent, be rational, and be decisive. Each must attend carefully to the data emerging in the dialogue, must inquire intelligently into the data, come to understand it, and formulate that understanding in mutually understandable concepts; each must then rationally reflect, marshal the evidence, and eventually pass judgment on the truth or falsity, certainty or probability, of his or her understanding. It is only after this rational judgment is passed that any true knowledge is achieved in the dialogue. After the passing of judgment, there is the final step of considering possible courses of action, evaluating them, making a decision about which course of action to follow, and then translating that decision into action. In all of this, as I argued, the participants in the dialogue must be equal partners, with none being privileged over any others, for it is only on the basis of this equality that any individual in the dialogue may reach intellectual and, perhaps also, moral conversion.

I am wide open to dialogue in this book. I have to be, given both the theological and the sociological positions I embrace in it and in my theological life. I could well be the man I spoke of at a third-story window getting only a restricted third-story perspective on the landscape outside the window, and, lest I be that man, I have to be open to the complementation of perspectives provided by women and men at sixth-, ninth-, and twenty-first-story windows. In theological parlance, this book is situated in the category of *quaestio disputata,* the disputed question, so beloved of the medieval Scholastics. The Scholastic Master had three tasks: *lectio* or commentary on the Bible; *disputatio* or teaching by objection and response to a theme; *praedicatio* or proclamation of the theological word.[22] Peter Cantor speaks for all of them when he argues that "it is after the *lectio* of scripture and after the examination of the doubtful points thanks to the *disputatio, and not before,* that we must preach."[23] It is important for the reader to be aware that this book is *lectio* and *disputatio* before it is theological and pastoral *praedicatio.*

It is important also for both reader and theologian-author to understand what has been undertaken in this book. Theologians speak *from* the church; they do not speak *for* the church. It is not for the theologian standing alone to formulate the teaching or the moral practice of the communion-church; that is a task for the entire body of believers acting in faithful dialogue and consensus. The theologian, however, does have a task on behalf of the church. It is the task of "interpreting the documents of the past and present Magisterium, of putting them in the context of the *whole* of revealed truth, and of finding a better understanding of them by the use of hermeneutics."[24] In this book, attentive, intelligent, rational, and decisive human subjects, along with the scientific disciplines of theology and sociology, have been presented as part of that hermeneutic. What I have written is to be read as propositions submitted to the attention, intelligence, rationality, decisiveness, and response of my fellow believers in the communion-church, particularly of my fellow theologians in the high tradition. Their response may be critical, but not destructive of the communion that is the church instituted by Christ and constituted by the ever-active Spirit of Christ, the Spirit of "righteousness and peace and joy" (Rom 14:17; cf. Eph 4:3).

# Notes

## Prologue

1. Bernard J. F. Lonergan, *Method in Theology* (New York: Herder and Herder, 1972), xi.

2. Ibid.

3. Frederick E. Crowe and Robert M. Doran, eds., *Collected Works of Bernard Lonergan,* vol. 4 (Toronto: University of Toronto Press, 1988), 245.

4. Karl Rahner, "Practical Theology Within the Totality of Theological Disciplines," *Theological Investigations* (London: Darton, Longman, and Todd, 1972), 9:102. Emphasis in original.

5. Ibid., 105.

6. See John E. Thiel, *Senses of Tradition: Continuity and Development in the Catholic Faith* (New York: Oxford University Press, 2000), 100–128.

7. GS, 62.

8. Bernard J. F. Lonergan, "Moral Theology and the Human Sciences," *Method: Journal of Lonergan Studies* 15 (1997): 5–20.

9. Peter L. Berger, "Sociological and Theological Perspectives," in *Theology and Sociology: A Reader,* ed. Robin Gill (London: Cassell, 1996), 97. Emphasis in original.

10. ST, 1, 5, ad 2.

## One / Theology, Sociology, and Theologians

1. Anthony Giddens, *Sociology: A Brief but Critical Introduction* (New York: Harcourt Brace Jovanovich, 1987), 11.

2. Michael J. Baxter, "Whose Theology? Which Sociology?" in Michael H. Barnes, ed., *Theology and the Social Sciences* (Maryknoll, N.Y.: Orbis, 2001), 34–42.

3. Karl Rahner and Herbert Vorgrimler, *Concise Theological Dictionary* (Freiburg: Herder, 1965), 456.

4. The terms "foundational" and "dependent" revelation are common currency in the theological tradition. See Paul Tillich, *Systematic Theology* (Chicago: University of Chicago Press, 1967), 1:126–28; Gerald O'Collins, *Theology and Revelation* (Notre Dame, Ind.: Fides, 1968), 45–47. Rahner speaks of the "supernatural existential," God's *immediate* free offer of Godself to every human being, which is reflected

on and *mediated* in human, theological words. See "Concerning the Relationship Between Nature and Grace," *Theological Investigations* (London: Darton, Longman, Todd, 1965), 1:297–317; "Some Implications of the Scholastic Concept of Uncreated Grace," Ibid., 319–46; "Reflections on the Experience of Grace," *Theological Investigations* (London: Darton, Longman, Todd, 1967), 3:86–90.

5. Bernard J. F. Lonergan, *Method in Theology* (New York: Herder and Herder, 1972), xi.

6. Ibid., 133.

7. See Joseph Doré, "De la responsabilité des théologiens dans l'église," *Nouvelle Revue Théologique* 125 (203), 3–20.

8. Lonergan, *Method*, 282.

9. Paul Tillich, *Systematic Theology* (Chicago: University of Chicago Press, 1971), 1:1, 60.

10. David Tracy, *Blessed Rage for Order: the New Pluralism in Theology* (New York: Seabury, 1975), 45–46.

11. Roger Haight, *Dynamics of Theology* (New York: Paulist, 1990), 191.

12. Piet Fransen, *The New Life of Grace* (Tournai: Desclee, 1969), 15.

13. Rahner calls this notion of grace the primary one. See Karl Rahner and Herbert Vorgrimler, "Grace," *Concise Theological Dictionary* (London: Burns and Oates, 1965), 194.

14. Fransen, *The New Life of Grace*, 87.

15. See Maurice de la Taille, "Actuation créé par acte incréé," *Révue des Sciences Religieuses* 18 (1928): 252–68; Karl Rahner, "Some Implications of the Scholastic Concept of Uncreated Grace," *Theological Investigations*, 1:319–46; Robert W. Gleason, *Grace* (New York: Sheed and Ward, 1962), cc. 9 and 10. For a critique see Christopher Kiesling, "The Divine Indwelling in R. W. Gleason's *Grace*," *The American Ecclesiastical Review* 150 (1964): 263–84.

16. Rahner and Vorgrimler, *Theological Dictionary*, 161.

17. Karl Rahner, "History of the World and Salvation History," *Theological Investigations*, 5:98.

18. An ecclesial tradition, established in the controversy between Augustine and Pelagius and regularly verified ever since, is that women and men are free persons and are graced, not against their will, but only with their free cooperation (*cooperatio*). See DS, 373–97.

19. John Milbank, *Theology and Social Theory: Beyond Secular Reason* (Oxford: Blackwell, 1990), 210.

20. Robert M. Doran, *Theology and the Dialectics of History* (Toronto: University of Toronto Press, 1990), 453.

21. Ibid., 447.

22. Karl Rahner, "Practical Theology Within the Totality of Theological Disciplines," *Theological Investigations* (London: Darton, Longman and Todd, 1972), 9:102. Emphasis in original.

23. J. E. Goldthorpe, *An Introduction to Sociology* (Cambridge: Cambridge University Press, 1968), 3; cp. Peter L. Berger, *Invitation to Sociology: A Humanistic Perspective* (New York: Anchor Books, 1963), 16; Metta Spencer, *Foundations of Modern Sociology* (Englewood Cliffs, N.J.: Prentice-Hall, 1982), 4; Anthony Giddens, *Sociology: A Brief But Critical Introduction* (New York: Harcourt Brace Jovanovich, 1987), 8.

24. Giddens, *Sociology*, 9.

25. Jack D. Douglas, *Introduction to Sociology: Situations and Structures* (New York: Free Press, 1973), 4.

26. Spencer, *Foundations of Modern Sociology*, 57.

27. Lonergan, *Method*, xi.

28. Daniel Quinn, *Ishmael: An Adventure of the Mind and Spirit* (New York: Bantam/Turner Book, 1995), 40.

29. Theodore Roszak, *The Making of a Counter Culture: Reflections on the Technocratic Society and its Youthful Opposition* (New York: Doubleday, 1969), 215.

30. Peter L. Berger and Thomas Luckmann, *The Social Construction of Reality* (New York: Anchor Books, 1967).

31. Alfred Schutz, *Collected Papers*, vol. 1 (The Hague: Martinus Nijhoff, 1964–67), 230.

32. Bernard J. F. Lonergan, "Moral Theology and the Human Sciences," *Method: Journal of Lonergan Studies* 15 (1997): 5–20.

33. Jerry D. Rose, *Introduction to Sociology* (Chicago: Rand McNally, 1974), 21–36.

34. Doran, *Theology and the Dialectics of History*, 4.

35. Bernard J. F. Lonergan, *Insight: A Study of Human Understanding* (London: Longman's Green, 1957).

36. Ibid., 322–24; also Lonergan, *Method*, 9.

37. Lonergan, *Method*, 8.

38. Ibid., 13.

39. Ibid., 236.

40. Ibid., 238.

41. Ibid., 240.

42. Ibid.

43. Doran, *Theology and the Dialectics of History*, 41.

44. Ibid., 59.

45. See Bernard J. F. Lonergan, "Reality, Myth, Symbol," in *Myth, Symbol, and Reality*, ed. Alan M. Olson (Notre Dame, Ind.: University of Notre Dame Press, 1980), 36–37; "Questionnaire on Philosophy: Responses by Bernard Lonergan," *Method: Journal of Lonergan Studies* 2 (1984): 31.

46. Baxter, "Whose Theology? Which Sociology?" in Michael Barnes, ed., *Theology and the Social Sciences*, 34–42.

47. Lonergan, *Method*, xi.

48. Douglas, *Introduction to Sociology*, 4.

## Two / Theology and Sociology: Mutual Mediations

1. John Milbank, *Theology and Social Theory: Beyond Secular Reason* (Oxford: Blackwell, 1990).

2. Ibid., 207.

3. Ibid., 218.

4. Ibid., 210.

5. Ibid., 380.

6. Ibid., 246.

7. Ibid., 380.

8. David Martin, "Theology and Sociology: The Irish Flaneur's Account," *New Blackfriars* 78 (1997): 110.

9. John A. Coleman, "Every Theology Implies a Sociology and Vice Versa," in *Theology and the Social Sciences*, ed. Michael H. Barnes (Maryknoll, N.Y.: Orbis, 2001), 26.

10. Aidan Nichols, "*Non Tali Auxilio:* John Milbank's Suasion to Orthodoxy," *New Blackfriars* 73 (1992): 327.

11. Gregory Baum, *Essays in Critical Theology* (Kansas City: Sheed and Ward, 1994), 53.

12. Michael J. Baxter, "Whose Theology? Which Sociology? A Response to John Coleman," in Barnes, *Theology and the Social Sciences,* 36.

13. Ibid., 40.

14. That critique began expeditiously with Kieran Flanagan, "Sublime Policing: Sociology and Milbank's City of God," *Blackfriars* 73 (1992): 333–41. Flanagan judges that Milbank's "notion of 'ecclesiology' as 'sociology' is wrong-headed and naive" (340).

15. John Milbank, Catherine Pickstock, and Graham Ward, eds., *Radical Orthodoxy: A New Theology* (London: Routledge, 1999). Milbank's *Theology and Social Theory* is one volume in the Radical Orthodoxy project. Others are John Milbank, *The Word Made Strange* (Oxford: Blackwell, 1997); Catherine Pickstock, *On the Liturgical Consummation of Philosophy* (Oxford: Blackwell, 1997); and Graham Ward, *Barth, Derrida, and the Language of Theology* (Cambridge: Cambridge University Press, 1995).

16. Milbank et al., *Radical Orthodoxy,* 4.

17. DS 3008.

18. DS 3009.

19. DS 3010.

20. John Paul II, *Fides et Ratio,* n. 55.

21. Milbank, *Theology and Social Theory,* 208.

22. Milbank et al., *Radical Orthodoxy,* 2. Emphasis in original.

23. R. R. Reno, "The Radical Orthodoxy Project," *First Things,* February 2000, 42.

24. Ibid.

25. Nichols, "*Non Tali Auxilio,*" 331.

26. Reno, "Radical Orthodoxy," 44.

27. Robin Gill, *The Social Context of Theology: A Methodological Inquiry* (Oxford: Mowbrays, 1975), 7.

28. Lonergan, *Method,* 133.

29. Ibid., 268.

30. Doran, *Theology and the Dialectics of History,* 452.

31. Robin Gill, ed., *Theology and Sociology: A Reader* (London: Cassell, 1996), 229–30.

32. Karl Rahner, "Practical Theology Within the Totality of Theological Disciplines," *Theological Investigations* (London: Darton, Longman and Todd, 1972), 9:102. Emphasis in original.

33. Bernard J. F. Lonergan, "Moral Theology and the Human Sciences," *Method: Journal of Lonergan Studies* 15 (1997): 5–20. Emphasis added.

34. GS, 62.

35. Don S. Browning, *A Fundamental Practical Theology: Descriptive and Strategic Proposals* (Minneapolis: Fortress, 1991), 47.

36. See Alison Stokes, *Ministry After Freud* (Cleveland: Pilgrim Press, 1985), 51–62.

37. For further detail, see David Tracy, *The Analogical Imagination* (New York: Crossroad, 1981) and Paul Ricoeur, *Hermeneutics and the Human Sciences* (Cambridge: Cambridge University Press, 1981).

38. Browning, *A Fundamental Practical Theology,* 48.

39. Don S. Browning, Bonnie J. Miller-McLemore, Pamela D. Couture, K. Brynolf Lyon, and Robert M. Franklin, *From Culture Wars to Common Ground: Religion and the American Family Debate* (Louisville: Westminster/John Knox, 1997).

40. Stanley Hauerwas, *A Community of Character: Toward a Constructive Christian Social Ethic* (Notre Dame, Ind.: University of Notre Dame Press, 1981), 86.

41. See the books that appeared after that move: Stanley Hauerwas and William H. Willimon, *Resident Aliens: Life in the Christian Colony* (Nashville: Abingdon, 1989); Stanley Hauerwas, *Against the Nations* (Notre Dame, Ind.: University of Notre Dame Press, 1992); *Dispatches from the Front* (Durham, N.C.: Duke University Press, 1995); Stanley Hauerwas and William H. Willimon, *Where Resident Aliens Live* (Nashville: Abingdon, 1996).

42. David A. S. Fergusson, *Community, Liberalism and Christian Ethics* (Cambridge: Cambridge University Press, 1998), 66.

43. Robin Gill, *Churchgoing and Christian Ethics* (Cambridge: Cambridge University Press, 1999), 197.

44. Alasdair McIntyre, *After Virtue: A Study of Moral Theory* (London: Duckworth, 1985), 252.

45. Gill, *Churchgoing,* 197.

46. Ibid., 261.

47. Andrew Greeley, *The Catholic Imagination* (Berkeley: University of California Press, 2000); *The Catholic Myth: The Behavior and Beliefs of American Catholics* (New York: Scribner, 1990); *The American Catholic: A Social Portrait* (New York: Basic, 1977).

48. David Martin, *Reflections on Sociology and Theology* (Oxford: Clarendon, 1997), 22.

49. Ibid., 73.

50. Baxter, "Whose Theology? Which Sociology?" 34–42.

51. Martin, *Reflections on Sociology and Theology,* 101.

52. David Martin, *A General Theory of Secularization* (New York: Harper Collins, 1979).

53. Ibid., 227–28.

54. Ibid., 229.

55. See, for instance, John Fulton, ed., *Young Catholics at the New Millennium: The Religion and Morality of Young Adults in Western Countries* (Dublin: University College Press, 2000); Timothy J. Buckley, *What Binds Marriage: Roman Catholic Theology in Practice* (London: Chapman, 1997), 1–27; Michael Hornsby-Smith, *Roman Catholicism in England: Customary Catholicism and Transformation of Religious Authority* (Cambridge: Cambridge University Press, 1991).

56. David Martin, *Tongues of Fire: The Explosion of Protestantism in Latin America* (Oxford: Blackwell, 1990).

57. Martin, *Reflections on Sociology and Theology,* 6.

58. Rodney Stark and William Bainbridge, *The Future of Religion: Secularization, Revival and Cult* (Berkeley: University of California Press, 1985).

59. Patricia Wittberg, "Religion and Society — Two Sides of the Same Coin," in Barnes, *Theology and the Social Sciences,* 205–13.

60. Martin, *Reflections on Sociology and Theology,* 67.

61. Wittberg, "Religion and Society," 210–11.

62. Ibid., 211.

63. Gregory Baum, "The Impact of Sociology on Catholic Theology," in *Theology and Sociology: A Reader,* ed. Robin Gill (London: Cassell, 1996), 132.

64. William Butler Yeats, *The Variorum Edition of the Poems* (New York: Macmillan, 1968), 438.

65. Michael Polanyi, *Personal Knowledge: Towards a Post-Critical Philosophy* (Chicago: University of Chicago Press, 1958).

66. Ernst Cassirer, *An Essay on Man: An Introduction to a Philosophy of Human Culture* (New Haven, Conn.: Yale University Press, 1944), 26.

67. Alfred North Whitehead, *Symbolism: Its Meaning and Effect* (New York: Putnam's, 1959), 8.

68. Ibid., 74, 66.

69. Ernst Cassirer, *Language and Myth,* (New York: Harper and Row, 1946), 8. Emphasis in original.

70. Cassirer, *Essay on Man,* 36.

71. Paul Ricoeur, *The Symbolism of Evil* (New York: Harper and Row, 1967), 15.

72. Robert Bellah, *Religion and Progress in Modern Asia* (New York: Harper and Row, 1965), 172.

73. Clifford Geertz, "Religion as a Cultural System," in *Anthropological Approaches to the Study of Religion,* ed. Michael Banton (New York: Harper and Row, 1965), 4.

74. Herbert W. Richardson, *Toward an American Theology* (New York: Harper and Row, 1964), 64.

75. Karl Marx, *Early Writings* (New York: McGraw Hill, 1964), 43.

76. Sigmund Freud, *Totem and Taboo: Resemblances Between the Psychic Lives of Savages and Neurotics* (New York: Buccaneer Books, 1989); *The Future of an Illusion* (New York: Norton, 1966).

77. Emile Durkheim, "L'individualisme et les intellectuels," *Revue Bleue* 10 (1898): 7–13.

78. Max Weber, *The Protestant Ethic and the Spirit of Capitalism* (New York: Simon and Schuster, 1985).

79. Robert N. Bellah, "Theology and Symbolic Realism," in Robin Gill, ed., *Theology and Sociology,* 124.

80. Robert N. Bellah, *Beyond Belief* (New York: Harper and Row, 1970), 245.

81. Liam Hudson, *The Cult of the Fact: A Psychologist's Autobiographical Critique of His Discipline* (New York: Harper and Row, 1972).

82. Max Black, *Models and Metaphors* (Ithaca, N.Y.: Cornell, 1962).

83. Ian G. Barbour, *Issues in Science and Religion* (London: SCM, 1966).

84. Karl Rahner, "The Theology of the Symbol," *Theological Investigations* (London: Darton, Longman and Todd, 1966), 4:221–52.

85. Michael G. Lawler, *Symbol and Sacrament: A Contemporary Sacramental Theology* (Omaha: Creighton University Press, 1995).

86. Ian T. Ramsey, *Religious Language* (London: SCM, 1959).

87. Bellah, "Theology and Symbolic Realism,"125.

88. Ibid., 124–25.

89. Robin Gill, *The Social Context of Theology,* 37.

90. Ibid.

91. Ibid., 39.

92. Maurice F. Wiles, "Does Christology Rest on a Mistake?" in S. W. Sykes and J. P. Clayton, ed., *Christ, Faith, and History* (Cambridge: Cambridge University Press, 1972), 8.

## Three / Sociology of Knowledge and Theology

1. Karl Marx, *Selected Writings* (New York: McGraw Hill, 1964), 75.

2. Anselm Strauss, ed., *The Social Psychology of George Herbert Mead* (Chicago: University of Chicago Press, 1964), 217.

3. George Herbert Mead, *Mind, Self, and Society* (Chicago: University of Chicago Press, 1934).

4. Strauss, *The Social Psychology,* 222.

5. Gibson Winter, *Elements for a Social Ethic: Scientific and Ethical Perspectives on Social Process* (New York: Macmillan, 1966), 23. See especially 14–33.

6. Georges Gurvitch, "Microsociology and Sociometry," *Sociometry* 12 (1949): 13.

7. Georges Gurvitch, *La vocation actuelle de la sociologie* (Paris: Presses Universitaires de France, 1950), 159.

8. Alfred Schutz, *Collected Papers,* vol. 2 (The Hague: Martinus Nijhoff, 1964–67), 161.

9. Ibid.

10. Schutz, *Collected Papers,* 1:174. He deals with this questions in three places: 1:150–203, 315 ff, and 352 ff.

11. Schutz, *Collected Papers,* 1:230.

12. Alfred North Whitehead, *Symbolism: Its Meaning and Effect* (New York: Putnam's, 1959), 8.

13. Thomas Luckmann, *The Invisible Religion: The Transformation of Symbols in Industrial Society* (New York: Macmillan, 1967), 45.

14. Winter, *Elements for a Social Ethic,* 131.

15. William James, *Principles of Psychology,* vol. 2 (New York: Holt and Co., 1923), 283–324.

16. Ibid., 292.

17. Ibid., 293.

18. Schutz, *Collected Papers,* 1:230.

19. See Ibid., 232–33.

20. Sumner, *Folkways,* esp. chap. 1.

21. This opinion was first enunciated by William Isaac Thomas in his *The Child in America: Behavior Problems and Programs* (New York: Alfred A. Knopf, 1928), 572. The term "Thomas Theorem" seems to have been coined by Robert K. Merton in *Social Theory and Social Structure* (Glencoe, Ill.: Free Press, 1949), 179.

22. Martin, *Reflections on Sociology and Theology,* 49.

23. Peter L. Berger, *The Sacred Canopy: Elements of a Sociological Theory of Religion* (New York: Doubleday and Company, 1967); Berger and Luckmann, *The Social Construction of Reality: A Treatise in the Sociology of Knowledge* (New York: Doubleday, 1966).

24. Berger and Luckmann, *The Social Construction of Reality,* 60.

25. Winter, *Elements for a Social Ethic,* 109.

26. The use of "culture" in this broad sense to refer to the totality of human products is adopted from the practice of American cultural anthropology. Sociologists have tended to use it in a sense restricted to symbolic spheres. The broader acceptation seems to be more appropriate to the argument of this section.

27. Martin, *Reflections on Sociology and Theology,* 48.

28. Berger and Luckmann, *The Social Construction of Reality,* 47–128; Berger, *The Sacred Canopy,* 8–14.

29. Eric Voegelin, *The New Science of Politics* (Chicago: University of Chicago Press, 1952), 27.

30. See Berger and Luckmann, *The Social Construction of Reality,* 129–73.

31. Berger, *The Sacred Canopy,* 187.

32. Ibid., 45. See also his *A Rumor of Angels: Modern Society and the Rediscovery of the Supernatural* (Garden City, N.Y.: Doubleday, 1969) 35–60, and his translation of the Catholic axiom *extra ecclesiam nulla salus* to the sociological "no plausibility without the appropriate plausibility structure," Ibid., 47.

33. See his *Die Wissenformen und die Gesellschaft* (Leipzig: Neuer Geist, 1926) and his *Die Formen des Wissens und die Bildung* (Bonn: Cohen, 1925).

34. Bernard J. F. Lonergan, *Method in Theology* (New York: Herder and Herder, 1972), 217.

35. Lonergan, *Insight,* 344. Emphasis added. See also *Method,* 217–19.

36. *Sermo 52,* 16, PL 38, 360. For a detailed analysis, see Victor White, *God the Unknown* (New York: Harper, 1956) and William Hill, *Knowing the Unknown God* (New York: Philosophical Library, 1971).

37. ST, 1, 3, preface.

38. Mannheim, *Ideology and Utopia,* 255.

39. Ibid., 106.

40. Georges Gurvitch, *The Social Frameworks of Knowledge,* trans. Margaret A. Thompson and Kenneth A. Thompson (Oxford: Basil Blackwell, 1971), 12. Emphasis added.

41. Theodore Roszak, *The Making of a Counter Culture* (New York: Doubleday, 1969), 215. Roszak goes on to argue that it is precisely the scientific search for objectivity that is at the root of widespread human alienation.

42. Martin, *Reflections on Sociology and Theology,* 90.

43. Mannheim, *Ideology and Utopia,* 264.

44. Doran, *Theology and the Dialectics of History,* 446.

45. Lonergan, *Method,* xi.

46. Mannheim, *Ideology and Utopia,* passim.

47. See, for instance, Karl Rahner and Herbert Vorgrimler, *Concise Theological Dictionary* (London: Burns and Oates, 1965), 456.

48. Anselm, *Proslogion,* c. 2. Quoted in Gordon D. Kaufman, *God and Problem* (Cambridge, Mass.: Harvard University Press, 1972), 90.

49. Karl Rahner and Herbert Vorgrimler, *Theological Dictionary* (New York: Herder and Herder, 1965), 456.

50. This word means to interpret, to place a certain meaning on. I use it to insinuate two connected meanings: first, the character of theologians as fashioners of meaning within the faith community; second, the character of theology as those meanings theologians socially construct, both that theology which preceded and

provided the foundation for sacred writings called scripture, and that theology which succeeded those writings.

51. Gordon D. Kaufman, *God the Problem* (Cambridge, Mass.: Harvard University Press, 1972), 20–21.

52. See Lonergan, *Method* and *Doctrinal Pluralism* (Milwaukee: Marquette University Press, 1971); David Tracy, *Blessed Rage for Order: The New Pluralism in Theology* (New York: Seabury, 1975), and *The Analogical Imagination: Christian Theology and the Culture of Pluralism* (New York: Crossroad, 1987).

53. John McQuarrie, *Principles of Christian Theology* (New York: Scribner's, 1977), 1; International Theological Commission, "Theses on the Relationship Between the Ecclesiastical Magisterium and Theology" (Washington: United States Catholic Conference, 1977), 15.

54. See, DV, 1–20; and Pontifical Biblical Commission, "The Interpretation of the Bible in the Church," *Origins* 23 (1994): 498–524.

55. See, for instance, James H. Ebner, *God Present as Mystery: A Search for Personal Meaning in Contemporary Theology* (Winona, Minn.: St. Mary's College Press, 1976); Karl Rahner, *Foundations of Christian Faith: An Introduction to the Idea of Christianity* (New York: Seabury, 1978); Michael H. Barnes, *In the Presence of Mystery: An Introduction to the Story of Human Religiousness* (Mystic: Twenty-Third, 1984); Elizabeth A. Johnson, *She Who Is: The Mystery of God in Feminist Theological Discourse* (New York: Crossroad, 1992). Though he is not a Catholic theologian, Paul Tillich could be added to this list. See his *Systematic Theology,* I (Chicago: University of Chicago Press, 1951).

56. Karl Rahner, "Concerning the Relationship Between Nature and Grace," and "Some Implications of the Scholastic Concept of Uncreated Grace," *Theological Investigations* (London: Darton, Longman and Todd, 1961), 1:297–346.

57. Gregory Baum, *Truth Beyond Relativism: Karl Mannheim's Sociology of Knowledge* (Milwaukee: Marquette University Press, 1977), 76.

58. DV, 2.

59. Cyprian, *De Zelo et Livore* 12, PL 4, 646.

60. Cyprian, *De Bono Patientiae* 9, PL 4, 628.

61. DS, 301.

62. See Alfred Schutz, *Collected Papers,* 3 vols.; Mannheim, *Ideology and Utopia;* Berger and Luckmann, *The Social Construction of Reality.*

63. Mannheim, *Ideology and Utopia,* 296–97.

64. Ibid., 47.

65. Jürgen Habermas, *Theory and Practice* (Boston: Beacon Press, 1973), 79–80.

66. Baum, *Truth Beyond Relativism,* 43.

67. AAS 73 (1981), 4, 393.

68. Ibid., 5, 393.

69. John Paul II, *Redemptoris Missio,* AAS 83 (1991): 55.

70. Ibid., 56.

71. Jacques Dupuis, *Toward a Christian Theology of Religious Pluralism* (Maryknoll, N.Y.: Orbis, 1997), 365–66.

72. Pontifical Council for Inter-religious Dialogue and the Congregation for Evangelization of Peoples, *Dialogue and Proclamation,* 49, in *Osservatore Romano,* July 1, 1991.

73. See Johnson, *She Who Is,* 104–23.

74. Kaufman, *God the Problem,* 27.

75. Pierre Thibault, *Savoir et pouvoir: philosophie thomiste et politique aux XIX siècle* (Quebec: Presse de l'Université Laval, 1972).

76. Walter Kasper, *Theology and Church* (New York: Crossroad, 1989), 1.

77. Congregation for the Doctrine of the Faith, *Declaration on the Question of the Admission of Women to the Ministerial Priesthood* (Washington: United States Catholic Conference, 1977).

78. Baum, *Truth Beyond Relativism,* 53.

79. Ibid., 31.

80. Bryan Wilson, *Religion in Secular Society* (London: Pelican, 1969), 97.

81. Mannheim, *Ideology and Utopia,* 106.

82. AAS 73 (1981): 4, 393.

83. Ibid., 5, 393.

## Four / Theology, Sociology, and Scripture

1. What follows in this section was provoked by conversations with my friend and colleague, Bruce Malina, who is the pioneer of the social scientific approach to biblical interpretation. He provided me with a copy of an essay, "From the Jesus Faction to the Synoptic Gospels: The Synoptic Gospels as Third Generation Phenomena," which was delivered at the SBL/AAR Regional Meeting, Omaha, April 19–20, 2002, and from which this section received its impetus.

2. Marcus L. Hansen, *The Problem of the Third Generation Immigrant* (Rock Island, Ill.: Augustana Historical Society, 1938), 9.

3. Will Herberg, *Protestant, Catholic, Jew: An Essay in American Religious Sociology* (New York: Doubleday, 1955), 40–54.

4. Malina, "From the Jesus Faction," 5.

5. Benedict T. Viviano, *The Kingdom of God in History* (Wilmington, Del.: Michael Glazier, 1988), 13.

6. Hansen, *The Problem of the Third Generation Immigrant,* 9.

7. I reiterate the meaning of this word: to interpret, to place a certain meaning on. I use it again here to insinuate two connected meanings: first, the character of the theologian as construction worker within the Church; second, the character of theology as social construction, both that theology which preceded writings that came to be called scripture as well as that theology which succeeded them.

8. David H. Kelsey, *The Uses of Scripture in Recent Theology* (Philadelphia: Fortress, 1975).

9. See DV, 19.

10. Fiction: literary narrative which portrays imaginary characters or events.

11. The terms "foundational" and "dependent" revelation are common theological terms. See Paul Tillich, *Systematic Theology* (Chicago: University of Chicago Press, 1967), I, 126–28; Gerald O'Collins, *Theology and Revelation* (Notre Dame, Ind.: Fides, 1968), 45–47.

12. DV, 19.

13. I use this term to mean not a single sentence but the full literary unit, a passage or even an entire book.

14. PBC, III, C, 1, 517.

15. PO, 18.

16. James Barr, *The Bible in the Modern World* (London: SCM, 1973), 118.

17. Karl Rahner, *Inspiration in the Bible* (New York: Herder, 1961), 47–50.

18. PBC, III, B, 1, 515.

19. Roger Haight, *Dynamics of Theology* (New York: Paulist, 1990), 97.

20. PBC, 505.

21. John McQuarrie, *Principles of Christian Theology,* second edition, (New York: Scribners, 1977), 1; International Theological Commission, "Theses on the Relationship Between the Ecclesiastical Magisterium and Theology," Thesis 6, 2 (Washington: United States Catholic Conference, 1977).

22. See Karl Rahner, "Experiences of a Catholic Theologian," *Theological Studies* 61 (2000), 3–15; Tracy, *The Analogical Imagination.*

23. ST, 1, 1, 1.

24. See Frank Whaling, "The Development of the Word 'Theology,'" *Scottish Journal of Theology* 34 (1981): 289–312; John J. Burkhard, "The Use of Scripture in Theology and Preaching: Experience, Interpretation and Ecclesial Identity," *New Theology Review* 8 (1995): 30–44.

25. ST, 1,1, 2.

26. ST, 1,1,10.

27. The official Catholic preference for the literal meaning is universally ignored in the much-ballyhooed *Catechism of the Catholic Church,* which indulges freely in spiritual meanings with no reference to the literal. See Gerard S. Sloyan, "The Use of the Bible in a New Resource Book," *Biblical Theology Bulletin* 25 (1995), 3–13.

28. PBC, 512.

29. This twentieth-century shift is best described by Protestant theologian Emil Brunner in his *Truth as Encounter* (Philadelphia: Westminster, 1964), but the Second Vatican Council approved it as a thoroughly Catholic shift. See *Dei Verbum,* the Dogmatic Constitution on Divine Revelation.

30. DV, 2.

31. Haight, *Dynamics of Theology,* 76.

32. Lonergan, *Insight.*

33. See Lawler, *Symbol and Sacrament,* 5–28, for the implications of symbol; George Klubertanz, *Saint Thomas Aquinas on Analogy* (Chicago: Loyola University

Press, 1960), esp. 270–71, and David Tracy, *The Analogical Imagination* for the classic Catholic doctrine on analogy.

34. Haight, *Dynamics of Theology,* 79.

35. DV, 12.

36. Frances Young, *Virtuoso Theology: The Bible and Interpretation* (Cleveland: Pilgrim Press, 1993), 175. The British edition of this book was entitled *The Art of Performance: Towards a Theology of Holy Scripture* (London: Darton, Longman and Todd, 1990). I cite from the U.S. edition.

37. See J. David Pleins, "How Ought We to Think About Poverty? Rethinking the Diversity of the Hebrew Bible," *Irish Theological Quarterly* (1994): 280–86.

38. David Tracy, "On Reading the Scriptures Theologically," in *Theology and Dialogue: Essays in Conversation with George Lindbeck,* ed. Bruce D. Marshall (Notre Dame, Ind.: University of Notre Dame Press, 1990), 43.

39. Ernst Käsemann, "The New Testament Canon and the Unity of the Church," *Essays on New Testament Themes* (London: SCM, 1964), 103–4.

40. Augustine, *Sermo 52,* c. 6, 16, PL 38, 360.

41. ST, 1, 1, 8 ad 2.

42. Mannheim, *Ideology and Utopia,* 252–53.

43. PBC, 521.

44. *Providentissimus Deus,* AAS 26 (1893–94): 283; see also Vatican II's Decree on Priestly Formation, OT 16.

45. Lisa Sowle Cahill, "Is Catholic Ethics Biblical?" Warren Lecture Series in Catholic Studies, No. 20 (University of Tulsa), 5–6.

46. See, for instance, Edward Schillebeeckx, *Interim Reports on the Books Jesus and Christ* (New York: Seabury, 1979), 142; David Tracy, *Blessed Rage for Order.*

47. See Frances Young, *The Theology of the Pastoral Letters* (Cambridge: Cambridge University Press, 1994), 145–61.

48. PBC, 520.

49. Hans-Georg Gadamer, *Truth and Method* (New York: Crossroad, 1982), 325–41; see Edward Schillebeeckx, *God the Future of Man* (New York: Sheed and Ward, 1968), 7–8.

50. Tillich, *Systematic Theology,* 1:63.

51. Ibid., 1:64.

52. Haight, *Dynamics of Theology,* 192.

53. Kelsey, *The Uses of Scripture,* 186.

54. PBC, 521.

55. See, for example, Bruce J. Malina and Richard L. Rohrbaugh, *Social Science Commentary on the Synoptic Gospels* (Minneapolis: Augsburg, 1992), 50.

56. Karl Rahner, "Current Problems in Christology," *Theological Investigations* (London: Darton, Longman and Todd, 1965), 1:150.

57. Kelsey, *The Uses of Scripture,* 196.

58. See the discussion in Hans Kung, "Early Catholicism in the New Testament as a Problem in Controversial Theology," *The Council in Action: Theological*

*Reflections on the Second Vatican Council* (New York: Sheed and Ward, 1963), 159–95.

59. Cahill, "Is Catholic Ethics Biblical?" 5–6.

60. Frances Young, *Virtuoso Theology,* 3.

61. *Church Dogmatics,* 3:3,50.

## Five / The Church Emerging in the Human Community

1. Patrick Granfield, "The Rise and Fall of *Societas Perfecta,*" *Concilium* 157, Peter Huizing and Knewt Walf, eds.(New York: Seabury, 1982), 3.

2. AAS 54 (1962): 792; cp. GS, 62.

3. AAS 56 (1964): 621.

4. *The Documents of Vatican II,* ed. Walter M. Abbott (London: Chapman, 1966), 3–4.

5. LG, 48.

6. Yves Congar, "Reception as an Ecclesiological Reality," in *Election and Consensus in the Church,* ed. Giuseppe Alberigo and Anton Weiler *Concilium* 77 (1972): 62.

7. Edward Kilmartin, "Reception in History: An Ecclesiological Phenomenon and Its Significance," *Journal of Ecumenical Studies* 21 (1984): 34.

8. Gerard Philips, *L'Eglise et son mystère au IIe Concile du Vatican* (Paris: Desclée, 1966), I, 7, 59 and II, 24, 54, 159.

9. CL, 18.

10. See its Final Report, "The Church, in the Word of God, Celebrates the Mysteries of Christ," II, C, 1.

11. N. 1, in *Catholic International* 3 (1992): 761.

12. Jerome Hamer, *The Church Is a Communion* (New York: Sheed and Ward, 1965); see also Yves Congar, *Divided Christendom. A Catholic Study of the Problem of Reunion,* trans. M. Bousfield (London: Bles, 1939); Henri de Lubac *Catholicism: A Study of Dogma in Relation to the Corporate Destiny of Mankind,* trans. L. Sheppard (New York: Longman's, Green, 1950); Marie Joseph Le Gouillou, *Mission et unité. Les exigences de la communion* (Paris: Desclée, 1960); Gustave Martelet, *Les idées maîtresses de Vatican II* (Paris: Desclée, 1966).

13. Yves Congar, "The People of God," in *Vatican II: An Interfaith Appraisal,* ed. John H. Miller (Notre Dame, Ind.: University of Notre Dame Press, 1966), 199.

14. Edward Schillebeeckx, *L'Eglise du Christ et l'homme d'aujourd'hui selon Vatican II* (Paris: Mappus, 1965).

15. LG, 1.

16. Ibid., 8.

17. Ibid., 48 and 49.

18. *Acta Synodalia,* II/1, 455.

19. *AAS* 55 (1963): 848.

20. *The Tablet,* November 7, 1987, 1203.

21. See *Confessions* I, 1, PL 32, 661.

22. Walter Kasper, *Theology and Church* (London: SCM, 1989) 151.

23. Pier Cesare Bori, *Koinonia: l'idea della communione nell' ecclesiologia recente et nel Nuovo Testamento* (Brescia: Paideia, 1972), 107–19.

24. LG, 2.

25. AG, 3.

26. LG, 4.

27. Ibid., 33–38.

28. See *The Documents of Vatican II,* ed. Abbott, 99.

29. GS, 32.

30. LG, 9; cp. AG, 19.

31. CL, 19.

32. *The Church is a Communion,* 175. Emphasis in original.

33. Jürgen Moltmann, *The Spirit of Life: A Universal Affirmation* (Minneapolis: Fortress, 1992), 118.

34. LG, 4.

35. Ibid., 9.

36. See, for instance, Mannes D. Koster, *Ekklesiologie im Werden* (Paderborn: Schöning, 1940), who argues that people of God is the best image of the church.

37. Robert Kress, *The Church: Communion, Sacrament, Communication* (New York: Paulist, 1985), 66.

38. LG, 9.

39. Karl Rahner, "Membership of the Church According to the Teaching of Pius XII's Encyclical *Mystici Corporis,*'" in *Theological Investigations* (Baltimore: Helicon, 1967), 2:83.

40. Yves M. J. Congar, "The People of God," in *Vatican II: An Interfaith Appraisal,* ed. Miller, 199.

41. LG, 9.

42. Ibid., 10.

43. Ibid., 9.

44. SC, 5.

45. LG, 9.

46. Neils Dahl, *Des Volk Gottes* (Oslo: Dybwad, 1941), 278.

47. Here I abstract completely from the disputed questions as to which Letter(s) the Apostle Paul actually wrote. It makes no difference to any thesis in this argument.

48. Heinrich Schlier, "Leib Christi," in *Lexicon für Theologie und Kirche,* ed. Joseph Hofer and Karl Rahner (Freiburg: Herder, 1957–65), VI, 908.

49. LG, 7.

50. See Jean-Marie R. Tillard, *Church of Churches: The Ecclesiology of Communion* (Collegeville, Minn.: Liturgical Press, 1992), 37–38.

51. LG, 26.

52. N. 11, in *Catholic International* 3 (1992): 764.

53. LG, 23; cp. Can 386.

54. John Paul II, "Address to the Roman Curia," *AAS* 83 (1981): 745–47.

55. See "The Church: Local and Universal," a study commissioned and received by the Joint Working Group between the Roman Catholic Church and the World Council of Churches (Geneva: World Council of Churches, 1990).

56. See "L'Eglise locale parmi les autres églises locales," *Irenikon* 43 (1970): 512.

57. LG, 26.

58. Lucien Cerfaux, "Les images symboliques de l'eglise dans le Nouveau Testament," in *Vatican II: Textes et Commentaires* (Paris: Cerf, 1967), 256.

59. Bernard Cooke, "Synoptic Presentation of the Eucharist as Covenant Sacrifice," *Theological Studies* 21 (1960): 25; see also X. Leon-Léon-Dufour, "Prenez! Ceci est mon corps pour vous," *Nouvelle Revue Théologique* 104 (1982): 225–27.

60. *Enarr. in Pss. 56, 1*, PL 36, 662; compare *Sermo 341*, PL 39, 1499–5000; *Sermo 455*, PL 38, 265; *Enarr. in Pss. 60, 2–3*, PL 36, 724.

61. LG, 12.

62. I am fully aware of the contrived nature of the word "communional." I select it deliberately over "communal" to provoke reflection on, first, the word and, then, the dynamic reality of the church which is communion.

63. See John D. Zizioulas, *Being as Communion* (New York: St. Vladimir's Seminary Press, 1985), 209–14.

64. Miller, *Vatican II,* 200.

65. In his *Vrai et fausse réforme dans l'église* (Paris: Cerf, 1950), 43, n. 35, Congar states it is not certain who coined the phrase *ressourcement,* but in the same book he says it was Pope Pius XI who first called for a return to the sources (p. 337). He also traces the origin of the process and the phrase to a passage from Charles Péguy (602), a quotation that we will have cause to quote again in chapter 6: "a [true] revolution is a call from a less perfect tradition to a more perfect tradition, a call from a shallower tradition to a deeper tradition, . . . an investigation into deeper sources; in the literal sense of the word a 're-source.' " For an excellent exposition of *ressourcement,* see Marcellino D'Ambrosio, "Ressourcement Theology, Aggiornamento, and the Hermeneutics of Tradition," *Communio* 18 (1991): 530–55.

66. LG, 8.

67. Ibid., 10.

68. Ibid., 12.

69. DV, 2.

70. See also Deut 26:5–9.

71. Gustavo Gutiérrez, *The Power of the Poor in History* (Maryknoll, N.Y.: Orbis, 1983), 8.

72. Ibid., 13.

73. *Joint Declaration on the Doctrine of Justification* (Strasbourg: Institute for Ecumenical Research, 1997).

74. DS, 1532.

75. I use this contrived term throughout to underscore the demand made on those who say they are followers of the Christ to live a life like Christ, a life that acknowledges reciprocation between God and the least and acts accordingly.

76. Xavier Leon-Léon-Dufour, *Sharing the Eucharistic Bread: the Witness of the New Testament,* trans. Matthew O'Connell (New York: Paulist, 1987), 82–95.

77. John Paul II, CL, 18.

78. Par. 1, in *Catholic International* 3 (1992): 761.

79. See its Final Report, *The Church, in the Word of God, Celebrates the Mysteries of Christ,* II, C, 1.

80. Gerard Philips, *L'Eglise et son mystère au IIe Concile du Vatican* (Paris: Desclée, 1966), I, 7, 59 and II, 24, 54, 159.

81. See Jerome Hamer, *The Church Is a Communion* (New York: Sheed and Ward, 1964); Michael G. Lawler and Thomas J. Shanahan, *Church: A Spirited Communion* (Collegeville, Minn.: Liturgical Press, 1995).

82. See Henri de Lubac, *Corpus Mysticum: l'eucharistie et l'église au moyen âge* (Paris: Aubier, 1944).

83. LG, 7. Emphasis added.

84. See Michael G. Lawler, *Symbol and Sacrament: A Contemporary Sacramental Theology* (Omaha: Creighton University Press, 1995), 29–62.

85. See David N. Power, *The Eucharistic Mystery: Revitalizing the Tradition* (New York: Crossroad, 1992), 30–32.

86. Clement of Alexandria, *Paedagogus* 2, 12, PG 8, 541.

87. Puebla Final Document, n. 382, 707, 733. The Puebla conference is analyzed in contextual depth in John Eagleson and Philip Scharper, eds., *Puebla and Beyond* (Maryknoll, N.Y.: Orbis, 1979).

88. Tissa Balasuriya, *The Eucharist and Human Liberation* (Maryknoll, N.Y.: Orbis, 1979), 22. Emphasis added.

89. LG, 8.

90. *De Zelo et Livore* 12, PL 4, 646.

91. *De Bono Patientiae* 9, PL 4, 628.

92. CL, 32.

93. I borrow the term "underside" from Jorg Rieger, *Remember the Poor: The Challenge to Theology in the Twenty-First Century* (Harrisburg, Pa.: Trinity Press International, 1998), 1–5.

94. These terms are derived from Doran, *Theology and the Dialectics of History,* 418–19.

95. See Karl Rahner, *The Church and the Sacraments, Inquiries* (New York: Herder and Herder, 1964), 191–299; Otto Semmelroth, "The Integral Idea of the Church," *Theology Today: Renewal In Dogma,* ed. J. Feiner (Milwaukee: Bruce, 1964); Avery Dulles, *Models of the Church* (New York: Doubleday, 1974).

96. LG, 48.

97. Doran, *Theology and the Dialectics of History,* 420.

98. AAS 38 (1946): 149.

99. LG, 31.

100. AAS 64 (1972): 208.

101. CL, 15.

102. See, for example, "Unity in the Church's Mission with Diversity in Apostolates," *L'Osservatore Romano* 723, n. 8, February 22, 1982, 6; "On Liberation Theology," *Origins* 8 (1979): 600; "The Church in Rural Africa," *Origins* 10 (1980): 23; "Specialis Filia Romanae Ecclesiae," *Catholic International* 4 (1993): 5.

103. See, for instance, CL, 4; also his Address to the Bishops of Switzerland and his Address to the Priests of Switzerland, AAS 71 (1985): 56, 64, 67.

104. Karl Rahner, "Current Problems in Christology," *Theological Investigations* (London: Darton, Longman and Todd, 1965), 1:150.

105. *Council Daybook*, Session 3, 303–4.

106. Gerard Philips, *L'Eglise et son mystère au IIe Concile du Vatican* (Paris: Desclée, 1966), I, 7, 59 and II, 24, 54, 159.

107. CL, 18.

108. *Catholic International* 3 (1992): 761.

109. LG, 1.

110. LG, 48.

111. Cyprian, *De Zelo et Livore*, 12, PL 4, 646.

112. CL, 32.

## Six / Reception and *Sensus Fidei*

1. See John E. Thiel, *Senses of Tradition: Continuity and Development in the Catholic Faith* (New York: Oxford University Press, 2000), 100–128.

2. Karl Rahner, "Practical Theology Within the Totality of Theological Disciplines," *Theological Investigations* (London: Darton, Longman, and Todd, 1972), 9:102. Emphasis in original.

3. Ibid., 105.

4. Cited in Yves M. J. Congar, *Vrai et fausse réforme dans l'église* (Paris: Cerf, 1950), 43, n. 35.

5. See, for instance, Joseph Doré, "De la responsabilité des théologiens dans l'église," *Nouvelle Revue Théologique* 125 (2003): 3–20.

6. GS, 62.

7. In this book, I embrace the ambiguity of the word "virtual," and argue that it can be specified only by dialogue and consensus in the Church. I have no doubt that 86 percent of any population is virtually all of it, but is 80 percent or 75 percent or 68 percent? Only dialogue and consensus can decide.

8. The foundational work on reception was done by Yves Congar, "La réception comme réalité ecclésiologique," *Revue des Sciences Philosophiques et Théologiques* 56 (1972): 369–403, and Alois Grillmeier, "Konzil und Rezeption: Methodische Bemerkungen zu einem Thema der ökumenischen Discussion der Gegenwart," *Theologie und Philosophie* 45 (1970): 321–52. See additional bibliography in Richard R.

Gaillardetz, *Teaching with Authority: A Theology of the Magisterium in the Church* (Collegeville, Minn.: Liturgical Press, 1997), 252–53.

9. See Second Vatican Council, DV 11–20; Congregation for the Doctrine of the Faith, *Mysterium Ecclesiae*, 5, AAS 65 (1973): 402–3; John Zizioulas, "The Theological Problem of Reception," *Centro Pro Unione*, 26 (Fall 1984): 6.

10. Herman J. Pottmeyer, "A New Phase in the Reception of Vatican II: Twenty Years of Interpretation of the Council," in *The Reception of Vatican II*, ed. Giuseppe Alberigo, Jean-Pierre Jossua, and Joseph A. Komonchak (Washington, D.C.: Catholic University of America Press, 1987), 27–43.

11. Giuseppe Alberigo, "The Christian Situation after Vatican II," in *The Reception of Vatican II*, ed. Alberigo, Jossua, and Komonchak, 3.

12. This claim is explained in detail in Herman Sieben, "On the Relationship between the Council and the Pope up to the Middle of the Fifth Century," *Concilium* 167 (1983): 19–24.

13. Walter M. Abbott, ed., *The Documents of Vatican II* (London: Chapman, 1966), 99.

14. GS, 32.

15. Eusebius, *The History of the Church from Christ to Constantine*, trans. G. A. Williamson (New York: New York University Press, 1966), 183.

16. J. Stevenson, *A New Eusebius* (London: SPCK, 1957), 356–57.

17. See Lawler, *Symbol and Sacrament*, 222–23.

18. *Epist. Ad Magnesios*, 2, PG 5, 758; *Epist. Ad Smyrneos*, 8–9, PG 5, 714; *Epist. Ad Polycarpum*, PG 5, 718.

19. *Epist. Ad Trall.*, 12, PG 5, 683.

20. *Epist. Ad Smyrneos*, 8, PG 5, 714.

21. Cyprian, *Epist. LXV*, 3, PL 4, 396.

22. Cyprian, *Epist. LXIX*, 8, PL 4, 406.

23. John D. Zizioulas, "The Development of Conciliar Structures to the Time of the First Ecumenical Council," in World Council of Churches, *Councils and the Ecumenical Movement* (Geneva: WCC, 1968), 41.

24. LG, 26.

25. Eusebius, *History of the Church*, 233.

26. Giuseppe Alberigo, "The Christian Situation after Vatican II," in *The Reception of Vatican II*, ed. Alberigo et al., 5.

27. Jerome, *Dialogus Contra Luciferianos*, 19, PL 23, 172.

28. Yves Congar lists a whole series of examples of reception in his classic essay "Reception as an Ecclesiological Reality," in *Election and Consensus in the Church*, ed. Giuseppe Alberigo and Anton Weiler *Concilium* 77 (1972): 45–58.

29. Alois Grillmeier, "The Reception of Chalcedon in the Roman Catholic Church," *The Ecumenical Review* 22 (1970): 383–11.

30. Richard Hanson, "The Achievement of Orthodoxy in the Fourth Century A.D.," in *The Making of Orthodoxy*, ed. Rowan Williams (Cambridge: Cambridge University Press, 1989), 151.

31. Zizioulas, "The Theological Problem of Reception," 4.

32. See Yves Congar, *After Nine Hundred Years* (Westport, Conn.: Greenwood Press, 1959); Jean-Marie R. Tillard, *The Bishop of Rome* (Wilmington, Del.: Michael Glazier, 1983); J. Michael Miller, *What Are They Saying about Papal Primacy?* (New York; Paulist, 1983); Patrick Granfield, *The Limits of the Papacy* (London: Darton, Longman, and Todd, 1987); Michael G. Lawler and Thomas J. Shanahan, *Church: A Spirited Communion* (Collegeville, Minn.: Liturgical Press, 1995), 88–113.

33. Congar, "Reception as Reality," 51.

34. See Yves Congar, *Power and Poverty in the Church* (Baltimore: Helicon, 1964), 40–134.

35. See J. Robert Dionne, *The Papacy and the Church* (New York: Philosophical Library, 1987).

36. John T. Noonan Jr., "Development in Moral Doctrine," *Theological Studies* 54 (1993): 662.

37. DS 906.

38. DS 716.

39. DS 753.

40. Noonan, "Development in Moral Doctrine," 664.

41. Cited in Charles E. Curran, "Authority and Dissent in the Roman Catholic Church," in *Vatican Authority and American Catholic Dissent,* ed. William W. May (New York: Crossroad, 1987), 29.

42. Pius IX, *Quanta Cura,* in Claudia Carlen Ihm, *The Papal Encyclicals 1740–1878* (Raleigh: McGrath Publishing, 1981), 383.

43. Brian Tierney, *Origins of Papal Infallibility 1150–1350: A Study on the Concepts of Infallibility, Sovereignty, and Tradition in the Middle Ages* (Leiden: Brill, 1972), 277.

44. UR, 3.

45. For discussion of these and other examples of change in Catholic moral teachings, see Charles Curran, ed., *Change in Official Catholic Moral Teachings* (New York: Paulist, 2003).

46. Ladislas M. Orsy, "Reception of Law," in *Encyclopedia of Catholicism,* ed. Richard P. McBrien (San Francisco: Harper Collins, 1995), 1082.

47. Margaret A. Farley, "Moral Discourse in the Public Arena," in *Vatican Authority and American Catholic Dissent,* ed. William W. May (New York: Crossroad, 1987), 177.

48. Ibid.

49. Thiel, *Senses of Tradition,* 47.

50. John Henry Newman, *On Consulting the Faithful in Matters of Doctrine* (New York: Sheed and Ward, 1961), 73.

51. Jean Guitton, *The Church and the Laity* (New York: Alba House, 1965), 29.

52. John Henry Newman, trans., *Select Treatises of Saint Athanasius in Controversy with the Arians* (London: Longmans Green, 1903), 261.

53. Samuel D. Femiano, *Infallibility of the Laity* (New York: Herder and Herder, 1967), 23.

54. Yves Congar, *Lay People in the Church* (Westminster, Md.: Newman, 1967), 288.

55. Vincent of Lerins, *Commonitorium Primum* 2, PL 50, 640.

56. ST, IIa-IIae, 2, 3, ad 2. See J. de Guibert, "A propos des textes de Saint Thomas sur la foi qui discerne," *Révue des Sciences Religieuses* 9 (1919), 30–44; C. H. Joyce, "La foi qui discerne d'après Saint Thomas," *Révue des Sciences Religieuses* 6 (1916): 433–55.

57. Cited in Avery Dulles, "*Sensus Fidelium,*" in *America,* November 1, 1986, 240.

58. DS 3074.

59. Augustine, *De Praed. Sanct.,* 14, 27, PL 44, 980.

60. LG, 12. Emphasis added.

61. FC, 5. Emphasis added.

62. Pottmeyer, "A New Phase in the Reception of Vatican II," 30.

63. Augustine, *De Baptismo,* VII, 53, PL 43, 243.

64. Pope Leo the Great, *Epist. 14,* 2, PL 54, 672.

65. Pope Gelasius, *Epist. XIII,* PL 59, 63.

66. See Gerard Bartelink, "The Use of the Words *Electio* and *Consensus* in the Church (Until about 600)," *Concilium* 77 (1972): 147–54.

67. LG 12, in Austin Flannery, *Vatican Council II: Constitutions, Decrees, Declarations* (Dublin: Dominican Publications, 1996), 17.

68. See, for instance, DS 3011 and 3065; LG 18, 22, 25.

69. Austin Flannery, *Vatican Council II: The Conciliar and Postconciliar Documents* (Collegeville, Minn.: Liturgical Press, 1992), 363.

70. Francis A. Sullivan, *Magisterium: Teaching Authority in the Catholic Church* (Dublin: Gill and Macmillan, 1985), 164.

71. Yves Congar, "Reception as an Ecclesiological Reality," *Concilium* 77 (1965): 60.

72. See, for example, Tillard, *Church of Churches;* Lawler and Shanahan, *Church: A Spirited Communion;* Dennis M. Doyle, *Communion Ecclesiology* (Maryknoll, N.Y.: Orbis, 2000).

73. Sullivan, *Magisterium,* 112.

74. Congar, "Reception as an Ecclesiological Reality," 62.

75. Edward Kilmartin, "Reception in History: An Ecclesiological Phenomenon and Its Significance," *Journal of Ecumenical Studies* 21 (1984): 34.

76. LG, 12.

77. Ibid., 25.

78. Walter Kasper, *Theology and Church* (New York: Crossroad, 1989), 1.

79. See Congregation for the Doctrine of the Faith, *Mysterium Ecclesiae, 5,* in AAS 65 (1973): 402–32.

80. GS, 4.

81. Ibid., 62.

82. Ibid., 36.

83. Ibid., 62.

84. FC, 5.

85. Martin, *Reflections on Sociology and Theology,* 69.

86. Gill, *Churchgoing and Christian Ethics,* 1. Emphasis added.

87. LG, 12.

88. Pius XII, *Divino Afflante Spiritu,* AAS 35 (1943): 297–325; Pontifical Biblical Commission, *Instructio de Historica Evangeliorum Veritate,* AAS 56 (1964): 712–18; Second Vatican Council, *Dogmatic Constitution on Divine Revelation,* in Austin Flannery, ed., *Vatican Council II: The Conciliar and Postconciliar Documents* (Collegeville, Minn.: Liturgical Press, 1992), 750–65; Pontifical Biblical Commission, *The Interpretation of the Bible in the Church,* Origins, January 6, 1994.

89. See Karl Rahner, "Current Problems in Christology," *Theological Investigations* (London: Darton, Longman, and Todd, 1965), 1:150.

90. Avery Dulles, *"Sensus Fidelium,"* in *America,* November 1, 1986, 242.

91. DS 1532.

92. Juan Alfaro, "Faith," in *Sacramentum Mundi: An Encyclopedia of Theology* (New York: Herder, 1968), II: 315.

93. *Joint Declaration on the Doctrine of Justification* (Strasbourg: Institute for Ecumenical Research, 1997), 61.

94. Yves Congar, *Lay People in the Church* (London: Chapman, 1957), 51.

95. See Gerard Philips, "Dogmatic Constitution on the Church: History of the Constitution," in *Commentary on the Documents of Vatican II,* ed. Herbert Vorgrimler (London: Burns and Oates, 1966), 107.

96. Cited from Yves Congar, "Moving Towards a Pilgrim Church," in *Vatican II Revisited: By Those Who Were There,* ed. Alberic Stacpoole (Minneapolis: Winston, 1986), 135.

97. AAS 55 (1963): 848.

98. *The Tablet,* November 7, 1987, 1203.

99. LG, 26.

100. Ibid., 15.

101. Anglican-Roman Catholic International Commission (ARCIC), *The Final Report* (London: SPCK, 1982), 5.

102. Cited from *L'Osservatore Romano,* English Edition, July 29, 1971. This phrase, "the Church is a communion," was the title of an earlier treatise by Jerome Hamer (New York: Sheed and Ward, 1965).

103. Ibid., July 28, 1976.

104. Ibid., August 26, 1976.

105. CL, 18.

106. *Catholic International,* 3 (1992): 761, n. 1.

107. See its final report, "The Church, in the Word of God, Celebrates the Mysteries of Christ," 2, C, 1.

108. Gerard Philips, *L'Eglise et son mystère au IIe Concile du Vatican* (Paris: Desclée, 1966), I: 7, and 59, II: 24, 54, and 159.

109. Yves Congar, "The People of God," in *Vatican II: An Interfaith Appraisal,* ed. John H. Miller (Notre Dame, Ind.: University of Notre Dame Press, 1966), 199.

110. Edward Schillebeeckx, *L'Eglise du Christ et l'homme aujourd'hui selon Vatican II* (Paris: Mappus, 1965).

111. LG, 12. Emphasis added.

112. Cited from *L'Osservatore Romano,* English edition, July 29, 1971.

113. *Catholic International,* 3 (1992): 761, n. 1.

114. See the Synod's Final Report, "The Church, in the Word of God, Celebrates the Mysteries of Christ," 2, C, 1.

## Seven / Sociology, Divorce and Remarriage, Contraception

1. Patrick H. McNamara, *Conscience First: Tradition Second* (Albany: State University of New York Press, 1992); Robert A. Ludwig, *Reconstructing Catholicism for a New Generation* (New York: Crossroad, 1995); William V. D'Antonio, James D. Davidson, Dean R. Hoge, Ruth A. Wallace, *Laity American and Catholic: Transforming the Church* (Kansas City: Sheed and Ward 1996); James D. Davidson, Andrea S. Williams, Richard A. Lamanna, Jan Stenftenagel, Kathleen Maas Weigert, William J. Whalen, and Patricia Wittberg, *The Search for Common Ground: What Unites and Divides Catholic Americans* (Huntingdon, Ind.: Our Sunday Visitor, 1997); William V. D'Antonio, James D. Davidson, Dean R. Hoge, and Katherine Meyer, *American Catholics: Gender, Generation, and Commitment* (Lanham, Md.: Rowman and Littlefield, 2001); Dean R. Hoge, William D. Dinges, Mary Johnson, and Juan L. Gonzales Jr., *Young Adult Catholics: Religion in the Culture of Choice* (Notre Dame, Ind.: University of Notre Dame Press, 2001).

2. D'Antonio et al., 43.

3. George H. Gallup Jr., *Religion in America 1996* (Princeton: Princeton Religion Research Center, 1996), 44.

4. D'Antonio et al., *American Catholics,* 43.

5. Ibid. 76.

6. Hoge et al., *Young Adult Catholics,* 59–60.

7. See, for instance, Michael Hornsby-Smith, *Roman Catholicism in England: Customary Catholicism and Transformation of Religious Authority* (Cambridge: Cambridge University Press, 1991); Timothy J. Buckley, *What Binds Marriage?: Roman Catholic Theology in Practice* (London: Chapman, 1997); John Fulton, ed., *Young Catholics at the New Millennium: The Religion and Morality of Young Adults in Western Countries* (Dublin: University College Press, 2000).

8. See Judith S. Wallerstein and Joan B. Kelly, *Surviving the Breakup: How Children and Parents Cope with Divorce* (New York: Basic Books, 1980); Judith S.

Wallerstein and Sandra Blakeslee, *Second Chances: Men, Women, and Children a De-cade After Divorce* (Boston: Houghton Mifflin, 1989); Judith S. Wallerstein, Julia M. Lewis, and Sandra Blakeslee, *The Unexpected Legacy of Divorce: A 25 Year Land-mark Study* (New York: Hyperion, 2000); Andrew J. Cherlin, P. L. Chase-Lansdale, and C. McRae, "Effects of Parental Divorce on Mental Health Throughout the Life Course," *American Sociological Review* 63 (1988): 239–49; N. Zill and C. Schoen-born, *Developmental, Learning, and Emotional Problems: Health of Our Nation's Children, United States, 1988* (Washington: National Center for Health Statistics, No. 190, 1990).

9. Harold T. Christensen and Kenneth E. Barber, "Interfaith versus Intrafaith Marriage in Indiana," *Journal of Marriage and the Family* 29 (1967): 461–69; Robert T. Michael, "Determinants of Divorce," in *Sociological Economics,* ed. L. Levy Garboua (Beverly Hills, Calif.: Sage, 1979), 223–68.

10. Justin McCarthy, "Religious Commitment, Affiliation, and Marriage Disso-lution," in *The Religious Dimension: New Directions in Quantitative Research,* ed. Robert Wuthnow (New York: Academic Press, 1979), 179–97; Evelyn L. Lehrer and Carmel U. Chiswick, "Religion as a Determinant of Marital Stability," *Demography* 30 (1993): 385–404.

11. Barna Research, "Born Again Adults Less Likely to Cohabit, Just as Likely to Divorce," *http://www.barna.org,* August 6, 2001.

12. Michael Hout, "Divorced and Remarried Catholics in the United States: De-mography, Attachment, and Participation," A working paper provided to me by the author. A summary version appeared in *America,* December 16, 2000.

13. William V. D'Antonio, "The American Catholic Laity in 1999," *National Catholic Reporter,* October 29, 1999, 12. See also William V. D'Antonio et al., *American Catholics: Gender, Generation and Commitment.*

14. Hout, "Divorced and Remarried Catholics."

15. Francis X. Murphy, "Of Sex and the Catholic Church," *Atlantic Monthly* 247 (1981): 44–45, 48–57.

16. Congregation for the Doctrine of the Faith, "Concerning the Reception of Holy Communion by Divorced and Remarried Members of the Faithful," *Origins,* October 27, 1994.

17. Raymond F. Collins, *Divorce in the New Testament* (Collegeville, Minn.: Liturgical Press, 1992), 205. Those who desire to survey the opinions, may consult Joseph Fitzmyer, "The Matthean Divorce Texts and Some New Palestinian Evi-dence," *Theological Studies* 37 (1976): 197–226, and A. Myre, "Dix ans d'exegese sur le divorce dans le Nouveau Testament," in *Le Divorce* (Montreal: Fides, 1973).

18. See Michael G. Lawler, *Marriage and Sacrament: A Theology of Christian Marriage* (Collegeville, Minn.: Liturgical Press, 1993), 92–93.

19. J. D. Mansi, ed., *Sacrorum Conciliorum Nova Collectio* (Paris: Welter, 1903–27), II, 672. Emphasis added.

20. Charles J. Hefele, *History of the Christian Councils* (Edinburgh: Clark, 1883), I, 410.

21. See Origen, PG 13, 1237; and Jerome, PL 22, 563.

22. Basil the Great, *Epistola LXXVIII,* PG 32, 804–5.

23. James A. Coriden, Thomas J. Green, and Donald E. Heintschel, *The Code of Canon Law: A Text and Commentary* (Mahwah, N.J.: Paulist Press, 1985), 742.

24. *Catechism of the Catholic Church* (New York: Paulist, 1994), n. 1640. Emphasis added.

25. AAS (1930): 552.

26. GS, 48.

27. GS, 50.

28. DS 1807 and footnote.

29. FC, 5.

30. See *History of Vatican II,* 3 vols. ed. Giuseppe Alberigo, English version edited by Joseph A. Komonchak (Maryknoll, N.Y.: Orbis, 2000).

31. *Stromatum,* 2, 23, PG 8, 1086 and 1090. See also *Paed.,* 2, 10, PG 8, 498.

32. *Divinarum Institutionum,* 6, 23, PL 6, 718.

33. *De Nupt et Concup,* 2, 32, 54, PL 44, 468–69; also *De Bono Coniugali,* passim, PL 40, 394.

34. *De Bono Coniug.,* 9, 9, PL 40, 380.

35. Ibid., PL 40, 375. Emphasis added.

36. ST, 3 (Suppl.), 65, 1, c.

37. See Urban Navarette, "Structura Juridica Matrimonii Secundum Concilium Vaticanum II," *Periodica* 56 (1967): 366.

38. William V. D'Antonio et al., *Laity: American and Catholic,* 79. Corroborating evidence is supplied by Davidson et al., *The Search for Common Ground,* 47.

39. See Andrew M. Greeley, William C. McCready, and Kathleen McCourt, *Catholic Schools in a Declining Church* (Kansas City: Sheed and Ward, 1976), 35; D'Antonio et al., *Laity: American and Catholic,* 140; Davidson et al., *The Search for Common Ground,* 131.

40. Hornsby-Smith, *Roman Catholicism in England,* 177.

41. Those who are interested in that debate and its arguments can profitably begin in Charles E. Curran and Robert E. Hunt, *Dissent in and for the Church: Theologians and Humanae Vitae* (New York: Sheed and Ward, 1969) and Germain Grisez, John C. Ford, Joseph Boyle, John Finnis, and William E. May, *The Teaching of Humanae Vitae: A Defense* (San Francisco: Ignatius Press, 1988).

42. HV, 11.

43. Cited in Clifford Longley, *The Worlock Archive* (London: Chapman, 2000), 233. Emphasis added.

44. Norbert J. Rigali, "On the *Humanae Vitae* Process Ethics of Teaching Morality," *Louvain Studies* 23 (1998): 3–21.

45. Longley, *The Worlock Archive,* 232.

46. For detail on this, see Janet E. Smith, *Humanae Vitae: A Generation Later* (Washington, D.C.: Catholic University of America Press, 1991), 11–33.

47. Richard McCormick, *Notes on Moral Theology 1965–1980* (Lanham, Md.: University Press of America, 1981), 164.

48. Joseph Selling, "The Development of Catholic Tradition and Sexual Morality," in *Embracing Sexuality: Authority and Experience in the Catholic Church,* ed. Joseph Selling (Aldershot, Hants.: Ashgate, 2001), 153.

49. AAS 22 (1930): 548–49.

50. Dietrich Von Hildebrand, *Marriage* (London: Longmans Green, 1942), v.

51. Ibid., 25. Emphasis in original.

52. Heribert Doms, *The Meaning of Marriage* (London: Sheed and Ward, 1939), 94–95.

53. See Michael Lamb and Abraham Sagi, *Fatherhood and Family Policy* (Hillsdale, N.J.: Erlbaum, 1983); Ronald J. Angel and Jacqueline L. Angel, *Painful Inheritance: Health and the New Generation of Fatherless Families* (Madison: University of Wisconsin Press, 1993); Jean Bethke Elshtain, "Family Matters: The Plight of America's Children," *Christian Century* 110, no. 21 (1993): 710–12; Sara McLanahan and Gary Sandefur, *Growing Up with a Single Parent* (Cambridge, Mass.: Harvard University Press, 1994); David Blankenhorn, *Fatherlessness in America: Confronting Our Most Urgent Social Problem* (New York: Basic Books, 1995); David Popenoe, *Life Without Father* (New York: Free Press, 1996); Arlene R. Skolnick and Jerome H. Skolnick, *Family in Transition* (New York: Longman, 1999); Linda J. Waite and Maggie Gallagher, *The Case for Marriage: Why Married People Are Happier, Healthier, and Better Off Financially* (New York: Doubleday, 2000); Judith Wallerstein, Julia Lewis, *The Unexpected Legacy of Divorce: A 25 Year Landmark Study* (New York: Hyperion, 2000).

54. AAS, 36 (1944): 103.

55. AAS 43 (1951): 848–49.

56. Ibid., 846.

57. Selling, "Marriage and Sexuality in the Catholic Church," in *Embracing Sexuality,* ed. Selling, 185.

58. GS, 47–48.

59. *Acta Synodalia Sacrosancti Concilii Vaticani II,* vol. IV, Periodus Quarta, Pars I, 536.

60. John Breck, *The Sacred Gift of Life: Orthodox Christianity and Bioethics* (New York: St. Vladimir's Seminary Press, 2000), 63.

61. Ibid., 62. While preferring *mysterion* or *sacrament* and eschewing *covenant,* John Meyendorff, *Marriage: An Orthodox Perspective* (New York: St. Vladimir's Seminary, 1984), articulates the same meanings Breck associates with covenant. See, especially, 18–20, 33–42.

62. GS, 48.

63. Ibid. Emphasis added.

64. See Marcia Falk, *Love Lyrics from the Bible: A Translation and Literary Study of the Song of Songs* (Sheffield: Almond Press, 1982); Helmut Gollwitzer, *Song of Love: A Biblical Understanding of Sex* (Philadelphia: Fortress, 1979).

65. GS, 49.

66. GS, 48.

67. GS, 50. Emphasis added.

68. The foregoing information may be found in more detail in Murphy, "Of Sex and the Catholic Church," 49–52.

69. See, for example, George Gallup Jr. and Jim Castelli, *The American Catholic People: Their Beliefs, Practices, and Values* (New York: Doubleday, 1987); Andrew M. Greeley et al. *Catholic Schools in a Declining Church* (Kansas City: Sheed and Ward, 1976).

70. Augustine, *De Praed. Sanct.*, 14, 27, PL 44, 980. See also LG, 12.

71. Rahner, "Practical Theology," 102.

72. GS, 50.

73. FC, 5.

74. Bishop P. Francis Murphy, "Let's Start Over: A Bishop Appraises the Pastoral on Women," *Commonweal,* September 25, 1992.

75. See *America,* August 31, 1996, 8. Emphasis added.

76. *The Tablet,* January 9, 1993, 30.

## Epilogue

1. Karl Rahner, "Practical Theology Within the Totality of Theological Disciplines," *Theological Investigations* (London: Darton, Longman, Todd, 1972), 9:102. Emphasis in original.

2. ST, 1, 5, ad 2.

3. Ibid.

4. GS, 32.

5. LG, 9; cp. AG, 19.

6. Yves M. J. Congar, "Reception as an Ecclesiological Reality," *Concilium* 77 (1965): 62.

7. Michael G. Lawler, *Marriage in the Catholic Church: Disputed Questions* (Collegeville, Minn.: Liturgical Press, 2002), 162–92.

8. *Catechism of the Catholic Church,* 2423. Emphasis added.

9. Paul VI, *Octogesima Adveniens* 4, AAS 63 (1971): 403 ff.

10. Congregation for the Doctrine of the Faith, *Instruction on Christian Freedom and Liberation* 72, AAS 79 (1987): 586.

11. John Paul II, *Sollicitudo Rei Socialis* 41, AAS 80 (1988): 571.

12. Ibid., 1. Emphasis added.

13. This notion of individual responsibility is analyzed by Jean-Yves Calvez in his essay, "Morale sociale et morale sexuelle," *Etudes* 378 (1993): 642–44.

14. *Sollicitudo Rei Socialis,* 3.

15. Calvez, "Morale sociale et morale sexuelle," 648. Emphasis added.

16. *Sermo 52,* PL 38, 360.

17. ST, 1, 3, preface.

18. Karl Rahner, "The Hiddenness of God," *Theological Investigations* (London: Darton, Longman, and Todd, 1979), 16:238.

19. Elizabeth A. Johnson, *She Who Is: The Mystery of God in Feminist Theological Discourse* (New York: Crossroad, 1992), 105.

20. Pontifical Council for Interreligious Dialogue, *Dialogue and Proclamation* (Rome: Typis Polyglottis Vaticanis, 1991), n. 49.

21. Encyclical Letter, *Ut Unum Sint,* n. 28.

22. See Jean-Pierre Torell, *St. Thomas Aquinas,* vol. I (Washington, D.C.: Catholic University of America Press, 1996), 54–74.

23. Peter Cantor, *Verbum Abrreviatum,* 1, PL 205, 25. Emphasis added.

24. International Theological Commission, *Theses on the Relationship Between the Ecclesiastical Magisterium and Theology* (Washington, D.C.: USCC, 1977), 6. Emphasis added.

# Index